Protecting the Right to Teach and Learn

Protecting the Right to Teach and Learn

POWER, POLITICS, AND PUBLIC SCHOOLS

EDITED BY
James K. Daly
Patricia L. Schall
Rosemary W. Skeele

FOREWORD BY JOHN S. MAYHER

Teachers College, Columbia University
New York and London

Published by Teachers College Press, 1234 Amsterdam Avenue, New York, NY 10027

Library of Congress Cataloging-in-Publication Data

Protecting the right to teach and learn : power, politics, and public schools / edited by James K. Daly, Patricia L. Schall, Rosemary W. Skeele ; foreword by John S. Mayher.
　　p.　cm.
Includes bibliographical references and index.
ISBN 0-8077-4005-5 (cloth : alk. paper)—ISBN 0-8077-4004-7 (pbk. : alk. paper)
　　1. Academic freedom—United States. 2. Education—Political aspects—United States. 3. Public schools—United States. I. Daly, James K. II. Schall, Patricia L. III. Skeele, Rosemary W.

LC72.2 .P76　2001
371.1'04—dc21
　　　　　　　　　　　　　　　　　　　　　　　　　　　　　00-059993

ISBN 0-8077-4004-7 (paper)
ISBN 0-8077-4005-5 (cloth)

Printed on acid-free paper
Manufactured in the United States of America

08　07　06　05　04　03　02　01　　8　7　6　5　4　3　2　1

We dedicate this book to Jim Moffett for his inspirational life and his visionary writings. We also dedicate our work to all educators who have confronted challenges to academic freedom. Through their struggles, they have protected their students' right to learn.

Contents

Foreword

MOST NEW TEACHERS, and even a lot of us who should know better, go on teaching in the naive belief that we are essentially protected from anyone who might threaten to take away our pedagogical prerogatives. We choose our books, and plan our curricula, and teach our students as though we, and they, lived in an educational vacuum. If questioned, we might mumble something about academic freedom, but most of us haven't thought very much about what that entails, practically or legally. And those of us in teacher education rarely disturb the pedagogical peace by warning our students of the potential pitfalls that could lie ahead as they leave our halls and enter public school classrooms.

This book is a wake-up call for the educationally somnolent. James Daly, Patricia Schall, Rosemary Skeele, and their co-authors have done us all a favor by showing that, yes—it can happen here. It can happen here whether one is teaching in a suburb or a city, in the north or the south, or whether one is experienced or a relative beginner. Some of the tales they tell here are of award-winning teachers and schools suddenly assaulted by ? ? ? By whom, exactly, is part of the story they have to tell, to show that these disputes pit neighbor against neighbor, and, in the process, threaten not only the individual teachers and administrators who are challenged but the school, the district, and the larger community.

Whether in their major case study of the community they call River Haven, or in the shorter profiles of teachers under siege, none of these stories should make any teacher or teacher educator feel safe. They reveal some fundamental clashes of values over the nature of schooling and the purposes of education. And since these clashes have been aggravated if not caused, by changes in the culture at large, it seems likely that as the culture keeps changing, the climate of anxiety and distrust that leads to these challenges will only intensify. Therefore every prospective teacher—as well as those of us currently feeling secure in our classrooms—should read this book in order to understand and help to anticipate the challenges we may soon face and to find ways to confront them when they occur.

In my own work, I've recognized the power of educational stasis and the resistance to change that it creates so that schools continue from generation to generation to be largely unchanged. Attempts to fundamentally change the nature of teaching and learning in schools require a deep change of mind and lots of shifts of role. They require that we rebuild our conceptions of how children learn and how teachers teach toward an active, constructivist, and meaning-centered pedagogy. And while I've recognized how difficult this is, I've tended to underplay how dangerous it can be.

As teachers and principals try to imagine and implement these deep changes, they may find themselves challenged by those who feel that the culture has already changed too much. That children and adolescents are increasingly out of control. That we need more order, discipline, and control, and that schools should encourage teacher (and parental) authority, not give children the tools to question authority, to think critically, and to make their own choices about what they read and write and how they are going to live.

The teachers and administrators whose stories are told in this book, in contrast, recognize that future citizenship in a democracy requires just those capacities. Further, they know that to live in the twenty-first century, children cannot have an education designed for the nineteenth century. The moral of the stories that Daly, Schall, Skeele, and their colleagues tell is not that we should pull back and stay with the tried and true. It is rather that we should be prepared to educate the whole community as well as our students, to understand that our beliefs and practices are controversial and therefore will cause controversy, and to help our students and colleagues understand the rights and responsibilities that come with academic freedom.

As these authors have shown us, these are beliefs worth fighting for, and their analyses and examples will help us. Having read their cautionary notes, we will be better able to prepare for the battles to come, as well as to do the job we must do to advocate for our beliefs, so that we can educate the culture to the benefits as well as the costs of change.

John S. Mayher
New York University

Acknowledgments

WE WOULD LIKE to acknowledge our families, friends, colleagues, students, technical assistants, and kind strangers who contributed to the development and completion of this book. The time and cost of completing a study of this type required support, encouragement, and assistance from many sources. We would especially like to thank the people of River Haven who welcomed us into their homes and graciously shared their thoughts, opinions, and passions.

We give our respect and compassion to Jan Cole, Janet Cooper, "Karen Hunter," Cissy Lacks, Gloria Pipkin, and Gretchen Klopfer Wing—educators who stood up for what they believed in, endured challenges, and generously shared their struggles with us and our wider audience of readers.

We thank our contributing authors—John Mayher, Jack Nelson, William Stanley, and Joan Naomi Steiner. It will quickly become evident to readers how much their work enriched this book.

Our gratitude to Cathy McClure, our development editor, who helped shape and revise the manuscript, making it a more readable book. Brian Ellerbeck, our editor, gave us valuable comments and suggestions as we planned, wrote, and rewrote the manuscript. We appreciate his guidance, support, and enthusiasm for our work.

Words don't begin to express our gratitude to Nancy Waddell, our Sherlock Holmes. Her tireless sleuthing helped us track down people, phone numbers, and other important information for our case study. We thank Terry Campbell, a formidable gatekeeper, who protected us from endless interruptions.

Our special gratitude to Brother Denis Sennett of the Friars of the Atonement, who welcomed weary researchers with food and shelter. We are grateful to Seton Hall University for providing financial support for our research. Our special thanks to Dr. Robert Hallissey, Director of Grants and Research, for his encouragement and support.

We appreciate the efforts of our colleagues Marshall Strax and Richard Ognibene, who read drafts of this book. Their comments and suggestions in the formative stages of our manuscript helped make the book much better.

JAMES K. DALY

I wish to express my gratitude to my parents, Virginia A. Daly and the late James Daly, and to my brother Bob and sister-in-law Nancy. Their support throughout my career has been appreciated. I have been fortunate to have had outstanding teachers and mentors, and I am particularly grateful to Jack L. Nelson and Ken Carlson. It is especially for Christopher and Elizabeth Daly that I dedicate the efforts behind this book, in the hopes that they may always have teachers who possess a passion for challenging and nurturing them and who are given the freedom to teach well.

PATRICIA L. SCHALL

I thank my husband, Peter J. Wosh, for his support, patience, and advice during the writing of this book. He read and responded to drafts of chapters and always helped me to "keep the faith" when I was tempted to lose it through many revisions of the manuscript. I also owe a debt of gratitude to my mother, Margaret Champi Schall, who taught me to love stories, and my grandmother, the late Rose Coccia Champi, who instilled in me an appreciation for talk and words, passions that have served me well in my personal and professional life. I am indebted to my father, the late Edward M. Schall, Jr., for giving me a sense of humor that gets me through the daily challenges. I am grateful to my sisters, Rose and Bonnie, my brother, Bo, and my uncle, Albert Champi, for sharing the good and bad times together as a family. I regret that my aunt, Lucy Champi Mineo, passed away just before seeing her niece's name on a book, something she would have loved.

I thank my mentors at New York University, especially John Mayher, Gordon Pradl, and Bee Cullinan, for enabling me to develop an uncommonsense vision for teaching and learning. I also appreciate the research skills I learned from Joe Giacquinta. This book would not have been possible without the support of these special teachers.

ROSEMARY W. SKEELE

Special love and thanks to my best friend, Marty Skeele, and my son, Colin Skeele. Marty cooked, edited, delivered packages, encouraged, and so much more, giving me the time to pursue this research. Colin played quietly, answered phones politely, became a great teenager, and did all the little things for which a busy mom is grateful.

Teachers, mentors, and friends who motivated me throughout my life deserve my gratitude. Like a visitor to Oz, I was given the desire to learn, as well as the courage and the confidence to take risks by a cast of very unique characters. Those who appear first in my mind are my parents, the late Helen and Joseph Weiss; my family, Joe and Kathy Weiss and Karen, David, and Jillian Sabella; Robert Latzer, English professor; Pauline Gurtner, art professor; Bruce Waldman, my first real "boss"; Dave Barnard, head of my master's program at the University of Wisconsin-Stout; and many wonderful students who are now friends. This assortment of wizards convinced me to believe and envision my own road.

WE GRATEFULLY ACKNOWLEDGE Seton Hall University for its financial support of this research project through the University Research Council and the Office of Grants and Research Services.

Protecting the Right
to Teach and Learn

Introduction

JAMES K. DALY, PATRICIA L. SCHALL,
& ROSEMARY W. SKEELE

TOGETHER WE HAVE BEEN involved in a myriad of educational experiences for almost 90 years. In inner-city, suburban, and rural schools, as well as in juvenile justice facilities, we have taught elementary school, middle school, high school, and adult learners, as well as university undergraduate and graduate students. We are currently responsible for the professional development of preservice and inservice teachers. All these experiences have compelled us to rethink schooling and the role of the teacher. This book represents much of that thinking.

Coming from three different disciplines, we were drawn together by a common interest in censorship and its relationship to academic freedom. An English teacher, a social studies teacher, and a school library media specialist—all committed to defending the rights of teachers to teach and the rights of students to learn. Preserving academic freedom is our common cause. Everyone has the right to learn in an environment that is open to multiple possibilities and perspectives. No individual, group, or political body should be able to restrict these rights. Through the years our cause seemed to take on new meaning as we watched the number of challenges increase and observed that the thrust of the challenges began to encompass pedagogy. Ideas and materials, especially books, have always been targets for the censor. However, we noticed more and more challenges to teaching methods from individuals and groups across the political and religious spectrum.

Anyone who has attended a school seems to have an opinion about how schools work. When parents return to school with their children, the landscape looks different. They raise questions and often express their discomfort and confusion. Where are the spellers? Where are those workbooks? No phonics? Where are Puff and Spot? Individual concerns became national outcries as some voices were heard and accommodated, resulting in restraints and constraints on the teacher's autonomy.

There is no national consensus on the mission of schools. In our diverse and democratic nation, we recognize that people will have competing expectations for schools. Addressing challenges produces an environment filled with creative tension that requires dialogue. This dialogue permits us to examine these conflicting expectations. To achieve fundamental change in schools, this dialogue is essential.

We have written a book about challenges to pedagogy because it is both necessary and timely. This book was designed to build educators' confidence as professionals; encourage the development of informed rationales for their practice; provide awareness of techniques for handling challenges; help develop the capability to articulately defend their choices; and encourage educators to become informed, confident change agents in restructuring schools. This book has practical applications for teacher educators, preservice and inservice teachers, educational administrators, and stakeholders in a position to develop policy for schools. Board of education members, collective-bargaining units, unions, community members, and families all could benefit from reading this book.

FACING CHALLENGES

Today, more people than ever before have an impact on life in elementary and secondary classrooms. It is reasonable and prudent to anticipate attempts to challenge educational decisions in an era of well-orchestrated challenges. Educators need to intelligently articulate an honest, convincing rationale for the choices they make for their classrooms, or they will lose the power to choose. Teacher educators should avoid teaching simple technical proficiency alone; they should also model the kind of learning that will help their students develop the critical and speculative stances needed to face challenges from a public perhaps rightfully skeptical of what they perceive as the latest educational "fad."

This book is intended to help inservice and preservice educators, school administrators, and others concerned with what happens in schools to build a solid foundation of knowledge about challenges to pedagogy. This knowledge will help inform the choices they make in their classrooms and schools. Without this knowledge, educators and communities remain vulnerable to attack, and their choices can easily be characterized as whimsical, politically motivated, or personal. We hope to help our readers understand and define challenges, determine why they occur, develop an awareness of what is typically challenged, envision the aftermath of these challenges, and understand the rights and responsibilities of academic freedom.

Constructing an Informed Philosophy

We view pedagogy as a protected academic freedom. It is essential for teacher educators to prepare teachers to exercise that academic freedom responsibly. A constructivist approach to learning that engenders reflective, inquiry-oriented practice will help teachers develop the knowledge and experience to articulate and defend their choices. Without this ability, teachers are easily relegated to the role of technicians, mechanically carrying out plans made by others. Students of these technician teachers ultimately suffer because they become the victims of a routine education. Such an education, devoid of choice for both teacher and student, fails to prepare people to assume a functional role in a democratic society. We share the conviction of those who redefine teachers as "transformative intellectuals" (Freire & Macedo, 1987).

In this book we explore a challenge to whole language in a particular school district. The River Haven story opens the door to an exploration of the complexities that surface from challenges to pedagogy. We have heard the voices of the challenged in River Haven resounding in cities and towns throughout the country. We explore the impact of these challenges on the preparation of teachers and on their philosophies and practices. We offer our point of view on the critical thinking and decision-making roles of teachers. We would argue that teachers who are reflective practitioners are better positioned to defend their choices to challengers and create the kind of dialogue that leads to understanding.

As we examine the role of teachers as reflective practitioners, we simultaneously consider the role of learners. The ways in which people view education and the metaphors used for learning may be linked to the issue of censorship. As we explore definitions of learning, we begin to see some interesting tensions emerging. If we believe that learners are empty vessels passively waiting to be filled with knowledge, learning becomes a process of transmission. If learning is a simple process of transmission, then what is learned as well as how it is learned become critical because the transmitter of knowledge can also transmit a worldview. This view of learning resembles brainwashing because the learner simply absorbs knowledge and whatever else is transmitted with it. The learner appears powerless to act on this knowledge.

If students are empty vessels, then teachers become controlling figures who can communicate their worldviews along with the multiplication tables. This understanding of learning can be particularly troubling to those who worry that the lives and minds of children are being molded by those they suspect espouse an ideology they do not share. To an experienced, reflective educator, notions like this may seem rather naive. Apple (1982) argues that anyone who has taught recognizes the myth of complete passivity in learners, who often ignore, reinterpret, or openly reject overt and covert messages presented by educators.

If one views learners as active beings who construct, interpret, and reconstruct, the nature of learning is very different. As Kelly (1955) says, learners are scientists who hypothesize about how the world works and apply the new understandings they have gained to reshape the mental constructs they use to make further predictions. Here the learner has more control of the process of knowing; and the teacher, in the words of Giroux (1988), promotes not only academic achievement, but also endeavors to "empower students so they can read the world critically and change it when necessary" (p. xxxiv).

Another interesting tension arises here, however. Do all stakeholders in education want learners to be capable of critically reading and changing the world? Do all parents want children who will challenge their convictions? Do corporate executives value workers who question the established system of control that governs the company? Do all teachers or administrators really want students who will resist the knowledge or the means of knowing sanctioned by the school?

We believe that students are active inquirers in the process of learning. Like Donelson (1994), we contend that if learners are denied the right to question, inquire, and challenge, education becomes indoctrination. We explore, among others, the theoretical perspectives of Giroux, Freire, Goodlad, and Apple to provide support for our positions. The topics we examine in these chapters—teachers as reflective practitioners, organizational constraints, the dialogic character of teaching and learning, and linking theory and practice—will help educators develop an informed philosophy for teaching and learning.

Censorship and Academic Freedom

Censorship wears many faces, assumes various forms, and emerges from different political, religious, and philosophical camps. More than 2,000 organizations have been identified as censors (People for the American Way, 1994), many of them equipped with well-funded research teams and the legal expertise to launch deliberate, effectively orchestrated attacks on schools. Censorship often goes unrecognized or unidentified until a door is shut, a learning style is abandoned, or a book is missing from the shelf. For example, the National Right to Read Foundation, Phyllis Schlafly's Eagle Forum, Norma and Mel Gabler's Educational Research Analysis, the Christian Coalition, and the National Association for Christian Education's activist arm, Citizens for Excellence in Education, all distribute literature that calls for expunging whole language from the curriculum (Weaver & Brinkley, 1998). We do not intend to imply that censorship is strictly a weapon of the political or religious right, though many of the cases documented in the United States can be attributed to the right. Jenkinson (1985) maintains that 95% of all attacks emerge from politically conservative and religious associations, with a significant increase having followed the 1980 presidential election (Arons, 1981; Jenkinson, 1985; Jones & Semler, 1983; Pincus, 1984; Seiferth, 1984). Arons (1981), Pincus (1984), and Giroux (1987) agree that more attacks come from the right: "As part of the existing political assault on public services and social justice in general, schools are increasingly being subordinated to the imperatives of neoconservative and right-wing interests that would make them adjuncts of the workplace or the church" (Giroux, 1987, p. 26).

While we note that most challenges tend to emerge from right-wing organizations, we also recognize that censors span the political spectrum. Left-wing groups have also acted as censors in their attempts to purge the curriculum of what they perceive of as racism, sexism, or distortions in the portrayal of other underrepresented groups (Donelson, 1994). Simmons (1994) acknowledges the debate on so-called political correctness and attributes its rise to the civil and equal rights movements. However, regardless of where we stand in this debate, we can see that it has had an impact on curricular choice in schools. Witness the ongoing censorship of *Huckleberry Finn*, for example. Described as "classic racism" (Donelson, 1997, p. 24), it is often challenged because it includes Black dialect and the use of terms considered derogatory to African Americans. Simmons asserts that groups who seek political correctness may be denying others their right to free speech when they seek the inclusion or exclusion of certain materials from the curriculum of schools.

As we discuss censorship, we also address the role of teachers and other educators as censors, especially when they consciously avoid controversial ideas, books, or strategies for fear of repercussions. Teachers include and exclude materials and strategies as they construct their courses of study. This invites the question of whether or not creation of canon is a form of censorship. Goodlad (1984) compares teachers to birds in a cage with the door open and a cat (society) poised just outside the door. Many teachers are well aware of public scrutiny, and society's expectations of what constitutes legitimate learning experiences often have an impact on choices they make about learning.

Academic freedom has the potential to protect the teacher from much of the official, external censorship as well as from the temptations of self-censorship. The American concept of academic freedom has evolved from the German model of the early 1800s (Hofstadter & Metzger, 1968). The autonomy of the German universities permitted the rise of two aspects of academic freedom, *Lernfreiheit* and *Lehrfreiheit*. *Lernfreiheit* refers basically to an absence of institutional restrictions on the student. Hofstadter and Metzger describe the German student as free to sample courses as desired, with passage of a final examination as the only requirement. *Lehrfreiheit* addresses the freedom of the professor to examine evidence and report findings in lectures or in published form.

In the United States, the concept of academic freedom has begun to focus on a concern for both professor and student. It has typically been seen more as a professional right emerging from the nature of the scholar involved in research, scientific conceptions of the search for truth, and a perception of service to the community (Hofstadter, 1955; MacIver, 1955). In its Joint Statement on Rights and Freedom of Students, the American Association of University Professors (AAUP; 1967) addressed the need for recognizing the student's right to learn as a distinct and necessary freedom. This combined view of academic freedom has been a powerful protection for those who would resist censorship on the university level. However, censorship is a serious threat in preuniversity schooling, where traditions of academic freedom are not very strong.

We view censorship as inappropriate control over decision making in schools, a control that ultimately restricts what and how students learn. We have found that people disagree on when challenges cross the line and become censorship. Even in our own case study, this was apparent. We exercise caution as we define censorship because we do not wish to imply that all challenges to the choices educators make are necessarily bad. Community members and families have the right to question what students are learning and how they are learning it. If the questioning leads to open dialogue about learning and creates the kind of cognitive dissonance that compels educators and those who challenge them to reflect on their stances and choices, the resulting tension might engender collaboration and constructive change. Genuine interaction of this nature nicely meshes with the dialogic character of effective learning. The conflict that arose in River Haven represents a missed opportunity for dialogue.

As democratic educators, we should acknowledge the multiple perspectives of the community in the structuring of curriculum, since what happens in schools is not the exclusive property of teachers and students.

However, we would argue that challengers cross the line and engage in inappropriate control or censorship when they prevent learners from receiving an education that will make them involved, discriminating citizens who possess the intellectual competence and aspirations to struggle for lives that are self-determined and meaningful (Aronowitz & Giroux, 1993).

Carlson (1977) believes that many censorship battles are metaphysical and not open to logical persuasion, compromise, or reconciliation. In such cases, those involved become locked into a values conflict centered on the rights of open inquiry in a pluralistic democracy and the imposition of certainty from those who claim to possess absolute truth (Brodinsky, 1982; Park, 1980; Robinson, 1981; Welch, Medeiros, & Tate, 1981). We also believe that any group that abuses power to impose its beliefs on schools is equally dangerous. Educational challenges often lead to arguments about concern for the public good, and everyone involved in the conflict assures themselves that they know what's best for learners. The acrimony and the casualties resulting from the discord and division that characterized the struggle in River Haven could have been avoided. Challenges can set schools, teachers, students, and communities adrift or they can create possibilities for renewal and change. In this book you will read about the consequences of failing to engage in open dialogue and silencing voices in the school and community.

THE SUM AND SUBSTANCE

The impetus for our research and the essence of this book is a case study that we have been involved with for more than 6 years. At a conference in 1993, we learned of an elementary school principal who had been removed from her school through a series of charges by parents that began with a challenge to the principal's whole-language philosophy. This challenge included "enormous community tension and divisiveness" (People for the American Way, 1997, p. 3) as well as rhetoric characteristic of conservative political or religious groups. Our past experiences with curricular challenges made us keenly aware that far-right "complainant rhetoric is nearly identical from state to state" (Jones, 1993–1994, p. 16). We developed a growing curiosity that led us into a close relationship with the people in a town we call River Haven. We were anxious to find out what happened and use this information to prepare teachers to better understand the nature of challenges and to develop strategies for dealing with them.

THE RESEARCH METHOD

We changed all the names and places described in our case study to protect the anonymity of the community and its people. We used ethnographic methods to conduct our research. Ethnography helped us reconstruct a story from multiple perspectives, including our own interpretation of the events (Babbie, 1999; Lofland & Lofland, 1995). Our aim was to shed light on the strife in this seemingly tranquil town and study the people involved with the conflict surrounding the Rock Spring Elementary School. We used the evidence we gathered to analyze the culture of the community and its schools, as well as to develop an understanding of the controversy. We wanted to gain a clearer understanding of how the dispute originated and how it progressed to its conclusion during the summer of 1999. Our data included observations, interviews, and documents, which we analyzed for themes. We searched for consistent evidence in the data to confirm or reject our tentative conclusions. We also used triangulation to cycle evidence from various forms of data, confirming and denying our hunches (Eisner, 1998). Together we discussed and debated our individual interpretations to account for what happened in River Haven. Sharing our different perspectives increased our confidence in our conclusions (Bogdan & Biklen, 1998; Glesne, 1999; Lofland & Lofland, 1995).

We conducted the study over a 6-year period by observing people in their environment, interviewing them, and striving to understand them from their point of view. We researched the town and its socioeconomic profile and history at local libraries, in government offices, and in conversations with the residents. We talked to real estate agents, local clergy, town employees, and any others who wanted to discuss the issues with us. Gaining access to information, for the most part, was not difficult, since the people of River Haven grew to know us and accept our presence around their town. With the exception of some school administrators and the Rock Spring Elementary School teachers, most of those involved on either side of the dispute were willing and anxious to talk to us. They trusted that we would attempt to remain detached from the conflict and to analyze the situation fairly. We examined the essential character of the town, its people, and their roles in the conflict. We attempt to present a balanced report on the River Haven conflict, draw conclusions, and discuss the implications that the controversy had for teachers, administrators, boards of education, community members, families, and others who find themselves facing similar challenges.

OUTLINE OF BOOK

In Part I, Chapters 1 through 3, we use the case study as an illustration to examine what can happen in communities when a challenge becomes a crisis. On the surface this does not appear to be a conventional censorship case; yet the controversy clearly illustrates what happens when schools and communities are in conflict over educational choices. Our research uncovered a complex situation that far exceeded the boundaries of a challenge to whole language. We encountered a far broader and deeper opposition to the philosophy and pedagogy that had manifested itself in a challenge to whole language and evolved into an attack on a particular administrator. We believe that the stories of the people of River Haven can provide other educators with insight into the nature of challenges and ways of dealing with them.

Part II of this book contains chapters by contributors. Jack Nelson and William Stanley believe that today threats to academic freedom at all levels of education seem at least as serious as they have been at any time since the concept became established in the twentieth century. In Chapter 4, they write about protecting the right to teach and to learn in a democracy. By tracing the historical development of teaching, Nelson and Stanley explain why there are differences between the intent of academic freedom and its actual practice in schools. They stress that academic freedom is an essential component of our democratic culture. They delve into the often-controversial subject of tenure and its important role in helping to maintain academic freedom. Believing that a democratic society requires teachers and students to have the freedom to investigate ideas, they describe the many threats that currently give us excellent reasons to renew our commitment to academic freedom. They help us to understand how public support for education, extreme ideologies, and the national standards movement impact students, teachers, the curriculum, teaching materials, and pedagogy.

Educators need to hear the voices of colleagues who have been challenged. In Chapter 5 we present the stories of teachers who faced or continue to face significant challenges to pedagogy. The experiences of elementary and secondary teachers representing different disciplines offer valuable lessons about the realities of censorship. We hear the voices of five resilient women who have endured challenges or litigation.

Jan Cole, a sixth-grade teacher in Colorado, was accused of witchcraft. Her experiences with the religious right deserve our attention. In Texas, Janet Cooper's contract was not renewed. Puzzled, she learned that school board members objected to her use of a simulation in a history class. Cissy Lacks, a writing teacher from Missouri, was fired for encouraging students to use language of their choice in scripts they wrote. Florida English teacher Gloria Pipkin saw years of collegial curriculum development disappear when a small group of parents began an attack on the books and then the methods used in junior high English classes. Her experience with censorship intensified when she was excoriated in the media and received death threats. Gretchen Klopfer Wing taught civics in North Carolina. She was challenged by a newspaper reporter for taking classes to a criminal trial at a local courthouse. Educators are enduring similar experiences all over the United States. Listening to their personal narratives puts a human face on the disembodied facts and statistics that typically describe educational challenges.

The theme of Part III of this book is the politics of school reform and the implications of institutional change for teacher education. Joan Naomi Steiner, in Chapter 6, addresses less overt, but equally potent, challenges to teachers. She describes the way schools mold, shape, and reshape those working within them. Steiner profiles three school districts to illustrate how they face change. In her stories, she shares her own experiences in these districts, analyzes the politics of curricular and pedagogical change, studies the nature of internal institutional barriers, and examines the strategies teachers use to mitigate them.

In Chapter 7, we describe the role and responsibilities of teacher educators as they prepare teachers to face challenges to the choices they make in their classrooms. Teacher educators need to introduce their students to the rights and responsibilities of academic freedom, help them recognize the continuing struggle to analyze its role in public schools, and encourage them to discover the protections that enable teachers to go beyond routine practices and procedures. The curriculum of teacher education programs should provide the opportunity for students to acquire the knowledge and skills necessary to communicate their philosophies and pedagogical choices to the larger community. We reflect on what all of this means for those who would be teachers. We believe that it is disingenuous to prepare persons for teaching without having them explore the protections of academic freedom, the stories of colleagues confronted with challenges, and the political and institutional barriers they might face. In this chapter we envision a synergy that results from the combined knowledge and experiences presented throughout the book. With a vision for teaching and learning that draws on a democratic social tradition, we propose specific changes in the arrangements that currently characterize schools.

Appendices A, B, and C provide information to accompany the case study. They will help readers understand the events and will be a quick

reference to the people mentioned in our story. Appendix D is an annotated list of major organizations that provide resources for educators who
need support when facing challenges.

REFERENCES

American Association of University Professors. (1967). *AAUP joint statement on rights and freedom of students.* Washington, DC: Author.

Apple, M. W. (1982). *Education and power.* Boston: Routledge & Kegan Paul.

Aronowitz, S., & Giroux, H. A. (1993). *Education still under siege* (2nd ed.). Westport, CT: Bergin & Garvey.

Arons, S. (1981). *Value conflict between American families and American schools* (Final report to National Institute of Education). Amherst: University of Massachusetts.

Babbie, E. (1999). *The basics of social research.* Belmont, CA: Wadsworth.

Bogdan, R. C., & Biklen, S. K. (1998). *Qualitative research in education: An introduction to theory and methods* (3rd ed.). Needham Heights, MA: Allyn & Bacon.

Brodinsky, B. (1982). The new right: The movement and its impact. *Phi Delta Kappan, 64,* 87–95.

Carlson, K. (1977). *Censorship: Cases and categories.* Paper presented at the annual meeting of the American Educational Research Association, New York.

Donelson, K. (1994). Ten steps toward the freedom to read. In J. S. Simmons (Ed.), *Censorship: A threat to reading, learning, thinking* (pp. 231–242). Newark, DE: International Reading Association.

Donelson, K. (1997). "Filth" and "pure filth" in our schools—censorship of classroom books in the last ten years. *English Journal, 86*(2), 21–25.

Eisner, E. W. (1998). *The enlightened eye: Qualitative inquiry and the enhancement of educational practice.* Upper Saddle River, NJ: Prentice Hall.

Freire, P., & Macedo, D. (1987). *Literacy: Reading the word and the world.* South Hadley, MA: Bergin & Garvey.

Giroux, H. A. (1987). Introduction. In P. Freire & D. Macedo, *Literacy: Reading the word and the world.* South Hadley, MA: Bergin & Garvey.

Giroux, H. A. (1988). *Teachers as intellectuals: Toward a critical pedagogy of learning.* South Hadley, MA: Bergin & Garvey.

Glesne, C. (1999). *Becoming qualitative researchers: An introduction* (2nd ed.). New York: Longman.

Goodlad, J. I. (1984). *A place called school: Prospects for the future.* New York: McGraw-Hill.

Hofstadter, R. (1955). *Academic freedom in the age of the college.* New York: Columbia University Press.

Hofstadter, R., & Metzger, W. P. (1968). *The development of academic freedom in the United States.* New York: Columbia University Press.

Jenkinson, E. B. (1985). Protecting Holden Caulfield and his friends from the censors. *English Journal, 74,* 26–33.

Jones, J. (1993–1994, Winter/Spring). Countering the "far right." *The Principal News, 21*(3), 8, 16, 21.

Jones, T. N., & Semler, D. P. (Eds.). (1983). *School law update—1982.* Topeka, KA: National Organization on Legal Problems of Educators.

Kelly, G. (1955). *The psychology of personal constructs.* New York: Norton.

Lofland, J., & Lofland, L. H. (1995). *Analyzing social settings: A guide to qualitative observation and analysis* (3rd ed.). Belmont, CA: Wadsworth.

MacIver, R. M. (1955). *Academic freedom in our time.* New York: Columbia University Press.

Park, J. C. (1980). Preachers, politics and public education: A review of right-wing pressures against public schooling in America. *Phi Delta Kappan, 61,* 608–612.

People for the American Way. (Eds.). (1994). *Attacks on the freedom to learn 1993–94.* Washington, DC: Author.

People for the American Way. (Eds.). (1997). *A right wing and a prayer: The religious right in your public schools* (Executive Summary). Washington, DC: Author.

Pincus, F. L. (1984). Book banning and the new right: Censorship in the public schools. *The Educational Forum, 49,* 7–21.

Robinson, S. (1981). Freedom, censorship, schools, and libraries. *English Journal, 70,* 58–59.

Seiferth, B. B. (1984). Censorship: Challenges, concerns, and cures. *Viewpoints.* (ERIC Document Reproduction Service No. ED 241 413).

Simmons, J. S. (1994). Political correctness—the other side of the coin. In J. S. Simmons (Ed.), *Censorship: A threat to reading, learning, thinking* (pp. 55–61). Newark, DE: International Reading Association.

Weaver, C., & Brinkley, E. (1998). Phonics, whole language, and the religious and political right. In K. S. Goodman (Ed.), *In defense of good teaching: What teachers need to know about the "reading wars"* (pp. 127–142). York, ME: Stenhouse.

Welch, I. D., Medeiros, D.C., & Tate, G. A. (1981). Education, religion and the new right. *Educational Leadership, 39,* 203–208.

A Case Study of a Community in Conflict

THE THREE CHAPTERS in Part I comprise a 6-year longitudinal study of a community in conflict. In these chapters we explore what happens when doubts about the whole-language vision and practices of a principal and her cohort of teacher change agents merge with questions about her leadership style and personal character and escalate into a litigious school and community crisis.

As we will explain, it did not surprise us that whole language was a source of conflict in the town we call River Haven. Whole language, perhaps because it is often misunderstood or poorly explained to parents and other stakeholders in education, remains controversial throughout the nation. Routman (1996), commenting on an evolving understanding of whole language, defines it as

> a way of thinking, teaching, and learning in a social community where learners are continually supported to purposefully use language (reading, writing, speaking, listening, viewing, thinking, drawing, composing, making sense mathematically and scientifically, and so on) in order to inquire and to construct and evaluate their own understanding of texts and real-world issues. (p. 41)

While whole language clearly emerged as a problem in River Haven, it was not the only source of conflict. Our many interviews and conversations with individuals involved in the dispute uncovered a complex web of tensions.

In Chapter 1, we begin the case study with a brief history of the controversy and the town itself. We describe River Haven, offer impressions of the community both from our perspective and those of the participants in the study, and explore the concerns of the parents who challenged the principal and the teachers who were enacting curricular changes. In Chapter 2, we present the opinions of the parents who supported the principal and the changes she and her cohort of teachers were making and describe how community pressure led to substantial changes in the curriculum and the school environment in general. In Chapter 3, we conclude the case study with an in-depth analysis of the dispute. At the end of the book, in Chapter 7, we further consider the implications of the River Haven crisis for a wider audience of educators. All names of people and places in Chapters 1 through 3 have been changed to protect the privacy of the participants in this study.

REFERENCE

Routman, R. (1996). *Literacy at the crossroads: Crucial talk about reading, writing, and other dilemmas.* Portsmouth, NH: Heinemann.

The Best of Times . . . the Worst of Times: A Case Study of a Community in Conflict

JAMES K. DALY, PATRICIA L. SCHALL,
& ROSEMARY W. SKEELE

> It was the best of times, it was the worst of times, it was the age of wisdom, it was the age of foolishness, it was the epoch of incredulity, it was the season of Light, it was the season of Darkness, it was the spring of hope, it was the winter of despair.
>
> —Charles Dickens, *A Tale of Two Cities*

WE CROSSED THE RIVER and traveled on the two-lane road zigzagging along the mountainside. Panoramic views of water, sky, and green hills reminiscent of nineteenth-century paintings appeared around every bend in the road. The sleepy, even tranquil, setting belied the turmoil we were traveling to investigate. The story we are about to tell has its roots in a town that seems very much like many other exurban communities in the United States. Yet, as we will explore here, a community is more than the sum of its geography and socioeconomic profile. The confluence of people, geography, economics, views on teaching and learning, and the national political climate led to a costly 6-year battle, fought by an elementary school principal, her supporters and detractors, and the board of education. This battle, which was finally settled in June 1999, resulted in many casualties and inflicted wounds that will not easily or quickly heal. Dickens described the climate of the French Revolution as a time of contrasts and contradictions. The controversy we are about to recount took on the characteristics of small-scale civil war; and, depending on their stance in the war, the forces characterize the reign of an embattled principal of an elementary school as "the best of times" or "the worst of times," a genuine tale of two cities.

The volatile mix of parents, educators, and board of education members who represent both sides of the controversy portray the learning environment, the curriculum, and the principal as either visionary or venomous. It has been unusual for us to find anyone who has offered a balanced account of her tenure at the school. As researchers, we have struggled to construct a multidimensional profile of the dispute. Parents from both sides of the controversy have been eager to talk to us. Most current teachers have declined interviews, and some have led us to believe that they fear repercussions if they voice their opinions on the dispute. In fact, we received only one response to a survey mailed in return-postage-paid plain envelopes to all teachers currently working at the school. A retired superintendent, the district leader during the most tumultuous times of the dispute, early in our research refused our request for an interview and warned us to stay out of the district schools.

To construct the case study that follows, we have relied on interviews with the principal, parents on both sides of the dispute, two retired teachers from the district, an administrator associated with the district, and the current district union leader. In our discussion, we reflect the multiple perspectives of those we interviewed and analyze these perspectives. We also have reviewed a number of documents, such as newspaper articles, letters to the editors of local papers, library information on the town and school district, board of education minutes, court documents, and copies of petitions circulated in the community. We offer here a reconstruction from multiple perspectives and sources, a patchwork portrait of the school and community based on the resources available to us at the time of this writing. We also analyze these two often contradictory accounts, ultimately creating our own version of what transpired. We have changed all names to protect the privacy of the participants in what has been a very public controversy, a story covered in both professional and popular media.

A BRIEF HISTORY OF THE CONTROVERSY

The Rock Spring Elementary School in River Haven has been the site of a bitter controversy. The controversy appeared to surface in 1991, when a group calling themselves the Concerned Parents protested a variety of pedagogical perspectives and practices used at the school. Often cited as a basis for their dissatisfaction was the constructivist, whole-language philosophy promulgated by the principal, Karen Hunter, and a number of the faculty, a vision for learning and teaching that appears to have emerged in the school in 1984 and grew more pervasive through the years. We found little if any concrete evidence in this case that the resistance to whole language resulted directly from the widespread, well-orchestrated and -funded attacks by some elements of the American political and religious right. Yet the controversy mirrors the rhetoric and actions of these groups and clearly illustrates what happens when schools and families are in conflict over educational choices.

Reacting to the challenge from the Concerned Parents, the acting superintendent of schools, Dr. Dorothy Stout, and the board of education directed Karen to develop a curriculum plan (Plan for Excellence) intended to address the issues raised by the protesting parents. When the implementation of this plan failed to satisfy these parents, they sought her dismissal. The board of education subsequently hit Hunter with what at one point amounted to 125 charges, none related to whole language. This legal action split the community into warring factions. Parents, teachers, and administrators became embroiled in the fray. Community Partners in Education, community members who supported Hunter and her educational philosophy and practices, coalesced to oppose the Concerned Parents, some of whom not only wanted her dismissed from the school but also advocated stripping her of her certifications and barring her from the profession. The battle lines were drawn.

The litigation resulting from the charges dragged on for 6 long years. In that time, only 64 hearing dates were scheduled before a three-member panel, most of whom found it difficult to work the dates into their schedules. A major newspaper that covered the story described the hearings as "lackadaisical," with participants forgetting about meetings, showing up late, and breaking for lunch. As observers at one of these hearings on July 24, 1996, we concur with this characterization. The hearing we witnessed was slow to start and sparsely attended by a few of Hunter's supporters we recognized. It concluded at 11:40 A.M., with the next hearing scheduled for September 12, 1996. This pattern, apparently, was characteristic of the hearings that preceded and followed the one we saw. Finally, in June 1999 the school board and the principal settled the dispute out of court. The same newspaper reported that Karen agreed to a monetary settlement of $100,000 per year for 6 years and was granted the right to accept a position elsewhere. She also dropped her federal lawsuit against the district charging that they had interfered with her right to free speech. Some consider her the triumphant party; others believe the Concerned Parents won. However, in reviewing the history of the dispute, we find a sequence of events that tore apart a school and town. A superintendent's contract was not renewed. A tenured principal was removed from her position. A curriculum was rewritten without the support or consent of educators. Teachers and parents were intimidated and fearful, and children were caught in the middle and confused by the mixed messages they received from adults. Much effort and energy were expended, and an astounding sum of more than a million dollars—money that could have been better spent on educating children—was consumed in a 6-year conflict. We perceive no winners.

RIVER HAVEN—THE TOWN, THE PEOPLE, THEIR LIVES

River Haven, the site of this study, surrounds Grandville, a small, racially diverse city of approximately 4½ square miles and a population of around 20,000. While Grandville's history goes back to the Revolutionary War, it was most prosperous in the mid-nineteenth century, when it was the site of stove foundries and plow works. In the 1970s, the exodus of a major industry to a neighboring state contributed to economic decay and eventually led to some efforts at downtown revitalization. Roads, old buildings, and sections of land in the area are named for three centuries of failed entrepreneurs and enterprises.

River Haven, the largest municipality in the county, is one of several municipalities that are divided into smaller geographic areas known as hamlets and still smaller unincorporated areas without civic titles. Waterview, the school district that serves River Haven, includes part of Grandville, all of two villages, and one town. Each of these divisions differs in geographic area, population density, and demographics. As of 1999, about 2,400 children attended the three elementary schools (the Rock Spring School, the Martin Van Buren School, and the Franklin Delano Roosevelt School), one middle school, and one high school in the Waterview school district, a geographic area that does not share the same boundaries as any one municipality.

In the last 40 years, River Haven has experienced a significant population increase. Because vacant land was available, it proved attractive to builders, who began to develop the area and draw a population from Metropolis, a large city located about 50 miles from River Haven. Many of the bedroom communities closer to the city were already well established, often with prohibitively expensive homes. River Haven, with its growing stock of attractive and more affordable homes about an hour's commute from Metropolis, served as a magnet for many well-educated, upwardly mobile white-collar families, with commuting dads and stay-at-home moms. The homes these new families occupied tended to be larger and newer than previously existing homes. The area even developed its own name, distinguishing it from the rest of the town, but with no civic significance other than a separate post office.

While River Haven offered what appeared to be the quiet exurban lifestyle sought by the newcomers, it isolated them from easy access to many of the employment, cultural, and social opportunities indigenous to life in Metropolis. River Haven is not a "town" in the conventional sense of the word, and its geography encourages isolation. It is a hilly, boulder-strewn series of subdivisions, with winding roads and small developments of large homes scattered through the woods and open tracts of land around a large partially wooded, somewhat swampy preserve. Driving through the area we could not help but notice the lack of a downtown district or a central area for shared services. Residents of River Haven must rely on cars to access shopping and other conveniences.

The nature and history of River Haven invite a reexamination of popular notions of the term *community,* a concept that remains the subject of sociological debate (Tonnies, 1887/1957; Williams, 1988). In earlier studies, community was considered more place-dependent. Communities were associated with locales and their residents, people and places that provided support and the basis for a communal identity—a standard to hold dear and maintain (Dennis, 1968). Scholars today have advanced more subtle and nuanced definitions of *community,* divorcing it from the concept of residents and place. Common interests (Scherer, 1972), networks of people (Gans, 1962), democratic problem solving (Schuler, 1995), a sense of belonging and the capacity to meet personal needs (Herek & Greene, 1995) expand the definition of *community.* The evolution of virtual communities in cyberspace illustrates this concept (Watson, 1997). The conflict involving the Rock Spring Elementary School followed this sociological pattern as it led to the formation of internal subcommunities that coalesced around the members' reactions to the controversy. Solidarities developed to assure the survival of each subcommunity and its cause.

IMPRESSIONS OF RIVER HAVEN

As we reviewed the transcripts of the interviews and our experiences visiting in River Haven over a period of 6 years, it appeared to us that the nature and history of the town and of the locale served by Rock Spring School contributed to the climate that led to the dispute that divided the community. Karen Hunter spent considerable time offering us her reflections on the school and community and their role in the battle that ensued. At one point she interjected:

Sociologists would have a field day with this, they really would. I mean the dynamic is very complex. . . . It has to do with socioeconomic status and where you live, and it's very, very important in that school district. And there are well-defined boundaries, and they happen to be around elementary schools.

She asserted that the populations of the areas surrounding the three elementary schools were very different, and the "boundaries" she alluded to referred to more than geography. To illustrate, Geri O'Brien, a former member of the school board, cited a conversation she had with a parent who was critical of the families served by Van Buren Elementary School, since these families "raised children who are truck drivers." She continued, "interesting in our community that is so lily white to have these kind of segregation issues." We believe that her comments about "segregation" refer to socioeconomic stratification and the differences in parental expectations for children growing up in white- and blue-collar homes and communities.

Karen gave us her impressions of the history of the school district and school. River Haven is a White community, and the Waterview School District, according to her, was "gerrymandered" to exclude areas of Grandville that included a minority population. She believed that the district was avoiding the city of Grandville by "creating these little enclaves . . . all these little communities sort of tossed together. I mean no identity whatsoever . . . different than . . . an identifiable town and a place and a center of town." She classified River Haven as "a sprawling suburbia" that "lacks an image of who it is." She explained that when she was hired, her predecessor at Rock Spring, Ralph Valle, had offered his impressions of the history of the town and school. Recalling conversations with Valle, Karen remembered their shared sense that the school was

born out of the woods, which were basically summer camp houses 30 to 40 years ago for very wealthy people who came up from the city. With each new development, . . . it was like the westward expansion. It was like people coming through in their covered wagons and establishing a new community.

Karen also recalled:

We as a school had to integrate these waves of people who would come with no connections to the community, with no connections with one another, and . . . all those needs were dumped on the school, and the school had to accommodate to all of them.

Repeatedly we were told that the Rock Spring School population was atypical of the two other schools in the district. Cathy Young, a Community Partner with children at Rock Spring School and an active volunteer there, told us that "this was the part of town . . . that was better educated. You know, a little bit more financially well off, and this has been the troubled part of town for some odd reason." Like many of the residents in this area, she had moved here hoping to escape life in Metropolis and believing that money, education, and status would shield her and her neighbors from the problems they were fleeing. Still, she found that what appeared to be "the good life" yielded its own troubles. She attributed some of the controversies at Rock Spring School to the "unrealistic expectations" some parents had for their children.

Some residents of River Haven were first-generation college graduates who felt they had "made it" when they were able to purchase a home there. They wanted the best for their families and worked hard to achieve these goals, but they were willing to sacrifice it all for their children. Herman Bailey, a Concerned Parent with children at Rock Spring and, at one point, a member of the board of education, told us "I think she [Karen Hunter] eventually made critical mistakes and would face people like my wife and I who would be willing to sell their house." The Baileys felt so strongly about the situation at Rock Spring School that they were willing to leave a home they loved if they were not able to create change at the school. Herman speculated that they represented the Concerned Parents:

> We are indicative of some of the people who would eventually have to fight back against some of the things we are saying happened [at the school]; well, we'll either be your best friend or your worst nightmare. We are not people who are going to roll over and play dead.

The Baileys refused to relinquish easily or quietly what they had achieved, and their determination was typical of the Concerned Parents.

An administrator associated with the Waterview School District, who preferred not to be identified in any other way, also characterized the Rock Spring community as more upwardly mobile, confirming that

> in some ways the aspirations of that segment of the school district varied somewhat from some other segments of the district. It served a population of students where it was expected when those children entered kindergarten by and large they were going to college. It [Rock Spring] was an academically demanding school, and

yet the parents wanted creative programs for the youngsters. . . .
Good enough is not good enough at Rock Spring.

He believed that the educational approach varied from school to school
in the Waterview School District "primarily because the expectations of
the parents and the communities were somewhat different." Children en-
tering Rock Spring School had parental support and more advantages,
and their parents also had higher educational and career expectations
for them.

Karen commented that the community she served as principal
"thinks it is liberal, but actually is very conservative." She believed the
public schools faced many difficulties when parents expected the school
to respond like a private school and begin a child's preparation for "Harvard . . . in kindergarten." Karen blamed some of the excessive expectations that parents had for the Rock Spring School on local realtors who
sold houses touting it "as almost a private school" and the "showcase"
school in the district. She said:

> I think people were sold a bill of goods about that particular public
> school and came really with expectations that have been and con-
> tinue to be well beyond what a small elementary school could
> handle. I think it's a very important part of the culture of that
> school that has not played out very positively.

We also noted during our interviews that many of the newcomers had
attended parochial schools when they lived in Metropolis, a phenome-
non that Karen also believed contributed to their expectations about the
school and curriculum.

We remain convinced that, for a variety of reasons, the geographic
and socioeconomic separation of the River Haven community and the
Rock Spring School contributed to the problems that arose. The school
was geographically isolated from the other elementary schools in the district, and Karen felt that the separation "made it known that you . . . have
to do your own thing out there." Geri sensed that people who lived in
the other sections of the district viewed River Haven as a "demanding,
greedy kind of neighborhood" and "tended to isolate River Haven. . . .
People set us apart to a certain extent, and I think that helped to create a
certain environment."

Another difficulty Karen identified was that the families living in the
Rock Spring district "had no preparation for the isolation of living in that
community." There are no services, shops, or institutions other than the
Rock Spring School in River Haven. Karen lamented, "I think the school

district has really missed the mark in trying to integrate that community into the school district and also supporting the Rock Spring staff in how to do that better." However, she readily admitted that while she thought she was hired to be a professional, "to bring a professional focus to the school," she found that her leadership style, personality, and even her dress may have been seen as threatening to some of the moms. Geri took a stronger stance regarding the isolation faced by women in the community: "Having a strong woman . . . in a leadership position does not reflect well on those other women who go home and start to think about themselves and what they're doing in their lives."

Members of the community offered more information that gave us insight into factors that contributed to the conflict that divided the people of River Haven. Robin Fisher, a Community Partner with a child in the Rock Spring School, was shocked to discover that in River Haven, "People don't like you because of what you believe in, . . . I find that appalling that it exists in this community. . . . This should not be a personal issue even though it has become one, and it's pitting neighbor against neighbor."

Martina Canon, a Concerned Parent with three children at Rock Spring, reflected the intensity of the passions aroused by the controversy, emphasizing the impact of these feelings on both the school and community: "Teachers stopped talking to teachers. Parents stopped talking to parents. Parents won't allow their children to play with other children. . . . It's been very uncomfortable."

In the next section of this chapter, we offer impressions of the dispute from the perspective of the Concerned Parents. We recognize that in choosing passages from transcripts and highlighting events, themes, and other elements that seem important to us, we are writing our own version of the Rock Spring story.

THE VOICES OF THE CONCERNED PARENTS

We interviewed five Concerned Parents who expressed their anger and frustration with Karen, the curriculum, and the learning environment at the Rock Spring School. All five—three women and two men, including a husband and wife—were remarkably consistent in the nature of their complaints, the language they used to describe the situations and people they opposed, and their proposed solutions to the current problems. While they might have become involved in the dispute for different reasons, they shared a common set of convictions and goals, some of which could have emerged from their association with each other and other members of the Concerned Parents group. The same issues surfaced in almost every interview, and we offer here an account of these issues from the perspectives of the Concerned Parents we interviewed.

Basic Skills

Virtually every Concerned Parent we interviewed criticized the curriculum at Rock Spring for its lack of attention to basic skills. They felt that grammar, spelling, math skills, handwriting, and basic organization and study skills were neglected. Four of the five Concerned Parents we interviewed complained about, as two mothers described it, the "substandard," "unacceptable," and "pathetic" quality of the work that came home. Hillary Roland, a mother who described herself as the product of "13 years of Catholic school," claimed that she did not want a similar "rigid" education for her own children or she would send them to private school. Still, she believed "that there are some things that they should be learning and they were not." She argued that an educational "foundation" was being sacrificed in the name of "creativity." Martina Canon cited an instance when her fifth-grade son brought home a book report rated excellent by his teacher, a Hunter supporter. She described how her husband "sat down with a red pen" and marked "30 spelling and grammatical errors." She complained to the teacher and the current principal about the "unacceptable" quality of her son's work and argued that she wanted him to "live up to his potential. Whatever that potential is . . . and he's got to be held accountable for his work." David Morgan, a father of two children in the district, summed up the complaints in these words: "They [the Concerned Parents] wanted their kids to know spelling. They wanted their kids to do calculations by rote and get the right answer. They basically wanted what other schools were giving the parents." The Concerned Parents we interviewed consistently complained about the failure of the Rock Spring staff to address basic skills.

Textbooks

All the Concerned Parents we interviewed decried the absence of textbooks and workbooks in the school. Hillary stated that some of the first rumblings in the district were heard in 1988, the year Karen returned from a summer trip to New Zealand to study whole language and received tenure. A group of fourth- and fifth-grade parents met with the principal and superintendent to communicate their displeasure about the absence of textbooks. Martina reflected all five Concerned Parents' comments on textbooks at Rock Spring: "You see Karen's thing was, anyone knows how to teach from a textbook. . . . You can have a monkey standing up in front of the classroom and they can teach from a textbook." She continued to say that she believed teachers should use "all kinds of resources" and rely on textbooks "for reference or maybe there's a particular chapter that will benefit the child from a textbook." She concluded her statements by claiming that the new teachers Karen hired had to be taught how to teach from textbooks when they were purchased under the Plan for Excellence. All the parents reiterated David's statement that once "whole language was introduced to the school, the textbooks disappeared from the scene." Herman Bailey perhaps used the strongest language, when he stated that textbooks were "outlawed in that school."

Several of these parents described as "hearsay" but repeated a story Martina told about how Karen, once she received tenure, "went into all the classrooms, and any teacher who had textbooks, she took them and literally threw them in the dump; and someone has pictures of the textbooks sitting in the dump." Herman insisted that the Concerned Parents were interested in quality textbooks, not "books from 20 years ago" but "books that could be used in correspondence with a whole-language philosophy." David repeated this wish with his insistence that they did not want "Johnny jump" textbooks for their children.

Special Needs of Children

Another frequently cited complaint, and one that ultimately led to many of the charges filed against Karen, was that children with special or individual needs were being neglected. Children of Concerned Parents in three of the four families we interviewed had experienced some kind of problem with academic and/or social development. All the parents of these children asserted that they felt frustrated by the lack of attention to their child's individual needs and the failure of the school staff to seriously address their anxiety about their children's progress. Many of them were irritated by what they said was Karen's habit of assuring them that the problems would solve themselves in time. As Anita Bailey, Herman's wife, recalled, they lost their patience with her insistence that: "It's developmental. It'll come. It'll come." Hillary criticized Karen's supporters, whose children, she claimed, were too young to have experienced problems in the school and who were benefiting from the Plan for Excellence curriculum. She said:

> They don't hear the horror stories. They don't have these people at the table saying, "I went into her five times and she told me he was

OK, and we just came back and we had him tested and he's dys-
lexic."

Discipline

The same parents decried the lack of discipline in the school. Herman
alleged that "fifth-grade children were overheard to say that no matter
what a Rock Spring child does wrong, they won't get in trouble." Hillary
claimed that Karen

> didn't believe in discipline at all. It was a free-for-all in that school.
> Children were hurting each other. The lunch room . . . because I
> was in that school a lot, was unbelievable. Kids were allowed to
> hurt each other. She did nothing about it.

All the Concerned Parents we interviewed recalled the misbehavior of a
boy, who they claimed was classified by the child study team in another
school district. David said that the child was "grabbing little girls and
grabbing them by the crotch, grabbing their butts, picking up their skirt"
and that Karen failed to seek any resolution to the problem until parents
threatened lawsuits and the child was sent to a school for emotionally
disturbed children.

Self-Esteem

Most of the Concerned Parents we interviewed complained that learning
and discipline were being sacrificed to a misguided focus on self-esteem
at Rock Spring School. Martina's comment typifies the objections: "They
are so big on self-esteem that it's to the point where the skills, the pride
in the work and the like are being sacrificed because of it, and I have a
real problem with that." She added later: "It is the parent who should be
the one building up the child's self-esteem and making him feel good
about himself." Hillary, echoing Martina's convictions, criticized the
"sloppy" quality of her son's work and complained that he "did not have
any basic skills." She described how she became the "bad guy" for compelling her child to rewrite book reports. She recalled how her son would
cry and ask "if it was OK with my teacher, why isn't it OK with you?"
She summed up her frustration: "The roles were reversed in that school.
The parents were the teachers, and the teachers at Rock Spring became
the nurturers and the people to give our children self-esteem. And that's
not the way it's supposed to work." David, speculating about self-esteem
and whole language at Rock Spring, said, "To a certain degree some chil-

dren may like this free-spirited, self-esteem type of do anything you want, and I'm not even sure what was practiced at Rock Spring was whole language the way it should be practiced." Only Herman made no mention of an inappropriate focus on self-esteem. In fact, one of the criticisms he had of his son's experience at Rock Spring was that his wife "spent quite a few years thinking something was wrong with him in terms of kids getting along with him, and a lot of what happened at Rock Spring to him was a lack of his self-esteem and other things."

Preparation for Secondary School

All these concerns about the curriculum and learning environment at Rock Spring ultimately merged in a general fear that the children were not adequately prepared for the more rigorous academic programs they would encounter in middle school and high school and for the responsibilities that awaited them in the more distant future. The Concerned Parents we interviewed were unanimous in their anxiety about Rock Spring students who were not, as Martina put it, "up to par . . . and able to move on." As Hillary asserted:

> I think they need foundations, and they need to learn the right way to do things. They have to learn because once they get to middle school, you are hit right in the face with the door. There are rules there. My child left fifth grade and she wasn't using cursive and they said, "We are taking 10 points off every time you print. We are taking 6 points off this math test because you used a pen instead of a pencil." So it was, we found a big difference once they got to middle school.

Hillary and Martina cited stories they had heard about middle school or high school teachers who could identify Rock Spring children by their lack of basic skills. Hillary claimed that the middle school teachers recognized that

> kids coming from Rock Spring did not have any research skills, did not know how to spell, did not know how to construct a sentence, did not have basic math skills. They left fifth grade carrying beans and macaroni in their pocket to figure out math problems.

Communication

Interwoven among all the complaints about curriculum and discipline was the Concerned Parents' conviction that Rock Spring School and some district-level staff—most of the teachers, the principal, and former super-intendents—failed to communicate effectively with parents. Virtually all the Concerned Parents we interviewed vociferously expressed their anger and resentment about this perceived communication breakdown. Martina implied that there was a history of administrators, even a popular one, who either soft-pedaled parental complaints or failed to address them at all. She alluded to letters of complaint parents had written to an apparently well-regarded previous superintendent, Fred Pacifico, who retired as the tide of discord was rising. David, perhaps confirming Martina's comment about Fred, characterized him as "good with people" and "one of those unique administrators who could compromise and bring people together and maintain the peace and talk his way out of many difficult situations."

While an administrator such as Fred, perceived as affable and non-confrontational, might be able to talk his way out of tight spots, Dr. John Paulsen, the superintendent who followed him, was criticized for his lack of this facility—although we wonder whether he chose not to exercise it in the face of the trouble he saw materializing. David described the district leader in this way:

> Paulsen, I don't know where he got his training from, but Paulsen just happened to rub everybody the wrong way. From his cowork-ers down to the teachers. You know he was just almost impossible to deal with. You know, he had his own style and it just didn't work.

Herman, recalling his early involvement in the Concerned Parents group, said he became active following the dismissal of a popular teacher, Veronica Manley, whom he described as "incredibly dynamic," an individual who "embodied a whole-language philosophy." He claimed he was invited to "join a group which was going to try to confront issues regarding the curriculum at Rock Spring." Paulsen was opposed to this effort, and, as Herman stated, "he got himself into a lot of other issues in the district, so he was bought out." He concluded, "Fortunately for us, he was history." The practice of politely sidestepping or consciously re-fusing to address complaints may have provided a backdrop for the antagonism toward a principal who was perceived as aloof and arrogant by many Concerned Parents.

It appeared to us that Karen began to make changes in an increasingly tense environment in which, according to the Concerned Parents, some families already felt ignored or excluded, and these conditions may have contributed to some of the resistance she encountered. All the Concerned Parents we interviewed felt that Karen failed to communicate effectively with families about a variety of matters, continuing what they perceived as a pattern of inadequate communication with school personnel, a pattern these parents claim was broken by Dorothy Stout, an administrator who was a veteran of the system and who consistently was praised by the group for her willingness to work with the community. Herman described her as "extremely approachable" and "very understanding."

Most of the Concerned Parents we interviewed expressed their confusion about whole language, and many of them wondered if some of the problems they perceived with children's performance in school could be attributed to it. Martina, speaking for herself and other parents she knew, explained that "we didn't have a clue" about what whole language was and that "we needed to be educated ourselves as to what this is." She stated that Karen began holding whole-language and mathematics workshops for families only after "repeated inquiry" from perplexed parents. David said that "every once and a while you would get something cut out of the *Times* or some professional journal. A one-page article on the glories of whole language, and that's all you'd see." Herman echoed David's convictions in almost identical language:

> When parents have brought problems or concerns to her [Karen Hunter], they were consistently told that any problems were the product of their imagination and that everything in the end would be all right. Parents were repeatedly told, "Trust me. Don't worry. Everything will work out," and so forth.

Hillary was convinced that Karen and some of the teachers regularly blamed the parents for their failure to understand what was happening in the school. She recalled an instance when a parent expressed concern for her child's progress and admitted that she did not understand whole language. She claimed that the teacher and Karen responded by sending home a book about misunderstood children and "some other piece of propaganda and something else that was placing the blame on the parent." Hillary suggested that Karen and the teacher made the parent feel ignorant, and "it got very ugly and nasty after that." David cited many instances of parents "not getting the information that [they] deserve." He claimed: "There were no tests coming back—there are no simplistic spelling or math tests. You never got to see the journals. Every time you go there and ask for something, you are told to trust me. Trust me."

David, who described himself as a former "major supporter" of Hunter, admitted that she could be "very eloquent" when she wanted to be, and he acknowledged that she often tried to address parents' concerns but became frustrated. He said, "At some point she would just give up and say 'just trust me.'" To illustrate his point, he recalled a meeting of parents when the issue of curriculum arose, and Karen put an end to the discussion—saying, "Curriculum is not a democracy"—and threatened to dissolve the parents group for the rest of the year if the topic arose again. He claimed also that the "nondiscussion mode" was enforced by the former PTA president, Geri, a friend of Karen's both in and out of school. David believed that most of the problems in Rock Spring stemmed from Karen's "bad management" practices. When asked if he thought anyone else in the district might have contributed to the growing crisis, he replied:

> Hunter's fault. Hunter's fault. Look, they're going to say. They come out with the apologetic—well, you know the board never corrected her. The superintendent should have corrected her. For Christ sake, this is a woman presumably with three years of experience, with a Ph.D. before she started the job, 10 years on the job, and now they are saying she should be helped? Either she's incompetent or she knows what she's doing. Now in my business or in any other business, if you mess up and you're a senior person, you get fired. You get tossed.

It should be noted that David also appeared to be irritated at Karen for her substitute teacher policy. She allowed no one who had children in the school to substitute teach, including David's wife, who held several teaching certifications. David addressed the issue of this policy three times during our interview with him.

Neglect and Mistreatment

Many of the complaints about lack of communication grew into more serious charges of actual neglect or mistreatment of parents. Anita Bailey believed that many parents "went on their own as a family when there was a situation, and time after time were knocked down." She added that eventually families began to meet and trade stories, because "the community is not that large and what goes around I think comes around." And the stories told by the Concerned Parents were linked by common allegations of neglect, mistreatment, and abuse. Martina asserted that what was happening to Karen had to do not with curriculum but with the dispute that resulted from parents' discovering other parents with similar problems and experiences who were willing to listen to their stories, people whose children were "in some way hurt by the action or lack of action of Karen."

Hillary was adamant in her charges that serious harm had been done to many children at Rock Spring. She referred to a "long history" of problems and insisted, "It didn't just happen because one day somebody just decided to persecute her [Karen]. Kids have been hurt. Kids have been hurt big time." She added that at first she did not believe the complaints because she had a friendly, "first-name-basis" relationship with Karen and "had been living in that school." She trusted that she could go to Karen with her concerns, which she did when she perceived that her child was not developing the skills she saw in a friend's child from a school in a neighboring district. Hillary suggested that Karen dismissed her concerns and told her that she "didn't understand the curriculum" and should not be comparing children of different sexes from separate districts. After this meeting, Hillary claimed that her relationship with Karen changed. She began to heed the warnings of parents who told her she would be "blacklisted" and the principal would "get you one way or the other." While she declined to offer details, Hillary concluded by saying:

> I won't get into it, but she did get us, big time. It sent a chill through me when she got us the way she got us. Vindictive is a good way to describe her. You do not question her. You do not cross her. If you do, you pay.

Angry Words

As we talked to the Concerned Parents and analyzed transcripts of interviews with them, we noticed that as they became more intensely involved in giving their accounts of lack of communication, neglect, and mistreatment, the language they used to describe events and individuals intensified and occasionally transformed into outright name-calling. The complaints about Karen's professional life and management style merged with issues related to her personality and gossip about her life outside the school. Furthermore, at times the dissatisfaction with Karen extended to those who supported her, both teachers and parents. As we have previously noted, we detected patterns in the content of what the Concerned Parents said about Karen and the language they used to say it. We suspect that some of these patterns emerged from ongoing association among the parents and regular discussion of issues of mutual concern.

Perhaps the most inflammatory discourse to emerge in our interviews with the Concerned Parents is what we will call the language of the cult or totalitarian leader. To a person, every Concerned Parent we interviewed used vocabulary linked to cults and totalitarianism to characterize Karen and her supporters. Describing Karen's relationship with the teachers and parents who support her, Herman stated:

> I would liken that to a group thing where a single person shapes the minds of a group of people. There is something insidious about her hold over some of the educational staff. Her influence over certain families, it's frightening. I mean any community can be a microcosm of a broader society, but I see too many examples in history where groups of people were compromised and to me it's frightening. . . . I mean, I'm not comparing it to Nazism or anything else.

Later in the interview, discussing teachers who had left Rock Spring because of Karen's management style and changes, Herman said, "They felt their professionalism was being compromised by the dogmatic doctrine espoused by Dr. Hunter." He described her style of staff supervision as "screening or surveillance of things that the teachers are doing." He concluded his discussion of her management style by comparing it to "the Israelis and the Arabs in terms of how they fight their wars, in terms of the centralized command theory versus the command in the field . . . the difference between Rommel and Eisenhower at D-Day."

Martina also decried Karen's followers, both parents and teachers, for their "cultlike behavior," which she found "very scary." She claimed that the parents who supported Karen were new to the school and were not acquainted with the history of problems, and she found it disturbing that these parents "so blindly follow behind her" and seem to care more about Karen than the children at Rock Spring. Discussing the teachers who supported Karen, Martina said:

> It was really funny, they all came out of the same cookie-cutter mold. They were all very small women. Very small, very thin. They all had like hair up to here. So any teacher who was hired who looked different from this, you know, we were all surprised, because they all looked like they were stamped from the same cookie cutter. They were all new teachers. New, young, enthusiastic, vulnerable, or moldable, or whatever the correct term would be, and they really looked up to Karen as a god to the point where a lot of

teachers seemed to follow her in a cultlike syndrome, which I find very disturbing, very scary.

Hillary commented on the fate of teachers who did not fit the mold Martina described: "She is a supreme being and you do not cross her. When teachers have crossed her, they have paid the price."

David underscored the "tension" and "undercurrents" that plagued the school just prior to Karen's suspension:

> Tremendous tension in the school throughout. I had teachers call me up and compare the school. Well, the joke in the spring of '93 was that this was Waco, River Haven. At a time when you had David Koresh up in Waco holing everyone up. And that was the tension some of the teachers felt at the school.

Throughout the interview, David reiterated that he had been a "major supporter" of Hunter, but he was disturbed by her penchant for running the school "with a control that was far beyond anything that you would expect of any business." He accused her of refusing to critically evaluate the curriculum in general and whole language in particular, which he called her "star piece." He labeled her as "a self-aggrandizing megalomaniac" who "set herself up as the only authority in education," and he implied that she was selfishly using Rock Spring School to develop a professional reputation for herself as a visionary educator. He added that Karen did anything possible to project a positive picture of the school, including, he had heard, reviewing report cards and sending them back to the teachers for editing if they failed to reflect her desired image of a model school. While David acknowledged that Karen "isn't an evil person by nature," he wanted nothing less than her expulsion from the profession. He added, "I not only want to see her out of here. I want her license lifted, and I wouldn't care if she never was in education again."

Some of the cult language the Concerned Parents used was also evident in the comments of one of the teachers who tangled with Karen. When we interviewed Marsha Bennett, a teacher who had transferred out of Rock Spring School to another school in the district, she commented on Karen's relationship with the teachers who supported their principal's vision and practices:

> I won't get into what the other teachers did to me. It became a cult. It became a sect. It became a following. And if you weren't in the chosen, what do sects do? They ostracize people. And if you weren't in their little cult and sect, you were basically ostracized.

And it all came from her. It's a very powerful thing because sects usually have a charismatic center, and she was the charismatic center.

It seemed evident to us, based on similarities in the language used by the Concerned Parents and by Marsha, that they had been communicating with each other.

We also detected in the interviews with some of the Concerned Parents a distrust of what they perceived as the "foreign" nature of Karen's brand of whole language, or simply a criticism of what they thought was her publicly funded travel to New Zealand to learn about it. Karen had received a grant for the trip. Still, Martina seemed irritated by the impression that Karen traveled "on taxpayers' money," and Hillary bemoaned her perception that Karen only "brought back half a program." While these complaints appeared to be focused primarily on anger at the waste of public resources or Karen's perceived inability to make the best use of her visit to New Zealand, Herman's complaints were more unusual. He worried about what could happen when someone takes "something from one part of the world" and expects "that it will take root." He added that while a "very rigid and narrow interpretation of whole language might work in New Zealand . . . it might work less well in River Haven, but basically it's not like the United States," a country he described as a "melting pot." He concluded his thought, saying, "I always wonder when something comes from another part of the world. You know what the relationship is? What the analogies and comparisons are?" At another point in the interview, Herman, commenting on a newspaper article about the Hunter hearings, said:

> When the Hunter hearing started, there was another article right next to it on Solzhenitsyn ends 20-year exile. And he was returning to Siberia, to Russia—and that's right next to Hunter. I guess that's just personal. I guess sometimes things just take a long time, but they come full circle.

At the risk of making the parents appear xenophobic, we still think it is important to highlight the unusual nature of some of their comments. In fact, in most of the parents' comments quoted here, there is an element of displeasure or distrust of what is perceived as foreign ideas either misinterpreted or applied out of context.

Personal Attacks

The criticism of Karen's professional life occasionally merged with situations in her personal life. Three of the Concerned Parents we interviewed either directly stated or implied that there was something suspicious about the way she was hired. When we asked Hillary how Karen had managed to make all the changes in Rock Spring School while the other schools did not seem to experience change, she said, "from what I understand, Karen Hunter got this job because her boyfriend was the assistant superintendent down in Mountain Crest and was good friends with Mr. Pacifico; he brought her up, and I don't think anyone questioned it." Martina repeated the same story:

> Karen Hunter's boyfriend, and all we know him as is "Andy Baby,"
> we don't know what his last name is, but Andy and Fred Pacifico
> were very, very good friends. Andy was the assistant superinten-
> dent of Mountain Crest. . . . Because of Andy and Fred's relation-
> ship, Karen was given the principal's position at Rock Spring
> School under the guidance of Fred Pacifico. So Fred gave her tenure
> after 3 years and let her do whatever she wanted. He gave her the
> school.

While Herman did not mention names and relationships, he offered a slightly different version of the same story, one that appears legally unlikely: "She got her tenure unusually fast. It took 2 years instead of 3 years. There was a person who was passed over, who expected to get the principalship. . . . There was some arrangement between Fred Pacifico and the assistant superintendent of Mountain Crest." An administrator associated with the Waterview School District flatly denied these speculations as nonsense and assured us that Karen was one of three candidates selected by a screening committee. The three were later interviewed by the board for the position. He added that Pacifico never knew Andy Monroe before Hunter was hired and that the two had only met a few times in social situations.

In the course of our research in the district, we visited Karen and Andy at the home they shared; and, while none of the Concerned Parents ever mentioned it directly, we continue to speculate about whether they were disturbed by the fact that a principal of a district school was living with a man. The administrator we interviewed agreed that Karen's lifestyle may have been an issue, and he added that he had also heard a rumor going around that she had had an affair with John Paulsen. While all of the Concerned Parents we met were educated, urbane people, we still suspect Karen's lifestyle may have assumed an exaggerated importance it might not have had if they had liked and respected her. But in a climate of antagonism, distrust, and rumors, it became one more juicy bit of gossip. The administrator we interviewed commented that Karen and Andy lived together and vacationed together and that, although she did not "go around advertising it, she never made a secret of it." He added that her lifestyle was her business, but all the rumors and talk did not surprise him, since "when you want to do damage to someone, you can come up with or believe what somebody else tells you because it supports what your real agenda is."

Criminal Charges

The Concerned Parents' most serious allegations amounted to criminal charges. Herman, discussing the nature of the charges against Karen, described some of them as "criminal in nature." David referred to some of the charges as "tampering with" or "falsification of" public records. He added that she had been accused of altering a school psychologist's recommendations and changing test scores. Martina and Hillary repeated these allegations. Martina said that the charges included accusations from "staff members who were instructed to change test grades, to leave paragraphs out of psychological evaluations so that children would not be classified." Hillary, when asked to account for how students who were reputedly doing poorly in language continued to achieve test scores as high as those in the other district schools, reported a somewhat different but related story:

> I know that in some tests, charts were left up in the room. In some fifth-grade classes . . . teachers were allowed to stay in their own classrooms and went back and told some children, "Why don't you look at that sentence again." I was told a story. Someone, a teacher in the building, walked by Karen Hunter's door one night and she had a pile of tests that had been taken and she had a pencil in her hand. There is no way my older child scored equivalent to the children in the other two schools. There is no way. There is absolutely no way. Children were allowed to retake tests. Our children in the fifth grade spent months preparing [for the tests]. In other schools they did not because they knew how to write an essay. Ours did not.

Since these charges of tampering with tests and reports were so serious, we asked the administrator we interviewed to comment on his impression of the validity of these charges. He claimed that he had no knowledge of any such activities and that nothing of that nature had occurred in his lengthy association with the district. When we asked him why the parents were dissatisfied with what seemed to us to be excellent test scores, scores as good as those in the other district elementary schools, he added that his knowledge of the nature of the community led him to believe that Rock Spring parents on both sides of the dispute had very high expectations of their children and that good test scores, test scores equal to those in the other district schools, would not be sufficient. He concluded: "Good enough is not good enough at Rock Spring. So if she changed test scores, she didn't do a very good job. I don't think she did, but I have no way of knowing that."

The Loss of Good Teachers and Teaching

Many of the Concerned Parents feared that the kind of education they sought for their children no longer existed at Rock Spring School. Contained within all their angry words, gossip, and personal attacks was a genuinely held fear that the curriculum and pedagogy were detrimental to learning and that the teachers the Concerned Parents perceived as outstanding were all leaving due to Karen's philosophy and management style. At least three of the Concerned Parents we interviewed alluded to good teachers leaving because, as Herman said, "their professionalism was being compromised by the dogmatic doctrine espoused by Dr. Hunter." Martina worried that the new teachers would not benefit from the "seasoning" possessed by the experienced teachers. All the Concerned Parents we interviewed bemoaned the firing of Veronica Manley, who was praised by all of them as a talented, humane teacher. Her dismissal clearly had a major impact on the Concerned Parents and appeared to exacerbate the dissatisfaction with Karen.

Karen herself recognized that firing Veronica Manley was, as she said, "politically suicidal." She explained that she decided to "bite the bullet, even knowing that it wasn't a good time to do it, even knowing that she had all the parent supporters." She added, "I just knew that potentially she was going to be damaging to what happened in the building." She reviewed her problems with Veronica, claiming that Veronica had returned to teaching after a long hiatus; and while everything was fine in her first year, she felt Veronica had "a lot to learn in those years and had been out of teaching." But as time progressed, Karen claimed Veronica purposely pitted parents against her to protect herself. She added that other teachers came to her and "started to say all kinds of things about what Veronica was doing, particularly to undermine them so that she would look good." When Veronica encountered problems with a difficult child, a boy whose behavior was described by three of the four Concerned Parents we interviewed, her situation became more problematic. Karen asserted that the trouble with the boy gave Veronica "the out for all her problems" and allowed her to blame her dismissal on complications with the child. Karen characterized the results of her decision to fire Veronica as "brutal," and she added, "I have suffered more as a result of that decision than probably anything else I've done over 10 years." In fact, it is curious that many of the charges brought against Karen related to special education; and a member of Veronica's family, who was a special education teacher in another district, had been seen visiting Rock Spring School unannounced on more than one occasion.

The Concerned Parents cited some names and estimated the numbers of teachers they claimed left the school due to their dissatisfaction with Karen's leadership; but in the course of our interviews with all the participants in this study, we were unable to determine an accurate number of teachers who had left. We were quoted estimates of anywhere from three to twenty-one teachers. We learned from a variety of reliable sources that some of the teachers had left the district and some had transferred to other schools within the district, including one, Marsha Bennett, who remained very popular with the Concerned Parents and was often lauded by them as an outstanding teacher. The administrator associated with the district commented on the perception that teachers were leaving due to Hunter. He claimed that the teachers who left did so for a variety of reasons, not just because they were dissatisfied with the principal and curriculum. However, he added, "There are different reasons why people leave, but it is absolutely true that some teachers, Marsha being one . . . who could not accept the changes that were taking place and asked to go to another building."

Marsha remained a key figure in this controversy. She lived in the community and was active in a social club with many parents of children in the school district. Karen described her as a formidable person for an administrator to handle, a woman with a "very strong personality" who "has a stance that probably reminds people of some of the teachers they had somewhere in the past." She added that Marsha was "very tough" and possessed "very high standards and she would convince parents that their children would not succeed in middle school unless they passed through the gate, through Marsha Bennett." After leaving Rock Spring, Marsha transferred to the Van Buren School and later to the Roosevelt School, and, according to Karen, "got those people over there stirred up." She characterized Marsha's behavior as unpredictable and described how she aired her concerns in "every imaginable place, grocery stores, the club." Karen concluded her discussion of Marsha by saying, "She is a very key person I think in all of what happened in the ensuing 6 years."

Karen herself accounted for eight teachers who left voluntarily during her time as principal. She openly acknowledged that five of them left because they did not support her philosophy and practices and resisted change. She claimed that one of the five was "very shaky with parents" and could not adapt to a departure from "the worksheet, workbook kind of stuff." Two others left because she refused to allow the departmentalization of the third grade. Another two, including Marsha Bennett, left because they were unhappy with her leadership. Of the remaining three teachers, one, according to Karen, left for health problems, and another left for what she thought amounted to a promotion; she was uncertain about the other but thought he left because he wanted to return to middle school teaching, although she admitted that other teachers and parents believed he left because of her. The union president, Ken Lodge, asserted that nine teachers had left Rock Spring "for basically one reason, and that was Karen Hunter." In the next chapter, we will hear the voices of the Community Partners, the parents who supported Karen.

REFERENCES

Dennis, N. (1968). The popularity of the neighbourhood community idea. In R. E Pahl (Ed.), *Readings in urban sociology* (pp. 74–92). Oxford: Pergamon.

Gans, H. (1962). *The urban villagers.* New York: Free Press.

Herek, G. M., & Greene, B. (1995). *AIDS, community and identity: The HIV epidemic and lesbians and gay men.* Thousand Oaks, CA: Sage.

Scherer, J. (1972). *Contemporary community: Sociological illusion or reality?* London: Tavistock.

Schuler, D. (1995). *New community networks: Wired for change.* London: Addison-Wesley.

Tonnies, F. (1957). *Gemeinschaft und Gesellschaft [Community and society].* (C. P. Loomis, ed. & trans.). New York: HarperCollins. (Original work published 1887)

Watson, N. (1997). Why we argue about virtual community. In S. Jones (Ed.), *Virtual culture* (pp. 102–132). London: Sage.

Williams, R. (1988). *Keywords.* London: Fontana.

The Season of Light, the Season of Darkness: A School and Curriculum Are Condemned

JAMES K. DALY, PATRICIA L. SCHALL, & ROSEMARY W. SKEELE

It is not mere cynicism on my part to say that perhaps the majority of the American public wants its children to spend school time doing false busy-work. It is a way of putting children on hold, in suspended animation, so that they will remain as we made them, as if children *belong* to parents. It took me years of work in curriculum development to understand that schools are as negative as they are because they are doing just what much of the public thinks it wants (and what many teachers themselves do not believe in).

—James Moffett, *Storm in the Mountains*

VOICES OF THE COMMUNITY PARTNERS

The parents who supported Karen Hunter and the changes she was making at Rock Spring School offer a rather different perspective on the school and curriculum. We interviewed six of these parents, including a woman who was a member of the Waterview Board of Education at the time we began our research. Two of the six parents were teachers, in either special education or elementary education, in neighboring school districts. The parents who supported Karen and her efforts at Rock Spring School at one point called themselves the Community Partners in Education. For the convenience of writing, we will refer to them as the Community Partners. These parents, many of whom offered a more multidimensional portrait of the school, still tell a contrasting story about life

40

at Rock Spring, and we present their perspective on how "the best of times" became "the worst of times." As is the case with the Concerned Parents, we had a difficult time determining how many people actually comprised the Community Partners group. Emily Mason, a founding member of the group and a mother who "religiously attended board meetings," estimated the numbers of active Community Partners at 40 or 50. Like the Concerned Parents, the Community Partners shared a common set of convictions and addressed a similar agenda of issues regarding the controversy in which they were embroiled. These convictions and issues surfaced in all our interviews with them, and we offer here a description of these concerns, told from their perspective, and retold by us as we analyzed transcripts and selected illustrative quotes.

A Visionary School

Within a remarkably short period of time, approximately 1 year, the Concerned Parents convinced Dorothy Stout, the acting superintendent of schools, most members of the board of education, and many residents of River Haven that the whole-language curriculum developed by Karen and her cohort of teachers was flawed and inadequate. They felt that it needed to be replaced with what amounted to a hastily developed, back-to-basics curriculum they called the Plan for Excellence, which we will describe in greater detail later in this chapter. All the Community Partners we interviewed regretted that a beautiful school had been ruined by the controversy. While all of them also agreed that there was room for revision and improvement, they still used positive language to describe Rock Spring School, prior to the Plan for Excellence and Hunter's suspension. Among the words they chose were: *award-winning, child-centered, visionary, caring, supportive, helpful, inspiring.* They praised the curriculum, the principal, the teachers, and the overall environment of the school.

Zena Brant, a mother of three children, two at Rock Spring at the time of the interview, characterized the school as "so child-centered and crackling with excitement." Emily, whose child had attended a preschool special education program, intentionally placed her son in Rock Spring, even though he could have attended special education classes in another school in the district. She claimed it was a difficult decision that she never regretted because of the "peer interaction . . . from constantly talking and learning from kids in a way that I think you can't learn by being talked at by a teacher in a large group" and because "the teachers were very helpful," allowing children to "read books at their own levels rather than having to read a basal reader that some of them couldn't read at all and some of them are bored by." Reflecting on her own education, she said she wished she had had a chance to learn in the way her son was learning, since she remembered "sitting at a desk and falling asleep over a text-book." She added that there was almost no need for gifted programs, since "each child was so enriched within the classroom that everyone was going at their own pace. The bright kids were never bored. The kids that needed a little extra help and the kids in the middle were happy." She referred to a report written by a consultant from a local university who praised Rock Spring School for its Best Practice approach to teaching and learning. Cathy Young, a mother of three children, two of whom attended Rock Spring at the time of the interview, praised the school because the kids enjoyed learning, something she had missed in her own education. She said, "The kids at Rock Spring didn't just go to school, come home, and stop. It always seemed as though there was something for them to learn or something for them to do that reinforced what they had learned." Cathy, who had a preschooler at the time of the interview, commented on the naturally paced approach to learning in the school:

> What reinforced it in my mind was having another child. Watching Billy be ready to do things made so much more sense than forcing it down his throat. I mean you would never try to force a child to walk. You would never try to force a child to speak, you know. So why do we then take kids and force them to do ditto sheets on commas that mean absolutely nothing to them? Why do we take kids and force them, you know, to do math sheets that were division and multiplication when they are not ready for it?

The Community Partners consistently extolled the skill and human-ity of the Rock Spring teachers and principal. Cathy characterized the teachers as "risk takers" who were "willing to go that extra mile to do something different or improve." Zena complimented the teachers on their "advanced degrees" and "continuing education." She believed that they looked to Karen for leadership and found her "absolutely wonder-ful and inspiring," an educator with "vision." Terry Kosc, a Rock Spring mother and a teacher in a neighboring school district, agreed, saying, "I personally believe that it's the teachers that make a school, and they have fabulous teachers in this school." She applauded programs that Karen and her teachers initiated, such as Expo Night, "where you walk through the school and the kids' work lines the walls. All the books they have written and everything. It is so beautiful and it is such a celebration." Also commenting on children's projects displayed on Expo Night, Emily said:

They had incorporated so many different aspects of their education into a simple art project . . . they made clay animals, they put them in their habitats. They did research on where they came from and so incorporated geography, biology, history, and all these into one project, and you could just see how much they learned.

Terry, when asked by a colleague why the Waterview Board of Education would not offer parents choice of district elementary schools as a way to resolve the dispute, speculated that they refused to institute choice because, "they are afraid that everyone is going to want to come to Rock Spring, which I think is going to happen. . . . I even think the Concerned Parents would want their kids to be at Rock Spring . . . [and] I think they are afraid of what that would say for their other schools and their other teachers." Terry also was personally grateful to Karen because she had seen her through a troubled time in her life. She said:

I had just been through a divorce, and my kids were having difficulty adjusting to a new school and a new life, and . . . I went to the teacher first. She spoke to Dr. Hunter and I kind of knew Dr. Hunter. So I spoke to her myself, and immediately he [her son] was seeing a social worker on a weekly basis until things seemed to be straightening out.

Robin Fisher, a mother and a special education teacher in a nearby district, respected Karen's knowledge of the children in her school: "I must say that she knew each and every child very well. She knew their strengths. She knew their weaknesses. I think she had a very good feeling for where they were going and where they were at." She worried that children were no longer "the focus in this school district at all," and she wondered how what she considered a well-educated community could not see the value in the "process of learning" that was characteristic of Rock Spring School under Karen's leadership. Zena summarized the Community Partners' feelings about the school: "There was a vision at the school. There was direction."

The Climate for Change

While Rock Spring appeared to be a visionary school for some parents, others found it strange and unfamiliar, like nothing they had known when they were growing up. Several of the Community Partners believed that the Concerned Parents were fearful of the changes they saw in their school and in schools in general. Cynthia Fields, a Rock Spring parent, contended, "I believe that . . . there are certain people that get very nervous if their kids aren't learning the same way we all learned 30 years ago." Emily described the resistance to the curriculum and practices at Rock Spring as "going against the current trend in education all across the country and wanting to go backward in time." She was certain that the program at Rock Spring was "sound in terms of professionals that we have spoken to." Terry, from her own experience in the classroom, commented on the internal and external impact on change:

> Karen came in with this sort of drastic change, and I am a teacher and I know in the school [where] I teach not everybody wants this; and . . . people leave with bitter feelings. And I know sometimes when people are doing different successful things, bitter feelings come out of that, if you are not ready to take the risk or even believe in doing that. So I think that it wasn't only parents. I think it was fed by teachers. Other teachers in the district.

Geri was saddened because the conflict "created a climate that doesn't welcome change." She thought that educators needed support and patience as they made change:

> If they make a mistake, you pick them up and dust them off. You give them good wishes and you try again. I don't know how you bring about change if it has to be perfect the first time out. And I don't know how you encourage people to be pioneers or to be adventuresome or any of those things that you need to be innovative in this kind of atmosphere.

Cathy aptly stressed the downside of attempting change in the face of resistance: "You know it's hard to think that you would want to embrace something new or do something new when you know the community will probably jump you for it."

Children with Problems

While some of the parental resistance might have come from the fear of change and unfamiliar classroom scenes, the Community Partners also attributed the dissatisfaction to other, more personal reasons. Some of the Community Partners believed that the parents who were most active in protesting curriculum and ousting the principal were people who had children experiencing problems in school. Zena said she knew parents from Rock Spring and other schools as well who found it "easier to blame the school" than look for potential problems in their children. Emily, whose own child had no problems in school, speculated that perhaps "some people did have tremendous problems with the curriculum" but added that their "personal problems" were "not my business." Robin attributed the dissatisfaction to "parents whose children were not achieving what they thought or perceived their child should be achieving." She thought it was easy for the parents to blame whole language for their children's problems, yet, in actuality, their difficulties demanded more than simple cause-and-effect explanations. Cathy, who acknowledged a problem with her own son's proficiency in reading that she thought was resolved by the third grade, maintained that the Concerned Parents felt that their children were always fine but "knew that there were kids at Rock Spring who were not getting it, as they say." She did add, though, that Herman Bailey's children had some problems and that the school staff "wanted to do more for his kids, and he wouldn't allow it." She found the situation ironic, since he was one of the parents who complained most about Karen's failure to address the needs of children who required special education.

Our interviews uncovered a number of the Concerned Parents—including Martina, Herman, and Hillary—who acknowledged that their children were having problems in school, difficulties that they believed resulted from the philosophy and methods that were dominant at Rock Spring. Martina, however, strongly contradicted the Community Partner parents' assumption that it was only parents of children with problems who complained. She said, "So another misnomer is that the changes at Rock Spring were made [by] the parents whose children had difficulties." She described an active member of the Concerned Parents whose "daughters are extremely bright" and "excel" in school. Terry interpreted the Concerned Parents' worries in another light. She believed that the complaints emerged not just from parents of children with problems, but from parents who thought "there wasn't enough competition, and that their children . . . were being nurtured too much. If that's possible—that kids can be nurtured too much."

Robin highlighted the issue of parental expectations for their children when she claimed that some of the dissatisfaction originated with "parents whose children were not achieving what they thought or perceived their child should be achieving." Cathy agreed with Robin:

> Some parents have very unreal expectations for their children. So I feel those people would not be happy with anything. I mean, I'm sure if it was a totally traditional program and their kids were drilled and had to write the times tables 25 times each night and

had to do spelling words 40 times each night . . . I don't think they would be happy either, but I don't think they would be happy because they are really not sure what they want for their children. But they know they have to expect the best for them. . . . But I think some people expect if their kids can't be CEOs or if their kids can't be, you know, great surgeons and so forth . . . then their children have failed them, and I think at Rock Spring some parents have pushed for classification of their children . . . because then it explains the limitations of their children.

The Myth of Poor Performance in Middle School and High School

Many of the Community Partners we spoke to dismissed as a myth the Concerned Parents' accusations that Rock Spring children failed to perform well in middle school and high school. A few of the Community Partners we interviewed already had children in the district secondary schools, and they criticized the Concerned Parents for spreading rumors about children's level of achievement. Terry, who had a child in middle school at the time of the interview, commented that her son was excelling in all his subjects and declared:

> And all I can say from my own experience, and I have heard rumors that the middle school people say this and that. But from my own experience . . . my son is in middle school. He is an A+ student when it comes to reading and writing.

While she acknowledged that she was speaking from her own experience with her son's success, she nonetheless maintained that many parents dreaded their children's transition into the upper elementary and middle school grades. She blamed the Concerned Parents for spreading and amplifying this fear, adding that "this is the propaganda that is being passed around." Zena explained how she tried to assuage the fears of parents who were convinced that their children would do poorly in middle school: "I begged them to call the middle school. Please don't just listen to what people say. Call them and ask them if the Rock Spring kids are doing badly; but they prefer to just gossip." She described her own child's success in middle school:

> I have a 12-year-old son who can write like crazy. I mean he writes so beautifully and his study skills are good and he does well in school and he does well at math and he loves to learn and he had

the most wonderful experience at Rock Spring. You show me that something is wrong with that before you go dismantling that.

Zena demanded "proof that anything was wrong" and was frustrated because, in her experience, "there was never any" hard evidence of problems, only rumors.

Karen blamed Marsha and some of the other teachers who had left Rock Spring for scaring parents into thinking their children were ill prepared for upper elementary grades, middle school, and high school. She claimed they made "disparaging remarks about the preparation of kids in the primary grades," which created problems for the teachers who taught at that level, mostly the newer teachers, and "fed a lot of anxiety in the community." Terry, reflecting on all the factions and hearsay, worried about "how my kids are going to come out of all of this" when they hear all the rumors circulating and see their parents in conflict with teachers, principals, and other parents. Like the Concerned Parents, the Community Partners feared for the welfare of their children.

Mismanagement of Resources and Personnel

The Community Partners all decried what they viewed as the board of education's and administration's use of irregular management practices and the irresponsible stewardship of public funds. Hearing these complaints, we felt we were listening to the flip side of the record of dissatisfaction with Karen, her management style, and her educational practices. Many Community Partners partially blamed Karen's problems on a lack of support from her superiors. Robin wondered whether Karen got off to a bad start at Rock Spring because she lacked the kind of professional support a new and less experienced administrator needed. She speculated about whether Karen had a reliable mentor she could turn to for support and advice. She added, "When you're a teacher, you look to your administrator for help and training, and where was this help? Where was this concern, or was she just left on her own?" Zena believed that Fred Pacifico supported Karen but doubted that "it was the kind of support she needed in terms of him getting involved in reaching out to these parents and trying to make them understand. I think he just kind of pushed them aside." After the ill-fated Paulsen was fired for failing to meet the demands of Concerned Parents, Dorothy, according to Zena, "had an agreeable ear for them in the administration, and they lobbied to have her made superintendent." With that accomplished, "the stuff hit the fan," according to Zena, and "everything really went crazy, and I understand that she [Dorothy] was very supportive of this campaign to

get rid of Dr. Hunter and very encouraging, you know." Emily also accused the board and Dorothy of failing to take an appropriate leadership
role as the crisis escalated. She declared:

> They never should have acceded to a special-interest group, which
> is what happened; and they are paying for it now. We all are paying
> for it. Most of all Karen is paying for it, but the children are paying
> for it. The taxpayers are paying for it. The parents who are fighting
> a lawsuit are paying for it. It's a shambles, but the board and the
> leadership are the problems here. It's not whole language. . . . I
> think this is a management problem.

Emily concluded that she objected to "the process" the administration
and board used to suppress and suspend Karen. She declared, "What
I'm taking issue with is the way the board and the administration have
handled this from the very beginning." Both Emily and Cathy called for
nothing short of hiring a new superintendent, an individual, as Cathy
said, "who believes in education, because I don't really get the feeling
that the one we have does . . . and I think she is so firmly entrenched with
the group that supports her that I don't think that she could be objective."
It is evident from these comments that the Community Partners were
convinced that Karen had inadequate professional support; and, to com-
pound the problem, they believed that the board and superintendent collaborated with one faction of parents to hasten her demise.

Interwoven with what amounted to accusations of administrative
malpractice were numerous protests about irresponsible stewardship of
public money. At one point in the dispute, a local newspaper carried stories about parents who were keeping track of the district's legal expenses
by displaying on a busy local road "thermometer" signs depicting the
rising costs of litigating the Hunter case. Geri groaned, "We have more
attorneys than we know what to do with." Terry regretted that money
spent on lawyers could have been put to good use in the schools. She
grumbled, "People are concerned about the money and what is being
spent here. My kid's class has one crappy computer. I mean we're talking
about a pretty affluent school district—one computer—that just doesn't
do the trick for me." Emily echoed Terry's remarks:

> We haven't even voted on the fund . . . for computer technology,
> and they are spending hundreds of thousands of dollars on the
> case against Karen. It's a big waste of all kinds of resources, when
> we should really be concentrating on getting the best educational
> program for our children.

Zena found it irrational that the district had to pay a publisher to reprint copies of an old textbook in the march back to basics that began with the imposition of the Plan for Excellence. Throughout our interviews with the Community Partners, we heard a chorus of complaints that resounded with regrets about wasted time, talent, and treasure.

Cooperation and Mediation as Alternatives

Five of the six Community Partners we interviewed wondered why the board of education had never attempted to use a more collaborative approach to problem solving or turn to formal mediation to settle the dispute with Karen. Robin thought it was sad that teachers and their principal had to be attacked in an attempt to rectify problems: "We could have worked together. Mutual respect . . . instead of what has come." Zena concluded, "I don't think you can remedy anything as long as people are being sued," and she recognized that the terms of mediation would differ depending on whether or not Karen returned to the school. Cynthia suggested that the board of education should "get a little help in learning to have peace." Emily recalled the Community Partners meeting with the board of education and documenting their suggestions in a letter to them and Dorothy. She explained:

> We met with the board and we offered many solutions. We offered mediation as one. We offered small-group discussions. Afterwards we wrote them up in a letter to her [Stout] . . . and shortly thereafter they pressed forward with a lawsuit against Cathy and Ron. So at that point talking to the district became very difficult, if not impossible.

She regretted that the Community Partners thereafter had to spend their time attending hearings and raising money to offset legal fees accrued fighting the gag order and numerous appeals that the board of education had filed against Cathy and Ron (discussed in the next section). She remained convinced that

> we could have worked together with mediators and so forth, facilitators to try to get some medium; and we could have perhaps kept the better parts of the program and worked on the weaker parts. . . . No school system is ever perfect, and it's really a shame that all of us had to put our energies this year into fighting lawsuits.

Geri never believed the board of education had any intention to resolve the dispute short of firing Karen. She said:

> I have had a feeling that there has been a whole lot of scheming going on. So I don't know always what is real and what is not real. I don't know how real our intent was to mediate . . . but at least there has been some discussion.

We think it is fair to say that most of the Community Partners viewed the failure to talk, mediate, and compromise as a waste of valuable time, effort, and resources, resulting in more squandering of monetary and human capital.

Silencing and Intimidation of Parents

All the Community Partners berated the Concerned Parents and school officials for silencing and intimidating Karen and her supporters. Every Community Partner we interviewed cited as the most extreme example of silencing the imposition of an injunction, commonly referred to as a "gag order," on Cathy Young and Ron Cluney, another parent and Community Partner, and an injunction against Karen and her attorney. Attorneys for the board of education went to court and claimed that Karen and the leaders of the Community Partners should be prevented from meeting and discussing the charges against her, since they involved minors who might be hurt if their names were revealed to the community. The Concerned Parents and their supporters on the board of education accused the Community Partners of discussing the charges against Karen and trying to determine the names of the families involved in the charges so that, as Zena claimed, "they could terrorize them . . . harass them and try to withdraw their charges." Cynthia described these accusations as "ludicrous," since the charges against Karen already had been published, without family names, in a newspaper, and "anyone can go to the microfilm and get a copy of it and see it for themselves." The courts consistently overturned these injunctions, but for 2 years the board's attorney requested them or appealed the court's decisions to dismiss them. Many of the Community Partners felt that their right to free speech was violated by the board's repeated attempts to secure these injunctions and its later decision to close a portion of the hearings for the same reasons.

Karen eventually released the charges against her, with the family names deleted. Zena effectively summarized the imposition and impact of the injunction: "They picked two people that they saw as the titular heads of the movement and trumped up charges against them and put a gag order against them, trying to scare everyone away." Describing the fear that resulted from the gag order, Zena, quoting a remark from Cathy and Ron's attorney, said:

> You have 10 birds on a telephone wire and you shoot two of them. What happens to the others? People got very scared, and I basically got very frustrated and I wasn't scared. I was angry and I was like, I don't care, let them come after me . . . that's when I started my newsletter, and it's interesting because this injunction just keeps getting thrown out of court and thrown out of court, but the board keeps renewing it. And so basically it's fear that you are going to have to end up having to hire yourself a lawyer and your home could end up being in jeopardy. . . . So the effect was devastating. The teachers were shut up and the parents were shut up. Some of them kept talking, but they were very afraid.

The newsletter Zena published to give voice to the silenced parents led to additional problems for her and some of her friends and acquaintances, and her newsletter eventually was answered by a newsletter published by the Concerned Parents. She mused, "I know that I have been snubbed by people I knew before. I guess when you publish a newsletter, you have got to take your licks." Zena was convinced that the gag order amounted to censorship. She added, "They say that the injunction against the parents is to stop the parents from distributing the charges. Which you couldn't miss the mark further. I wish they would start treating it as a censorship case." Cathy and Ron eventually recovered their legal fees by winning a lawsuit they filed against the board of education.

Zena was outraged at the hostile behavior and vitriol that she perceived were leveled at the Community Partners. She saw similarities between the strategies and rhetoric of the Christian Coalition and the Concerned Parents, who she claimed accused the Community Partners of "being communists" because they did not support using textbooks. Her strongest allegations came at the end of our interview, when we asked her if she thought what was transpiring amounted to censorship. She declared:

> They have gone after parents and free speech. . . . These people have this gag order against them because they had meetings in their house. And this is the McCarthy era, and myself and other people have offered to come forward and say, "Let us testify about what happened at those meetings at Ms. Young's house. Put the cuffs on. Ask me about it. Take me to court. Have your attorney ask

me about it. Have someone ask me about it." They won't do it. They just won't do it. . . . I think that's what makes this dangerous . . . the censorship issue.

We know that the talk of McCarthyism had made the rounds of the River Haven neighborhoods, since many of the Concerned Parents called it to our attention and labeled the charges ridiculous.

Intimidation and Silencing of Teachers

All the Community Partners we interviewed worried about the intimidation and silencing of the educators at Rock Spring School. Cathy thought the protests of Karen's supporters "went in one ear and out the other" when they met with members of the board of education. She was convinced that the board met with these Rock Spring teachers in small groups of three members one night and four the next to avoid making the meetings open to the public. Terry mentioned the changes that resulted from the Plan for Excellence, a back-to-basics curriculum imposed by the acting superintendent and board of education that reflected the demands of the Concerned Parents. She feared that because of the Plan for Excellence "teachers were teaching in a way that they were not committed to teach." She was disgusted by the "arm twisting" the administration and board applied to Karen and the teachers. She said it was "heartbreaking and frustrating" to see Karen "standing up there with overheads presenting her Plan of Excellence," a plan forced on her by parents, Dorothy Stout, and a board of education who "were sitting up there with these big smiles on their faces . . . sitting in the audience, and there was no way that Dr. Hunter developed this Plan for Excellence."

The Community Partners all perceived that the teachers' union had played favorites in the Rock Spring crisis, siding with the veteran teachers and abandoning those who supported Karen. As a teacher, Terry detected a familiar pattern in the union's actions, with Ken Lodge, the union leader, supporting the veteran teachers who opposed Karen. She believed the union was "supporting everyone else" but the teachers who liked Karen and shared her vision. Commenting on the isolation of these teachers, Terry added, "These teachers are like on an island, a desert island, with nowhere to turn." Cathy claimed the union viewed Karen's teacher supporters as "the poor relation." She criticized the union leader for abandoning the teachers who supported Karen in favor of "eight teachers who left Rock Spring because of this horrible creature." She suggested that he had warned them "that you'll all be brought up basically the same way

Karen is" and stated that she thought his warning silenced the teachers. She concluded, "So in that way, the censorship is there, too." Cathy also remained convinced that the union had abdicated its responsibility to support teachers as developers of curriculum when it failed to protest the writing and imposition of the Plan for Excellence. She thought that "because of their [the union's] feelings for Karen" and because she had hurt the teachers who left Rock Spring, "so, you know, screw her. Let her have a Plan for Excellence." Zena described the teachers as "intimidated and so frightened that they won't talk to anyone." While she said she couldn't "prove it," she remained convinced that the teachers could have been "told to be quiet" and "threatened by the administration, by the board, and by the teachers' union." Geri, who was on the board of education at the time, confirmed the parents' suspicions, saying, "There are teachers at the school who have been told by their union president that if they were not quiet about all this, if they were not good little teachers, there would be additional [charges and dismissals] in the school."

Many of the Community Partners accused Karen's detractors of having vendettas against her. Terry thought the whole dispute originated with "a vendetta against Karen Hunter." She described a phone call she received from Herman Bailey, who attempted to "manipulate" her into believing that Karen had "committed the acts that they now charge her with." As a teacher, she challenged what he was saying:

> He was really unable to answer my questions, because I could not understand how a principal has all this power to make these decisions he said she was making . . . he kept turning it around and trying to manipulate me. I know education and that's what bothered me about that phone [call]. I am sure there are many parents who don't know how kids are classified and don't know the channels you go through; and I could see people saying "yeah, yeah" and going along with what he was saying. And that scared the hell out of me.

At the end of our interview with her, Terry castigated the people she thought were falsely accusing Karen:

> It is very scary the politics that are going on, and it's scary that someone as lovely as Karen is being attacked this way. And I see her in my professional writing group. . . . Such a smart person! So it concerns me that she has to go through this and this can happen in this world.

She concluded that "this has been a vindictive attack, that Karen is a scapegoat for something completely different." Cynthia also attributed Karen's problems to "some people [who] have personal vendettas against her." Zena underscored Cynthia's comments: "There was absolutely nothing that would appease these people. And when they did change the curriculum, these people were still not happy . . . until Karen Hunter was out of that school. It was very personal with them." Cathy summarized her feelings about Karen's fate in the strongest language: "All I have done in this thing is gone with what I believe in my heart, and I believe that what they are doing to Karen in my heart is nothing short of a lynching."

The Need for Improved Communication

The only area in which we found any congruence between the complaints of the Concerned Parents and the Community Partners was on the subject of communication. Like the Concerned Parents, five of the six Community Partners we interviewed saw a need for improved communication between the school staff and the parents. Cynthia, echoing the language of Martina and Hillary, said:

> Manipulatives [were used] for math, no worksheets, and some parents were very antsy about that. And Dr. Hunter's answers, very soft-spoken lady, she would pat them on the back and say, "Don't worry, everything will be OK." And even from my perspective—loving the program, my son just flourished—I knew that there were very bright people in this community, and nobody wants a pat on the back and to hear it'll be OK. They wanted facts. They wanted studies that showed whole language works. And if there was any fault of Dr. Hunter's, I believe that people would agree that she didn't market the program.

Robin referred to "a lack of communication with parents" and noted that she, a teacher with a master's degree in special education, "could see that not enough information was coming home about what the kids were doing in the classroom." She initially became more involved in the school because "very few papers came home." While she praised the many "masterful" teachers at the school, she also thought that some of the teachers were new and inexperienced and did not yet recognize that they had to "reach each and every child," something she admitted was difficult for new teachers, a skill she said "comes with experience." She was convinced that the "lack of communication and the work that came home led parents to believe that their child was not being taught those skills."

Robin was satisfied that she had expressed her concerns to Karen and the teachers and that they "did work hard to rectify these concerns" and "they had improved their communication tactics."

Terry, also speaking as a parent and teacher, found herself in agreement with one item on the Concerned Parents' agenda. She blamed the central administration for some tactical errors they made at certain points. While she understood the argument about the flawed nature of standardized tests and the limitations of scores, she thought it was a mistake not to release the Rock Spring scores, which she described as "as good at least if not better" than the scores in the other elementary schools. The reluctance to release the scores, needless to say, made the parents suspicious; and their worry about test scores was compounded by an inadequate understanding of a new and unfamiliar approach to teaching and learning at Rock Spring. Robin, sympathetic to the fears of the Concerned Parents, said in their defense:

> As a teacher, I know that you have to be clear with parents, especially when you want to try something new and different. I think that was their big mistake here. . . . As a teacher I was thrilled, but I've been reading about it and studying about it and seeing it work for myself . . . if they had been educated [about the approaches to learning], perhaps it would have been different.

While Robin sympathized with the Concerned Parents' fears, she nevertheless continued to describe them as "set in their ways," and she wondered if their understanding of how children learn was permeable to new information.

Zena also sympathized with parents who did not have enough information and experience to understand a holistic approach to learning. She surmised:

> I think that number one there was a new system of learning in whole language that people didn't understand, and it was very difficult for some parents to understand what their children were doing in school when they didn't have a piece of paper showing them. . . . They needed something . . . the child could bring home and that they could see what the child was doing. . . . I think that when you sit down and read to your child or you go to the supermarket with your child and you look at the price of things or what time it is or you talk to your children and you see what they know and what they are learning, but these people apparently needed something more tangible . . . and I don't think it was presented to

them. There should have been an effort to educate people . . . this is how we are teaching your children. You don't have ditto sheets coming home, but this is how you can interact with your child and understand what your child is learning.

Later in the interview, Zena concluded, "When you do innovate, you have to educate people along the way. It's scary. New things are scary to people." Cathy hinted that the district's efforts to educate parents about new school endeavors were inadequate: "When they want you to know something in this district, they do a little song and dance, and they present, and that's how you hear about it, and then it disappears." Geri regretted the absence of sufficient dialogue between the school staff and parents: "So there was dialogue. Obviously it wasn't enough. Obviously." With parents on both sides of the fence claiming that communication between school and home was inadequate, it would appear that this was an issue that needed to be addressed.

More Angry Words

In talking to the Community Partners and in analyzing transcripts of our interviews with them, we noticed that they, like the Concerned Parents, used their own version of angry words when giving accounts of the Rock Spring debacle. Their language was steeped in imagery of disaster, disease, and mob rule. As we said previously, many of the parents spoke of vendettas against Karen. Terry described the Concerned Parents' tactics as "a vindictive attack" that made Karen "a scapegoat for something completely different." She seemed shocked at the behavior she was seeing, and she exclaimed in language reminiscent of mob attacks, "I think they just get each other going. You know, cheer each other on, and I don't know. I don't know where—because to me it's all so evil. I can't imagine where such evil comes from." At two points in our interview, Zena accused the Concerned Parents of resorting to McCarthyism: "They have given anonymous interviews to newspaper reporters where they accused us of being communists because we don't want books." Later she declared, "This is the McCarthy era." She alleged that they were "out for blood." Emily was infuriated at the board of education for the "atrocities" they committed against Karen. Cathy used perhaps the strongest language of all when she described the actions against Karen as "nothing short of a lynching."

The Community Partners also used disease and disaster imagery to describe the events that transpired during the community conflict. Attempting to describe how the trouble originated, Zena invoked visions of illness: "Because it's like a cancer. I couldn't tell you when the first cell started growing. I think though I don't remember a time when it didn't exist." At two points in our interview, Terry also used terminology evocative of profanity and natural disasters to describe the escalation of the attacks on Karen and the curriculum. She labeled whole language the "W word" and called the conflict a "tornado." She later claimed that the board of education was being "egged on" by parents who refused to be pacified by any efforts or explanations, and she described the board's failure to act in the face of the growing conflict as "definitely allowing this volcano to erupt" since it served their real purpose: getting rid of Karen. In the next section of this study, we describe the culmination of the community unrest in the demise of the principal and curriculum.

A SCHOOL AND CURRICULUM ARE CONDEMNED

What was perhaps the death knell for the curriculum and Karen's tenure at Rock Spring sounded during a midsummer meeting in July 1992. John Paulsen had been fired. The board appointed Dorothy Stout acting superintendent. Karen was vacationing in Europe. Most teachers were on summer break and unavailable. A group of Concerned Parents organized a semipublic display of children's work from the three elementary schools. Martina, Hillary, and Herman were instrumental in collecting and displaying the work. They also alluded to unnamed others who had participated in this effort, including, Hillary claimed, seven "certified teachers" from other school districts. All three Concerned Parents offered similar accounts of how the meeting evolved and what transpired that evening.

Hillary proudly admitted that she, at a board of education meeting, "stood up and demanded that they give us the opportunity to show them the differences between the three elementary schools." Martina reinforced this account, saying, "Then at one board meeting Hillary stood up and said, 'Why don't you please let us show you what we are talking about? You obviously don't understand the depth of the problem.'" At that point, the board agreed to allow them to set up the display of the children's work at the Rock Spring School.

Hillary, Martina, and Herman described their method of gathering, displaying, and inviting people to view the children's work. All three accounts of the event are basically the same. Martina said:

> So we canvassed Franklin D. Roosevelt, we canvassed Martin Van Buren, and we gathered work from the first through fifth grade for all the schools. . . . I remember we went to Rock Spring School and

we set up the work by grade level, and each board member and the [assistant] superintendent, Dorothy Stout, came by. They sat at each station and . . . we showed them.

She went on to describe the differences she noticed in work all the elementary school children at a given grade level do, such as butterfly reports. She claimed that "there was no substance there" and no attention to form in the Rock Spring papers. She also claimed that the Concerned Parents who organized the display used children's journals to demonstrate that they were not making any progress in spelling, since they could point to words they continued to spell wrong throughout the year. She added that she thought the board members were "shocked" since they finally "saw it in black and white."

Hillary explained her role in gathering the work:

And all I did was . . . contact people from Martin Van Buren and Franklin Delano Roosevelt and ask them for their children's work. We divided it up by grade level, and some of us took first grade and went over and kept a pile for Rock Spring. Kept a pile for Van Buren and kept a pile for Franklin D. . . . We combined all that information, and the board of ed then gave us a night and said OK. . . . At that point, the work was set up on the stage of Rock Spring School. We packed the auditorium with parents from all three schools. They came in and the board member and the [assistant] superintendent came in. They came up on stage and we allotted a certain amount of time and had the tables set up . . . that was when they saw we were not crazy people. That it was not just that we felt she had gone overboard in the teaching methodology.

When we questioned Hillary about the gathering and display of materials, asking if parents on both sides of the dispute were allowed to contribute their children's work, she added somewhat cautiously:

It was just us. We were trying to prove a point, and we just used our children's work. People may say that that is not fair. It may not be fair, but we had concerns. We didn't go and say give me the top work at Van Buren, give me the top work at Franklin D. Roosevelt. We did not; we just randomly [asked] people we knew and asked them for work.

Herman described the gathering and display of work in similar terms. He added, however, that some of the work had been collected from par-

ents who had signed the two petitions the Concerned Parents had circulated. He read the statements on both petitions, one signed by, he
claimed, 310 Rock Spring parents who were calling for "supplemental
tools to enhance the existing program." The second petition, which Herman claimed was signed by 182 people, stated:

> We the parents of Franklin Delano Roosevelt and Martin Van Buren
> are satisfied with our respective school programs and the existing
> teaching methodologies. Furthermore, we agree with parents of
> Rock Spring that all three of the elementary schools should have
> uniform teaching methods in the schools and we intend to support
> them in this pursuit.

He explained how the work that was collected from the three schools,
with the children's names and other identifying information "taped out,"
was displayed at tables where "people were assigned to sit . . . and it was
sort of a round robin where board members would sit at a table for a time
and then move to another."

David, a Concerned Parent who did not appear to be as actively involved in organizing the display at the meeting, referred us to Herman
for further information and offered his comments on what happened.
His account concurs with the basic outline of events cited by the other
Concerned Parents, and he also added what appears to be a disclaimer
in his remarks. He said, "the board was allowed to look at the work of
various students versus the work of other school students, but the public
wasn't. What was shown, how it was shown, whether it was biased,
whether it was prejudiced is beyond me saying because I didn't see the
materials either."

Karen's impression of the meeting, a secondhand account, since she
was in Europe, supports what the others said about the events that transpired. She believed it was "strategically planned," and she described it
as "an unbelievable night" and a "charade." She added that "the press
got to see it" and "the school board members got up to see it." She stated
that they displayed work the teachers had returned at the end of the year:

> And did a really fabulous job making it very scientific looking, and
> the parents were there explaining it to all of the board members
> who would come up to see it and the press, but no one in the audi-
> ence. No one, no other parents, and no staff members could see it.

She characterized the meeting as "a highly unusual thing" and remarked
that Herman Bailey stood up and delivered a report he had written on

the curriculum of Rock Spring School. She concluded, "He was their educational expert who had done an analysis of the program . . . about what was wrong with the program at Rock Spring School."

Ken Lodge, the union president and the only currently employed teacher we were able to interview, offered his perceptions on the meeting. He believed the furor about the Rock Spring children's work that led to the meeting erupted when a fifth-grade spelling test was published in a local newspaper. He claimed parents were infuriated with the simple words on the test, which made them wonder what the students at Rock Spring were accomplishing compared to the students at the other two schools. He stated, "Just the board was able to make the tour around the stage, and apparently, from what I gather, it was quite dramatic and shocking in terms of the quality or lack of in the comparison of the three schools." When we asked him if any teachers were involved in the display, he added, "It was July and . . . there weren't a lot of people in the audience, so I don't think it was very well publicized, or there'd be a lot more people there." When we asked if any teachers had complained about the meeting and what took place, he added:

> Well, sure. They had no part in the selection. I mean, how would you feel? It was done, it was done. I mean there was no crying about it. After the fact—start railing—then you become, well, that sounds like you're guilty and you should have done something beforehand so you could, you know, that's not right. You just let that sleeping dog lie is best.

According to Ken, the teachers' union neither took a stand nor was requested to take a stand on this issue.

Geri O'Brien, who was a newly elected board member at this time, stated she was the only board member who "expressed concern" about the display, which she said was viewed by the board members and the media. Describing the display, she commented:

> In the Franklin Delano Roosevelt children's work . . . clear attention is paid to presentation and to correction and to lists and to spelling and to worksheets and to workbooks, and the work displayed by the Rock Spring children showed just the opposite, showed incomplete notebooks, notebooks with doodling, notebooks with scribbles. I mean my own kids had notebooks like that. . . . What are we comparing, and how do you compare children like that? And how can you take the works out of context . . . to what purpose? But I

didn't realize what damage it could do. . . . This was very carefully organized.

Robin offered a version of what happened at the meeting that agreed with Geri's account:

The works of the children from the district were presented to the board on stage. And in my opinion, it was a very poor presentation because the work was taken totally out of context. No one knew whose work was chosen. Was it a fair comparison of students at the same ability level? Was the work a rough copy? Was it a finalized draft? . . . No teachers were allowed to see the work or parents told, you know, how they selected these . . . it was almost a hush-hush thing that no one really knew.

Cathy concurred with Geri and Robin:

What they did was take samples of kids' work from the three elementary schools and some of the writing journals from the kids at Rock Spring. Now the only people who were allowed to view it were the board of education and the press. No parents were allowed to see it; no teachers were allowed to see it. No one was allowed to see it. Quite honestly it could have been a kid in [the gifted and talented program] compared with a kid in special ed. It could have been the rough drafts, or as Jennie [my daughter] calls them, her sloppy copies . . . and another kid's finished work. No one ever knew.

All the parents who commented on the meeting believed that it led to the Plan for Excellence.

THE IMPLEMENTATION OF THE PLAN FOR EXCELLENCE

All the Community Partners regretted the changes in Rock Spring School due to the institution of the Plan for Excellence and the ultimate suspension of Karen Hunter; they were also saddened by what they perceived as a diminution of all that was special about the school and the loss of morale among the teachers. The Plan for Excellence focused on language arts, mathematics, assessment, and communications. For each of these elements, there were grade-level goals and objectives initiated to meet the demands of the Concerned Parents. Characterized by some as a basic skills curriculum, the Plan for Excellence included such familiar components as grammar, spelling, vocabulary, handwriting, phonics and decoding, "computational skills for the achievement of speed and accuracy," worksheets, and math standards activities. The assessment goal demanded more tests, quizzes, standardized tests, sharing of test scores with parents, homework corrected with explanations, increased reporting of individual and building results (children's performance), and identification and evaluation of at-risk students. The final goal addressed communications between parents and the school. It included curriculum statements, communication and coordination between grade levels, monthly classroom newsletters, school newsletters, school visitations, and parent surveys. It should be noted that the Plan for Excellence as initially developed retained some aspects of the previous curriculum such as portfolios and writing conferences.

Reflecting on these curricular changes, Zena complained that the Concerned Parents "dismantled" the school and "intimidated the teachers, and they have taken away the principal and sued the parents to the point where it is a very depressing place." Cynthia remained concerned that the escalation of the dispute and the coverage in the media convinced people "that Rock Spring is a place that has a sign across it that says CONDEMNED." She remained hopeful that, despite all the problems, the children at Rock Spring "are still getting a very good education and there still are wonderful things going on in that school and the teachers are still wonderful." Karen compared the changed atmosphere at the school to death and mourning. She said:

> There was just tremendous angst about what we were giving up. How we would have to do things. A recognition that we had to do it. But it was a death. It was a loss. It was a grieving process [for] what we had worked so hard to build.

The Community Partners criticized the Plan for Excellence, suggesting that the process of instituting the plan was questionable and that its impact on the school was devastating. Five of the Community Partners we interviewed agreed that the Plan for Excellence was forced on the teachers and principal and that it became more of a means to oust Karen Hunter than a systematic attempt at curriculum reform. Cathy described the Plan for Excellence as a last-minute effort by a group of parents, Karen, and whatever teachers could be gathered in July. According to her, they developed the plan in 1 week—writing, revising, and rehearsing for a public presentation.

Many of the parents on both sides of the dispute offered a similar version of the development of the plan. David, now a Concerned Parent but formerly a friend of Karen's, confirmed that they had had a week to prepare the plan and that he had been instrumental in writing it and helping Karen present it. He claimed that it was an attempt to give the Concerned Parents what they wanted: improved communication, textbooks, basic skills, and increased accountability. He characterized the plan as "a quick, ad hoc attempt to save Karen or get her out of a particular jam." He claimed it was not "a major overhaul of the system" and that it "went through a whole series of minor corrections back and forth between Hunter and Stout." Geri recalled David reassuring Karen, saying,

> Oh, you're gonna give them a little bit of what they want, and you're gonna make it look good. You're gonna use graphics and you're gonna use a slide show, and, Karen, you're gonna get dressed in a power suit and you're gonna go forward and you're gonna convince everyone that this is what they want.

Herman described the plan as a grassroots, democratic effort to bring about reform. Hillary called it "an improved program" that addressed what she and the other Concerned Parents saw as voids in their children's education. Martina had a positive impression of the plan and worried that it might be "in danger" if Karen ever returned to the school.

Karen generally concurred with the parents' version of the development of the Plan for Excellence. She agreed that David named and wrote much of the plan in cooperation with her and the few teachers and supportive parents she could round up in the middle of the summer. She added that she received from Dorothy a "directive in writing that I had to respond to" based on the letter of complaint the Concerned Parents had written and read at a spring PTA meeting and Herman Bailey's curriculum report, which he presented at the July meeting that featured the display of the children's work.

Karen had just returned from a vacation in Europe and found a letter summoning her to the acting superintendent's office the next day, where she met with Dorothy, the high school principal, and the principal of one of the other elementary schools. The other two principals claimed they were present at the meeting to offer her help. Within a week's time, she had to address, point by point, all the complaints in the Concerned Parents' letter and the Bailey report and, by September, develop an action plan to respond to these issues. Summarizing the frustration she felt in confronting this task, she said:

This was the edict. If I didn't do it, I would be insubordinate, and that was going to start up a whole host of things. I would say that was more difficult than anything I had to deal with. . . . Those moments of having to abandon 7 years of work in an instant, without teacher input, and having to be the author of what was supposed to be my plan. Dorothy didn't care if I had any teacher input at all. . . . It was awful! But thank God I had a supportive staff, and we met in houses in the evening. I think we worked around the clock for as many days as we had.

When Karen presented the Plan for Excellence to Dorothy, it was rejected for many reasons. She was asked to "tighten it even more" within the next week or week and a half prior to a public presentation of the plan. Karen suspected that the board of education was pressuring Stout to

fix the problem. . . . Give those parents what they want, and then they'll get off our back. And there was a lot of magical thinking, especially by Dorothy, that if we just give them what they want, this whole thing will just go away.

Karen believed that Dorothy would not have been motivated to pressure for the changes independently. She said, "Dorothy wasn't going to take this thing on in the first week [of her superintendency] and set it up in this kind of way. It just wouldn't have fit her style." She was convinced that the board was agitating to "get that Karen in line . . . she's gone far too much off the deep end with her staff. Just pull her in and we can give them everything . . . a little of this and a little of that." Karen remained frustrated and perplexed by this outlook. She added, "To us . . . it was a philosophy we were giving up. It didn't even matter about the practices so much." Unhappily, she put aside the philosophical stance they had adopted and responded to the administration's pressure to meet the parents' demands: "So we brought back all the textbooks. We bought them from a used book company we had sold them to, and we embarked on the most unbelievable task of setting up this program for September that you could possibly imagine."

Geri, from her perspective as a board member when the Plan for Excellence was implemented, without offering confidential details, said that the plan was discussed, reviewed, and minimally revised in an executive session prior to presenting it at a public session. The very next day, seemingly without board approval, Dorothy visited Karen at the school and continued to make revisions in the plan. Geri said:

Suddenly there were time sequences to evaluations and standardized testing. I mean it was a lot more specific than it had been. . . . I
was concerned that there was just no time . . . for any board action
or decision, and Karen was being told [by Dorothy] that this was
what she had to present to the public and the board. . . . And so I
confronted Dr. Stout at that point and told her that I expected that
the plan that was approved by the board was the plan that was presented to the board, and [I] actually went and sat in the lobby of
the district office the following morning while Dr. Stout was meeting with Dr. Hunter.

Geri concluded that the board of education had never actually voted on
the Plan for Excellence but that they wanted the public to believe that
there was unanimous support for the changes it represented. She wrote
a memo to the board making it clear that she did not support the Plan
for Excellence, although she hoped that it "would bring some peace to
Rock Spring School."

While the parents on both sides of the dispute agreed on the time
line and process of instituting the plan, they often disagreed about the
purpose and the results. Cathy said, "They were hoping beyond all hope
that this Plan for Excellence would be the straw that broke her [Hunter's]
back and she'd leave." She added:

It was Karen being told on Monday, I want something to help Rock
Spring by next Monday. And it was her scrambling with teachers. . . . It was like call all the teachers, see who we can drag in, see
what we can put together. It was parents helping out. We sat at
Rock Spring and Karen did like rough runs of presenting this to an
audience and the board of education. Because you know what was
going on. It was horrible. It was disgusting. And looking back on it,
nothing was ever proved that what was being done was wrong,
and yet you had to change.

Geri was particularly harsh in her assessment of the plan:

I am very concerned about the Plan for Excellence that we imposed
on the school because I just categorize that as a piece of garbage.
That's all it is. It had no background. It had no research. It had no
rhyme or reason. It had no evaluation. It had no plan for assessment, and it's never been reevaluated by the board of education,
even though the plan itself calls for that to happen.

Emily reinforced Geri's comments and the assertions of the other Community Partners:

> They essentially forced Karen to come up with the Plan for Excellence and apparently she was made to do this within a week's time . . . [and] from what I believe and what I hear from other parents . . . she complied with it and worked with this plan as well as she could. She did not try to make it fail or anything else. She tried to make it as successful as she could. Unfortunately, we don't know how successful that plan has been because it has never been revisited by the board of education. There is this plan in place and there is no assessment for it in the plan . . . and that is the way, unfortunately, our district handles . . . the educational reform it takes on.

While the Plan for Excellence might not have been evaluated, it was both formally and informally monitored. Based on testimony from parents on both sides of the dispute and Karen, it appeared that the acting superintendent and parents were observing and reporting on life in Rock Spring School. Karen commented that Dorothy was "a physical presence" in the school. She said, "She would drop in unexpectedly, unannounced." She believed Dorothy never

> really knew how to observe in classrooms. So to even go and monitor this would have been hard other than the superficial things. She was thrilled that all the textbooks were lined up . . . on the desks of one of the third-grade classrooms before the kids arrived.

However, Karen added that there was really no need for Dorothy to actually monitor what was going on in the school, since she could read the required monthly reports, and, more significantly, she regularly received informal feedback from the Concerned Parents. She asserted:

> She [Dorothy] didn't have to worry . . . because the parents were there monitoring it, and I know full well they were telling her everything that was going on in every classroom because that was their function. At that point, they had been empowered to kind of make sure it happened.

Geri confirmed and extended Karen's account of the monitoring. She claimed Karen "was being hounded, and that's the only word that really fits, by the central administration with these kind of visits by the central office army police to make sure she was softened up for the changes."

She alluded to a meeting she encountered by chance when she visited the board office while working on a committee project. She recalled:

> I walked into a meeting that was being held by a group of Concerned Parents and Debbie Marshall [the school psychologist], and I didn't realize at the time that the meeting had started an hour or two earlier . . . and I asked Dr. Stout about it afterward, because it was clear that all these parents were there and they had all kinds of workbooks and children's works with them again . . . and she told me that there were terrible problems at Rock Spring School with Karen, and she was preparing a memo for the board. And it was very serious. I asked her, how can you be preparing a memo for the board? When are you going to discuss it with Dr. Hunter?

Geri remarked that there would have been no time to discuss the matter with Karen, since the meeting with the parents took place on a Thursday and the memo would be sent in a packet to the board on Friday; and Dorothy knew that Karen was out of the district that day. Geri believed that her intervention led to an "abbreviated" memo that alluded simply to very serious parent complaints. After the board meeting, the district went, as Geri put it, "from parent meeting to attorney," and Karen was accused of, among other things, harassing a parent for speaking up at board meetings and threatening to "take action against her children."

One of the ironic side effects of the implementation of the Plan for Excellence, Geri claimed, was that the plan was "being implemented too well." She alleged that parents began to complain that "the teachers were going overboard, and there was too much homework, too much spelling." She added that she worried that Rock Spring School would become an "educational embarrassment" because "the other districts were moving forward with whole language, with assessments, with portfolios, with all kinds of innovative things, and we were moving back to standardized tests and back to basics." It was at that point when, "Almost simultaneously, it just seems too connected to me, suddenly the memos no longer talked about the program at Rock Spring School. They talked about the problem with Dr. Hunter."

A Community Divided

All the Community Partners repeated their concerns about the impact of the dispute on the children and families. Zena complained:

It's so terrible in the school because people are pulling their kids off of ball teams because they don't want them playing with Johnny from that street . . . I have seen such maliciousness . . . I spoke to a woman on a block where a lot of Concerned Parents live, and when she moved in they just swarmed on her and then found out that she had become friends with some people who were not on their side, and now she can barely go to the bus stop. It's just the degree of anger and it's amazing!

She added that "our kids are being affected daily." Emily, although she reaffirmed her belief in public schools, said she might consider sending her child to private school if things did not improve at Rock Spring. Terry wondered about the impact the dispute would have on children "raised in a totally divided community . . . knowing who's on this side and who is on that side. And knowing that their mommy doesn't like their teacher, but they are confused because they like their teacher." Terry was also anxious about the disappearance from the children's lives of a principal they liked. She said:

I don't think anyone has sat down and thought of the effect of all of this—Dr. Hunter disappeared out of their lives totally. She was not allowed to go . . . to the Rock Spring Fair. Not allowed to set foot on the property, go to graduation. Nothing.

Zena went on to say that many parents had to explain to their children what had happened to Dr. Hunter, and she was angry that Dorothy later "came in and lied to them," assuring them that "'We have a special job for Dr. Hunter in the central office,' and our kids sat there and said, 'What are you talking about?' because our kids knew what was going on." Terry concluded, "But it's just incredible to me that this can happen, but what it really comes down to, to me, is how are my kids going to come out of all of this?" Terry's concern was one shared by parents on both sides of the Rock Spring fence.

As we analyzed the transcripts of interviews with all the parents, we were amazed by the dichotomy between the descriptions of Rock Spring School. With the exception of perhaps one or two areas where we saw some congruence, which we will discuss further, it struck us that the parents were describing two different schools and two different principals. Terry thought these vastly different perspectives on the school and principal represented one of the biggest barriers to solving the dispute. She remarked, "The barrier I guess is that you're talking about people's hearts and just what people believe in. . . . You can't knock your head against a wall and tell people something they don't believe in."

Zena, when she first moved into the community, had heard stories about problems at Rock Spring. She recalled being told that students were not taught spelling and phonics, never had tests, and were not held responsible for the quality of their work. She called the principal to ask her about these issues, and Karen reassured her that what she had heard was not true and added, "I wish more parents would call me and ask me instead of just getting their information at the bus stop." And as time went on, Zena said that she recognized that skills were being taught. After that, she would tell critics, "I feel like our kids go to different schools because I don't really see this in the school," and she urged them to call the school for more information, rather than relying on gossip.

While the Concerned Parents had a vastly different perspective on what had gone wrong in their school and community, they, too, were frustrated by the divisions that resulted. It was clear to us that neither the Concerned Parents nor the Community Partners enjoyed the discord that tainted their community. Martina, although she blamed Karen for all the problems, nevertheless articulately expressed the feelings of many families on both sides of the dispute:

> It's going to take so long to heal that what's going to happen until we are healed? Are we ever gonna heal? I don't know. I don't know. I mean I still talk in terms of us and them, so I know other people do, too. For myself, I know that I personally have not stopped talking to anybody, have not in any way prevented my children from playing with anybody who they choose to play with, but I know that this is going on. And this disturbs me terribly that people are so shallow or, I don't know, so inhumane to their neighbor. I just don't know how people can act this way.

In the final chapter of Part I, we offer a more detailed analysis of the events in the River Haven conflict, and we consider the impact of these events on the future of the people and schools in the town.

REFERENCE

Moffett, J. (1988). *Storm in the mountains: A case study of censorship, conflict, and consciousness.* Carbondale: Southern Illinois University Press.

The Spring of Hope, the Winter of Despair: Analysis

JAMES K. DALY, PATRICIA L. SCHALL, & ROSEMARY W. SKEELE

When a local public school is lost to incompetence, indifference, or despair, it should be an occasion for mourning, for it is the loss of a particular site of possibility. When public education itself is threatened, as it seems to be threatened now—by cynicism and retreat, by the cold rapture of the market, by thin measure and the loss of civic imagination—when this happens, we need to assemble what the classroom can teach us, articulate what we come to know, speak it loudly, hold it fast to the heart.

—Mike Rose, *Possible Lives*

THE RIVER HAVEN CRISIS surfaced with a series of small complaints, tiny pebbles tossed in a pond, rippling out in ever-widening circles of conflict. A parent here or there worried about her child's spelling or was frustrated by an articulate young principal's habit of dismissing her concerns about her child's "sloppy copy" homework or inability to recite the multiplication tables by heart, the way she recalled she was able to do when she was the child's age. A group of veteran teachers, perhaps feeling marginalized or disrespected by young, johnny-come-lately teachers and a neophyte principal exploring the rhetoric and practice of progressive education, transferred to another school in the district, one with a strong union presence. From there, they relied on the power of the union and their privileged veteran status to incite in the schools and community resistance to the principal and the changes she and her cohort group were making. An established superintendent, a man who gave his principals considerable latitude to run their schools as they wished and who has been described as a "people person," was replaced by a man who was characterized by many individuals we interviewed as a feckless district leader who only seemed to exacerbate existing problems by mishandling parents who came to him with complaints. While he supposedly was hired to bring change, he ironically helped hasten a kind of change that ultimately benefited no one. The administrator who replaced him after he was fired was a veteran of the school system and a native to the area. Anxious to please and to stem the rising tide of discontent, she used and was used by one of the factions in the dispute. The board of education, among whose members were several lawyers, sidestepped any efforts to mediate the dispute and rushed head-on into expensive and extensive litigation. Throughout the course of the River Haven crisis, many participants in the dispute ignored formal policies and procedures, engaging in irregular and, at times, what we perceive as unethical behavior as they marched on from loathing to litigation in their effort to be heard and to have their way. In our estimation, this use and abuse of power escalated into a textbook case on how not to make change. In this final chapter of our case study, we attempt to analyze some key elements that make this case a significant one for stakeholders in education. The elements we have chosen to highlight are the political characteristics of public schools in general and the Rock Spring School in particular, the process by which change was made at Rock Spring School, the role and nature of the change agents and those who resisted change, and the impact of these actions on the eventual outcomes of this conflict.

THE POLITICS OF PUBLIC EDUCATION

As we analyze the Rock Spring controversy, we find it necessary to briefly consider the politics of public education. The public schools are political institutions designed and maintained to perpetuate specific political objectives. The success of the Common School Movement, effectively led by Horace Mann, was a fusion of the liberal Protestant Whig beliefs with the Prussian model of schooling (Tozer, Viola, & Senese, 1995). This model borrowed from an undemocratic European state seemed an appropriate vehicle for inculcating in the young a set of common values drawn from Christianity. Schools were not seen as a democratic arena embracing multiple cultural and pluralistic perspectives. Schools were and are political institutions. As such, curriculum is a political tool used to help achieve school objectives. Since schools are state supported, those objectives are significantly determined by the state. As the political agenda of decision makers shifts, so, too, do school objectives and curricula.

It is critical for all those integrally involved in the public schools to understand this political base for operating. T. Jackson Lears (1985) expands on C. Wright Mills's concept of a "power elite" by focusing on hegemony theory, maintaining that a small minority of citizens control political and economic institutions that shape civic beliefs, values, and behavior. Schools and curricula play important roles in socializing people into accepting the status quo. Exploring the negative and positive aspects of such a hegemony is best left to others, but considering it provides additional evidence of the political nature of schools. The growing recognition of the existence and the power of the hidden curriculum (Giroux, 1983) presents compelling indication of the political nature of schools.

Recognition of the nature of schools better equips those in the schools to deal with those from outside the schools armed with an agenda for change. Calls for change in schools are often more than they appear to be on the surface. Since the way we teach and what we teach both often carry messages and learnings far beyond what we anticipate, any attempts to modify, restrict, or eliminate content and practice must be recognized as potentially political actions as well as educational reforms. Awareness of the political nature of the school also permits people to recognize the power relationships involved in resolving challenges to pedagogy and content. The hierarchical model of power and decision making in schools, adopted from industrial management theories, places the ability to enact school change in the hands of a few. Those seeking change need not represent or even seek to win majority support for their views.

Throughout our years of interviews, site visits, and reading of hundreds of pages of newspaper articles, documents, and transcripts, it became evident to us that the themes of power and politics in the public schools permeated all aspects of the Rock Spring controversy. The Concerned Parents saw each conflict, from initial disagreements to communitywide issues, as a power struggle; and, often by bypassing people and established policies, they effectively reached and engaged those centers of power in the community, on the board of education, and in the schools and used them to accomplish their objectives.

Karen, the teachers who supported her, and the Community Partners, especially early in the dispute, seemed not to have considered the conflict beyond what it appeared to be on the surface: some unhappy parents, displeased with the progress made by their children. This lack of awareness seemed evident to us the first time we met them, when Karen and a group of parents spoke about their experiences on a panel at a conference for educators. They seemed surprised when many members of the audience at their session inquired about the possibility that right-wing political and religious groups might be at work in River Haven. It appeared that they had not considered this scenario or, if they had, had dismissed it.

It seemed to us that it was not until the turmoil escalated that the Community Partners began to see the similarities between their problems and more widespread national conflicts. As it turned out, we never found any hard evidence of any national groups at work, but we still think it would have been politically astute for the Community Partners to consider that since the West Virginia textbook wars of the 1970s there has been an aggressive targeting of books, materials, and methods in public schools. The current climate permits, perhaps even encourages, personal issues to escalate and prevail. The national press has been consistent in its reporting of alleged school failures, including various programs often referred to as whole language. As we previously stated, the discourse that critics of the Rock Spring School used echoed the language of censorship heard in other districts throughout the country (Jones, 1993–1994). It appears that no one took notice until it was too late.

Our observations suggest that as opponents mounted ever-expanding campaigns, the initial political naiveté of the Rock Spring teachers, the principal, and the Community Partners prohibited them from acting in more effective ways. In fact, there were parents and even teachers on both sides of the dispute who seemed unclear about the existence of policies and procedures in place for parents and community members to challenge materials or practices. It appears that the Concerned Parents ambushed the Community Partners, taking them by surprise with their calculated strategies, well-established links to sources of power in the Waterview district office and the board of education, and bold actions. The Community Partners even admitted to us that they were stunned by the speed and effectiveness with which the Concerned Parents moved every item on their agenda. They themselves realized that they had no plans in place until it was too late to respond to the Concerned Parents' successful strategies for modifying the curriculum, eliminating practices, and suspending a principal who still enjoyed the support of many of her staff.

THE PROCESS OF CHANGE

Geri O'Brien complained about River Haven's approach to change:

> We are probably a conservative school district. We don't embrace change. It comes somewhat difficult for us, and so we could stand

for some introspection in each of our schools. . . . But what worries
me is the way . . . we go about change. Over the past couple of
years . . . it's very surgical.

Our own research and experience in education leads us to believe Geri
is on target. Anyone who has been around education in any capacity for
a number of years recognizes how vulnerable schools are to a taste-and-
toss approach to new ideas and practices. How often have we heard
teachers say, "I tried it and it didn't work, so I gave it up."

No educator would argue that change is easy or fast, nor should it
be. Cuban (1984) somewhat humorously suggests that the *Guinness Book
of World Records* should include a page on failed school reforms. In his
extensive study of change in American classrooms, he found that classroom practices were "uncommonly stable at all levels of schooling touch-
ing students of diverse abilities and different settings over many decades
despite extensive teacher education" (p. 2). He offered for consideration
a number of explanations for the resistance to classroom change, including the basic nature of schools, which reflects the larger society's inclination toward uniformity and obedience; the organizational structure of
schools as well as the "architecture" of classrooms and the schoolday; and
the inclination of teachers to teach the way they themselves were taught.
A number of the parents and educators in River Haven insisted that the
district and community wanted change and hired administrators they
thought would bring a fresh perspective on teaching and learning; yet it
appeared to us that none of them could articulate exactly what they
wanted, nor did they have a workable plan of action for bringing about
change. The absence of a plan and expectations created problems for
those who were entrusted with the responsibility for change.

THE ROLE OF THE UNION AND VETERAN TEACHERS

The atmosphere in the building Karen entered as a new principal may
have militated against change. She recalled that, when she was hired, she
replaced Ralph Valle, a principal who was popular with the staff, a man
who had risen through the faculty ranks to become principal. Karen commented that "there was a big social life around the school. Lots of parties,
I'm told, and they would socialize and go out to dinners." Marsha Bennett confirmed this contention when she described the atmosphere of
Rock Spring School when she first arrived: "Many people socialized after school. It was a very warm feeling. I was greeted . . . and had a very
good feeling when I came into the building." Ralph, however, also had a

reputation for having a bad temper, and Karen commented that "when he made a decision, that's the way it was." She speculated that this administrative style had a negative impact on relations with the community. For reasons she claimed she did not fully understand, Karen surmised that the last few years of Ralph's tenure as principal were acrimonious, leading to what she described as a "rupture between the staff and the parent community" that "somehow got centered with Ralph in the middle of all that." She added, "So when I came on board, I think there was some relief that they [the staff] were out from under some of that with the community, and for a while I guess things were sort of status quo." She concluded by commenting on the irony in the way events played themselves out, saying, "I felt the doors to the community were closed when I arrived. Which is probably not too different from what they are today, so we have come full circle."

It appeared that a strong union faction, a corps of powerful veteran teachers, and a group of new teachers who shared or, by virtue of their nontenured status, could have felt compelled to share Karen's vision proved to be a volatile mix at Rock Spring School. Karen cited as a detriment to change in her early years as principal the strong union presence in the building:

> The teacher union leadership was all in that building . . . so there was a little bit of the "what-are-you-going-to-do-to-us attitude" simply because the union president was there. Several of the officers, the executive board. We were the hotbed of all the union activities . . . it became, well, maybe we can challenge that young principal and set her straight about her job and what's our job kind of thing.

Furthermore, as her problems unfolded, Karen's main source of support came from her contacts with some of the teachers at Rock Spring, who appeared to be powerless in the face of all the trouble, and from some area college faculty who wrote letters of support for her, letters that she appreciated but that had no impact.

In addition to the union leaders, there were powerful veteran teachers, such as Marsha Bennett, who resented Karen and felt disenfranchised by all the changes she was making. Marsha accused her of being rigid and administering the school with a "her way or no way" management style. She claimed that when Karen received tenure, she really began to make changes, adding that she kept all the decision-making power to herself, contrary to what Marsha believed was the current trend in education. She said:

[Karen had] a tremendous desire to keep power in one—in her. . . .
It had to come from her. Although she tried to make it seem as
though it came from the teachers, it came from her.

Karen and Marsha disagreed on many issues, including the use of textbooks, the importance of process and product in learning, and departmentalization versus self-contained classrooms. Even though Marsha believed she incorporated many elements of whole language in her
teaching, she still felt alienated by what she called Karen's proselytizing
and the "cultlike" adoration of the new teachers who supported her. Both
Karen and Marsha agreed that these philosophical differences led to a
split in the staff. The union initiated and ultimately dropped an academic
freedom grievance that Marsha and other established teachers filed
against Karen, and eventually many of the union leaders and other veteran teachers moved to another school. Many of the faculty who remained and who supported Karen were less experienced teachers and
more vulnerable to pressure from colleagues and the community.

As a new principal, Karen found that her desire to analyze the curriculum and examine practice proved challenging, mainly because of
the established culture of experienced teachers who were invested in the
teaching and learning philosophies and structures they felt worked for
them. She explained:

We had added pressure of the intermediate teachers who didn't
want to be involved in any change process, who were very committed to departmentalization and standards and homework and
books and really came from a perspective that these [the students]
are empty vessels we're just pouring in.

After Karen received tenure, she began making the kinds of changes that
threatened the familiar routines in the school. Believing in the benefits of
self-contained classrooms, she was determined to have the Rock Spring
teachers integrate all subjects in one classroom rather than specializing
in two or three curricular areas. With the help of the fourth-grade teachers, she ended the departmentalization that they had informally established at that grade level; and, believing that this change was successful,
she set her sights on ending a similar arrangement in the fifth grade.
She contended that the resistance of the veteran upper-grade teachers,
including Marsha Bennett, was significant. Eventually the upper elementary teachers filed a grievance against her, largely because she had informed them of the change back to self-contained classrooms by memo.
Marsha, who told us she habitually applied for transfers out of the build-

ing, described how distressed she was to receive this notification by memo:

> I went to the teachers' room and . . . in the mailbox there was an envelope. . . . I opened it and it said, "You will not teach departmental math. You will be teaching whole language. . . . If you need any help with this, contact me." And that was her idea of consensus and compromise. Her way or no way.

After receiving the memo, Marsha revealed that she called the superintendent's office and pleaded, "I don't care where I go, what I teach, but you've got to get me out of here." Karen described the reaction to her decision to end departmentalization at the fifth grade:

> Well, the roof fell in. Within 24 hours they were just basically marching on me, marching on the school, marching on Fred Pacifico's office, marching on the school board. We had a very difficult meeting with all of the parents. I guess the attack came from the fourth-grade parents moving to the fifth grade. Marsha Bennett's strategy was to get her current parents to . . . scare the fourth-grade parents [telling them what] they weren't going to get once this change was implemented, and she was very effective in raising the anxiety of so many people and has continued to do so. We had this large group meeting and everybody in the world came and I was the person who had to talk about why the changes were necessary. We started out with about 80 people. It was the most incredible moment of my career. I think of just facing what were very angry people and having to explain what this was about. They asked for a second meeting and by that meeting we had about 40 people and by the third meeting, if there was one, we were down to about 20. And Marsha then put in voluntary transfers to other schools in the district.

Marsha seemed to be pivotal in much of what occurred. She had come to Rock Spring because the district had closed a small elementary school, the Garfield School. She had been teaching for only 1 year at Rock Spring when the principal retired and Karen arrived. To complicate Marsha's feelings, a good friend from Garfield had applied and was rejected for the job now filled by Karen. Speaking of the teachers who transferred from Garfield, Karen recalled, "They were very angry." We suspect that Marsha must have been an irritant to Karen in many ways. Because Marsha was respected and established in the district, she felt free to cut deals for herself. For example, when she first arrived at Rock Spring, she was dissatisfied with her second-grade assignment. She went over Karen's head and contacted the superintendent directly, arranging to take a fifth-grade job that opened because, she claimed, Karen had "pressed the teacher so hard that he left." She acknowledged that Karen probably resented the way this change was handled.

A number of the veteran teachers were unhappy because their colleague from Garfield was passed over for a woman they viewed as a wet-behind-the-ears upstart from out of town. Ken stated:

> There was not a good atmosphere to work in . . . these were . . . veteran teachers that had many more years in the classroom than Karen Hunter ever had. She was a music teacher apparently with a minimal amount of classroom education and experience, and she was teaching these veteran people who were very well respected in the district and certainly very well respected at their local schools. She was telling them basically her view of education was the best way and only way.

Ken informed us that the veteran teachers had asked the union to intervene on their behalf:

> We had a grievance—we were going to file a grievance against her . . . for calling a meeting . . . in too short a period of time [without enough] notice. . . . We were going to file a grievance against her for . . . calling a meeting on a Friday before vacation. . . . We were going to file several grievances of an anticontractual nature.

It was interesting to hear that Karen Hunter, a supposedly dictatorial administrator who caused nine outstanding veteran teachers to leave the school, evoked such mundane reactions from the union. Ken claimed he had worked with two of the veteran fifth-grade teachers who frequently complained about the principal and her actions, and he stated that he brought their concerns informally to the superintendent at the time, with no result. Those teachers were very active in the union.

An administrator associated with the school district recalled, "Some of the long established teachers at Rock Spring left . . . because they wanted to teach their way, their style, their traditional methods, etc. Very, very, very strong, active teacher union members." He made an observation that often came to mind as we sought to understand the union's actions and motivations: "The teachers' union is never going to take the position that would be contrary to what those teachers wanted and felt."

He believed that the union took sides as the controversy grew, supporting some faculty members against others, and he asserted, "The other [veteran] teachers [in the district] are more active and more heavily endowed in the union than the [newer] Rock Spring teachers." In this context, it may make sense that the union took actions on behalf of teachers who left the school but remained silent during the summer of 1992, when the Concerned Parents organized the display of children's work that led to the Plan for Excellence.

Ken confirmed that no teachers were involved in the display of children's work. Furthermore, he added that the union was not asked to take a stand on the display, nor did it take a stand. He stated, "There was no position that the association took. We let it run its course." We asked whether other teachers in the district knew that parents had written a curriculum that was being forced on an unwilling principal and teachers, and we wondered what their reactions might have been. Disagreeing with our understanding of the events, he explained:

> No. I don't think the parents wrote the curriculum. The Plan for Excellence wasn't a curriculum as far as I recall. I don't even recall seeing this Plan of Excellence, unless it was brought to the executive board. But it was not a curriculum. It would not have been a curriculum. We would not have allowed parents writing curriculum.

When we reminded Ken that the Plan for Excellence specified what could be taught and how it could be taught, and even addressed assessment requirements, he demurred:

> If that was the case . . . well, I do recall some things that we will do two and [three] pages and everybody will be on the same page. That was . . . more of a thumbing their [the teachers] nose at the parents . . . OK, sure, you want it this way? We'll give it to you this way. That's what . . . Karen and some of the teachers who were in on it [did] and Karen got her side of the people . . . saying OK, we'll stop, put our finger in the dike by doing this. You want something? Here, we'll give it to you.

Ken seemed surprised that one of the Concerned Parents had been instrumental in conceiving and writing the Plan for Excellence, and he appeared mystified when he learned of Stout's initial rejection of the plan because it wasn't specific enough. Ken's only comment was, "Well, I was not privy to that." He additionally seemed unaware of the year-long monitoring of the Plan for Excellence by the superintendent, Concerned Parents, and the Community Partners, who discussed, with few or no teachers present, what was appropriate to teach and how to teach it. When we asked him if he knew of any teachers who were involved in the monitoring process, he replied:

> That was very much an internal . . . component to the whole elementary school set. And it was basically let us stand back—let's not get involved. Let them work on their own internal problems 'cause they're the ones that ultimately have to live with it. So let them— work with it, let them solve it. And basically that was our stance at that point.

We asked Ken how, in such a short period of time, parents had surfaced at a PTA meeting criticizing teachers, a superintendent had been dismissed, a public display of student work with no teacher involvement had taken place, the Plan for Excellence had been adopted, and a year-long monitoring process had ensued—all occurring with little or no teacher involvement. He interrupted us to state:

> I don't know if that was quite the case. Your last statement that the teachers weren't involved in the monitoring . . . I'm sure they had both grade-level meetings, school-level meetings . . . with the principal to monitor as it was going along.

We were curious if Ken knew whether any teachers were involved with the curriculum-monitoring group that was holding meetings in the evenings. "That met in the evening?" he asked, seemingly surprised. We explained that parents had informed us that community members were meeting in the evenings during the year to develop a report, as specified in the Plan for Excellence, and that it appeared to us that few if any teachers were involved. Ken replied:

> I'm sure there were so many complaints going back and forth during the last 4 or 5 years of this whole fiasco that, I mean, to sort out the number of complaints, when they were, who they were against, who was involved in the planning . . . I wouldn't even begin to sit down and try to sort it out.

While the complexity of events at the school makes this reaction understandable, it was curious that the union, at the minimum a watchdog for teachers, was unaware of and uninvolved in issues of such importance.

As outsiders, we were confused by both official and unofficial groups that formed and became involved in developing and monitoring the Plan for Excellence, with the charge to report back about specifics, such as number of spelling tests given, or to make suggestions as to what should be done in the curriculum. When we asked Ken if he could clarify any of these issues for us, he responded:

> I don't really know. I tried to divorce myself from all . . . the ifs and all the inner imaginations that were going on. It was just—it was rampant. It was unbelievable. Constantly articles in the newspaper and letters to the editor, and one newspaper had a very pro-Hunter bias and it was so evident it was pathetic. And, you know, . . . there were a lot of things that had to be said to counter those things, not only on my part but other people's parts, the other side.

As a teacher in another district school, Ken found the situation unbelievable. His reaction surely caused us to speculate on what it must have been like for those at the school who were faced with implementing the Plan for Excellence. It seemed remarkable that the president of the union had tried, in his own words, to divorce himself from all that was going on, and he added that during this time no Rock Spring teachers brought any complaints to his attention.

The actions of the union seem disingenuous to us. The union grieved the scheduling of a meeting on a Friday, they grieved insufficient notice for a meeting, but they failed to pursue academic freedom abuses where they were perceived to exist. It is difficult to understand why the union chose to make no comment on a staged display of student work and was silent when that display resulted in the imposition of a new curriculum. In Ken's words, the union chose to "let them work it out." And yet the union was not always silent. On behalf of the veteran teachers who left the school, it took action in response to what it perceived as a disparaging statement by a board member, Geri O'Brien. The union president seemed both proud and pleased that a letter of support he wrote for these veteran teachers and read at a board meeting "knocked the board dead" and "blasted" the local papers. But for the newer teachers at the Rock Spring School, whose vision, curriculum, and teaching methods were under siege, there was only silence.

We mentioned to Ken that some parents in the community reported to us that they believed the union was taking sides, championing the cause of a group of veteran teachers over the concerns of newer teachers. Ken responded:

We have our own perspective on things. . . . We have our own bi-
ases but we need to see a history and some of these parents don't
have the history . . . they see it as just a black-and-white issue. And
basically I have more obvious knowledge than any of these parents
do with the number of grievances, the people that have been let go,
the number of statements, the number of contract violations, just
on and on . . . it's affected teachers. So if that's taking sides, well, oh
well. . . . Parents just don't know this . . . they don't have that history
and they're not privy to all . . . those grievances and contract violations and the dastardly deeds that might have been done, and then
they think it's taking sides. Well OK, maybe it is. I don't apologize
for it.

It seemed that the union acted only when the veteran teachers who left
the school became angry. Karen was not surprised by the response of the
union. "The union represented the old Rock Spring faculty, OK," she said,
"the rest of the teachers were neophytes. . . . They didn't know whether
the union was for them, against them. They didn't even know how to use
the union to help them."

When we asked Ken if the controversy had an effect on teachers in
other elementary schools in the district, he stated:

No. It was a morning topic of conversation, what's going on next or
did you see the ad in the newspaper, you know, the letter in the
newspaper, the article in the *News*, did you see the *Gazette*, which
had a different perspective than the one that published the tests
that really got this ball rolling? And so every week there was a new
thing. And there was a parent group that came out with a newsletter countering the newsletter that the district put out.

Speaking of the impact of the dispute on teachers at all levels in the district, the union president expanded, "The lack of academic freedom affects teachers, the doing away with a . . . basal text and phonics skills that
some kids need." We reminded him that the one time a group of veteran
teachers had raised these very issues as challenges to their academic freedom, the union failed to file the grievance. It seemed that the union acted
only when the veteran teachers who left the school became angry. We
asked Ken if the union responded to the Rock Spring teachers, many of
whom, we were told, continued to support the principal and enthusiastically endorsed the curriculum prior to the Plan for Excellence. He explained:

They've made their point to the head building rep and . . . we respect their right to have . . . that opinion, to have sides. We felt it
was not in their best interest . . . to make a public display of taking
sides. When Karen was first taken out of the school and [the]
charges were filed . . . there was a very open display of pro-Karen
sentiment, wearing purple ribbons, rallying around the flag pole,
crying, running through the halls with shouting, making statements and we felt, the WEA [Waterview Education Association] felt,
it was not in their best interest to do so, that they should remain
neutral. That . . . there should not be any public display of emotion,
there shouldn't be anything stated and said to the kids in your
class, if you were one way or the other . . . [to] kids that go right
back home to Mommy and Daddy. And I counseled them to kind
of be careful about that. They weren't very pleased that I said that,
[that I] wrote them a letter. They weren't pleased . . . but when I
went over to explain why and was put on the hot seat . . . they appreciated that . . . the fact that I came over and . . . that I was concerned about them and that they could be next. As I looked around
the room I saw some nontenured people and I said, "You know,
your job is in jeopardy and there's a possibility of you being next,
you being called on the carpet. Just low-pedal it, soft-pedal it, you
know, no open emotions or displays one way or the other."

We told Ken that many of the other people we interviewed thought the
Rock Spring teachers were scared by what they saw happening in their
school, and he denied hearing about their fears. Of course, one wonders
how young teachers, indeed any teachers, could avoid some concern
when their union president warned them that their jobs could be next.
Having been counseled to remain neutral, and having seen what a vocal
group of parents were able to accomplish in a short period of time, their
silence does not seem remarkable.

As we had done with everyone else we interviewed, we asked the
union president about the national reports that this controversy involved censorship:

I read the newspaper article and they . . . basically had people interviewed from my perspective that had their own agenda. That basically was not a very well-written, unbiased article . . . I don't think
they got a tempering of viewpoints. . . . Censorship? No. This is . . .
a situation where parents are questioning the decline or the perceived decline of Johnny's ability to read . . . Susie's ability to do
math, and they are wondering why. And if Johnny can't read or

Johnny can't write . . . there must be some reasons. . . . And parents
say, "Well, you know, I learned by phonics. I learned by rules and
skills and procedures, and that's not being followed in whole language." . . . Then I think the parents have a right to question . . .
what they're doing. And that's what the whole country is doing.
That's what California did when they said this is ridiculous. And
they did away with it. And Texas said this is ridiculous, and they
did away with it. And they're going back to basics, back to skills . . .
and maybe we'll see in 5 or 6 years that the scores are going back
up and whole language will die on the vine.

Ken brought to the interview a copy of a newspaper article on how whole
language had been condemned as a failure in California, Florida, and
Texas. He continued his discussion of the shortcomings of whole language but attested that he used some aspects of it himself, what he described as "literature-based things," but he denied using "it as a total."
He preferred what he described as a "very eclectic approach," since he
believed there was "not just one way of doing things." While we would
agree that there is no single "right" way to educate all children, we still
wondered why a union president seemed so poorly informed about the
controversies surrounding attacks on whole language and the reading
wars in California and Texas.

Ken claimed to be an advocate for children and teachers:

I'm biased . . . I have a perspective that a lot of other people don't
. . . I've been in this for 28 years. I love what I do. I can't wait to go
to work in the morning. I'm an advocate for kids, and I'm an advocate for professionals treated as professionals. And . . . if any of
those two things get . . . knocked down, I'm going to fight.

His willingness to fight, however, certainly seemed selective and somewhat uninformed. We had already been told by an administrator associated with the district that a policy existed for parents who questioned or
wished to challenge school practices and materials, and we wanted to
explore why the union did not call for the enforcement of the policy. Ken,
seemingly unaware of the policy, remarked:

A written policy at the board level for challenging? No . . . no. I
think they'd have to go either to the teacher or to the principal.
There are some teachers that are accessible as, you know, we sit
here and some of us are more accessible than others and more ame-
nable to parental input, and others are more standoffish. That's just

human nature but a— there's no—there's no written policy of the board regarding the chain of command. It's generally taken for granted that if you have a problem with the teacher, you talk to the teacher. If you can't talk to the teacher because of one reason or another, personality conflict, go to the principal. If the principal wants to get the parent and the teacher involved, then that's fine. If . . . the person doesn't get any satisfaction from the principal, they can go to the superintendent. Some parents we know don't go to the principal or the teacher. They go directly to Dorothy. That's human nature, too, go to the top.

It did not appear to disturb Ken that parents had circumvented established procedures and had gone directly to the board of education with their complaints. He commented, "Yeah, that's probably true in a lot of other districts. I don't think that we would be any different."

When the Rock Spring teachers who supported Karen complained about the actions of the Concerned Parents, Ken counseled them to be careful. He wrote them a letter and came to the school to speak to them. Intended or not, his comments appear ominous and chilling. To a faculty concerned about parents'—and board of education members'—irregular behavior and activities, and to a faculty looking to find ways to address unprofessional conduct and unsubstantiated attacks on what and how they had been teaching, the president of their union said, "You know, your job is in jeopardy and there's a possibility of your being next, your being called on the carpet." So much for professional support.

If in fact the union was choosing to side with veteran union members, seeing the conflict as a chance to get back at a principal who had angered those veteran members, then the actions taken and not taken seem understandable. Principle seemed to take a back seat, whether it dealt with indiscriminate displays of student work, violation of district policies, unsubstantiated attacks on the practices and materials used by the teachers at the school under assault—even when academic freedom concerns of those very same veterans were initially raised. In the climate of distrust, hostility, gag orders, and parental monitoring, the union response appears to have been effective in disenfranchising teachers, making them powerless in the arenas in which they should have the most control—their schools and classrooms.

Since this study began, no teachers who supported Karen have agreed to interviews. A tentative meeting date and time was set up a few years ago, with teachers invited to join us after school. We were told that some might show up, but nothing was definite. The now-retired superintendent forbade us to enter any school buildings or grounds, so we hoped to meet some of the teachers at a parent's home not far from the school. We waited anxiously as school closing time approached. As the appointed hour came and passed, not one teacher joined us. The degree of their fear seemed legitimate, even though at that time we did not know of the "veiled threat" from the union president. Many Community Partners stated that teachers told them they were afraid to do or say anything after that warning. Again, as formal and informal gag order followed gag order, the teachers' voices remain unheard.

THE ROLE OF GENDER

As we discussed and wrote this case study, we came to believe that gender played a role in the controversy at Rock Spring School. We reiterate that all the people we interviewed were well educated and intelligent, and they probably would be surprised by our suspicion that the principal's gender and the gender of her teacher supporters might have had an impact on the events that played themselves out in the school district. Nevertheless, as we analyzed the transcripts of interviews, the language, concerns, and comments of many of the players in this drama led us to believe that, either consciously or unconsciously, gender was an issue that revealed itself in a number of ways.

Many of the Concerned Parents referred to the fact that Karen was living with a man they disparagingly called "Andy Baby," who was an administrator in a neighboring school district. At least two Concerned Parents insinuated that she had "slept her way to the top," securing her position only because her partner had intervened for her with Fred Pacifico, an allegation firmly denied by the administrator we interviewed. Would the parents have gossiped so much about Karen's living situation or implied that she did not get the job on her own merits if she had been a man? Was Karen facing a double standard that reveals barriers that women continue face when seeking or working in executive positions, even in a profession that remains female-dominated on the teaching level but male-dominated in administration (Skrla, 1995)? Even cosmopolitan Marsha Bennett, a career teacher whose longevity surely had given her many opportunities to see women advance in the field of education, remarked that she believed Karen was "fixated on weddings" and claimed that the only time Karen exhibited much of an interest in her as a person occurred when Marsha's daughter was getting married. She concluded that Karen "just couldn't have cared less" about some of the family problems she was experiencing at the time, "But weddings she was fixated on. I just don't know why. It just stands out in my mind. It has no bearing on anything. She just seemed fixated on that." We do think these remarks have a bearing on the way Marsha and others viewed Karen. We interpret Marsha's statements as an oblique referral to Karen's living situation. We remain convinced that Karen's status as a single woman with a live-in partner would not have been viewed the same way if she had been male.

Some of the language that was used to describe Karen, her teacher supporters, and their behavior during the crisis resounded with stereotypes associated with females. Martina called to our attention the physical stature of the young teachers who supported Karen, describing them as clones of their leader, "very small, very thin" women with "hair up to here" who "were stamped from the same cookie-cutter mold." Ken, a male power broker in the district, commenting on the behavior of the same young, female teachers—women who were his own colleagues and who had just learned that their principal had been suspended—described them as "crying, running through the halls with shouting," and he advised them against "any public display of emotion." Geri suggested that Ken warned Karen's supporters to "be good little teachers" and remain quiet and under control. Even Marsha believed that Fred Pacifico did not want to be bothered with her complaints about Karen because she thought he perceived the tension between them as "a cat fight, and that it was purely two women who didn't get along." She added that during meetings with Fred, a male colleague who accompanied her let her do all the talking, which led Fred to dismiss the problem as two women being unreasonable. Marsha's comments suggest that even she believed that her complaints had been trivialized as girl stuff. We even wonder if some of the problems with the female Concerned Parents resulted from a certain amount of jealousy and resentment because Karen was a well-groomed, professionally dressed, young female who had accomplished some significant career goals by the time she was 30 years old.

Karen herself reflected on whether or not she ever really had been a "comfortable fit" for the school and community where she was employed. She speculated:

> A good segment of the moms that are at home need a place to hang out . . . and perhaps they need a leader of that school who . . . did not take the professional stance I did, but rather more homesy, folksy, come on in, let's have coffee, maybe dress differently, and was not as threatening in any way, maybe made a space within the school and said, "Come on in. It's your place. Hang out here. Bring your kids." . . . I didn't understand that when I was hired. . . . The

only models I ever had were people who sort of took a professional stance. . . . I think it also has to do with the role of mothers and what's happening in a changing society and what's happening with the stay-at-home mom versus the working mom and the working mom's dilemma and a conflict about what her role needs to be. . . . And if they don't want to work or can't work or they shouldn't work, what then becomes meaningful work for them? And how that plays into feelings of inadequacy perhaps when they meet up with teachers who are working mothers, who to them somehow have made it. Or there are a lot of wannabe teachers in the mothers, stay-at-home mothers in the community.

Geri, who was present during the discussion about the community mothers, speculated that Karen "would have done much better if she had been a man." She was convinced that the mothers would have "accepted [her] leadership more readily," even if the behavior and stances had been identical. She concluded, "I think having a strong woman . . . in a leadership position does not reflect well on those other women who go home and then start to think about themselves and what they are doing with their lives." Some of the Concerned Parents accused Karen of wanting to make Rock Spring a model school and use her accomplishments as resume fodder for a more impressive job. Would a man have been criticized as severely for attempting to move up the career ladder? Karen was the only female among a cadre of male principals whom Geri, repeating Karen's words, characterized as "homesy, folksy" men. Karen thought that publicly the community members, due to "the sort of elitist status that everybody wanted," appeared to endorse an "extraordinary principal . . . and instructional leader," but privately, "emotionally and subjectively," they wanted something she, especially as a young woman with a strongly professional stance, could not provide.

It appears to us as outsiders in the role of participant observers that many of those involved in the Rock Spring dispute either failed to recognize or would deny that gender did indeed play a role in the way parents, teachers, and administrators dealt with each other. Their inability to see the gender bias in some ways is not surprising, since they were immersed in the situation and were "recipients and products of the culture they try to critique" (Patterson, 1995, p. 119). Karen, however, as a reflective educator, accustomed to taking a critical stance and using the kind of "double vision" Mayher (1990) advocates, was inclined to see the bias we, too, believe she confronted.

WAS IT CENSORSHIP?

The Rock Spring controversy drew national attention in the popular and professional press as a possible censorship effort aimed at whole language; and, in many ways, it resembled other censorship efforts across the nation. But was it censorship? The reported actions and rhetoric originally drew our attention to the situation. As we began our research, we thought we might find some of the expected right-wing political or religious groups at work. We were surprised to discover a far more complex set of circumstances that we never could have predicted.

Did censorship occur in River Haven? The members of the community and the educators involved were split in their opinions on this issue. One of the petitions circulated specifically called for an end to whole language. We asked everyone we interviewed whether the community conflict centered on, or was even peripherally involved with, an attempt to eliminate whole language. The Concerned Parents were well prepared to answer the question, and they completely denied this allegation. Many claimed that the educational philosophy and practices in place at Rock Spring were not whole language, but the principal's and the teachers' interpretation and adaptation of elements of whole language. And yet, we repeatedly heard the Concerned Parents call for a return to phonics, to traditional texts and teaching, to rote mathematical calculations, to tighter discipline and less nurturing, to more rigor and less attention to self-esteem, to practices more like the protesting parents had experienced in their own schooldays. The Plan for Excellence seemed to supply much of what the Concerned Parents demanded: essentially a basic skills-and-drills curriculum. Workbooks, systematic spelling tests, and basal readers reappeared. Parents imposed and monitored changes against the wishes of a principal, teachers, and a corps of parents who supported the program in place prior to the Plan for Excellence. Still, these changes fell short of the demands of the parents monitoring the plan. So we are left with the question: Was it censorship?

David Morgan, who was instrumental in writing the Plan for Excellence, denied that any censorship occurred:

> It is not a censorship case. There are . . . charges having to do with special education . . . falsification of records . . . [and] changing of school psychologist recommendations. So it has nothing to do with [censorship of] whole language.

Of course, it deserves attention that the charges came after the curriculum was changed and after the teachers were forced to follow the Plan for

Excellence. The Concerned Parents had won the curriculum victory, and the charges that followed may have been due in part to the fact that some Concerned Parents still were not pleased with the implementation of the plan. The target ultimately shifted from eliminating the old curriculum to removing the principal who was charged with overseeing the new curriculum.

Our conversations with many key players in the dispute led us to believe that it had a chilling effect on any effort to innovate in the district. Asked about the impact of the controversy on teachers in other district schools, even Marsha Bennett, a major critic of Karen and the Rock Spring curriculum, acknowledged that the furor had cast a pall on any discussion of whole language:

> What I do believe happened is that whole language as a concept closed down. And I think that a lot of people wouldn't even listen to anybody discussing the whole concept. . . . It became . . . the curse word. You don't want that. If it's labeled whole language, you don't want it. And I think people became almost more traditional.

Cathy feared that the teachers would be reluctant to innovate, since the Concerned Parents would "jump" anyone who attempted change. Cynthia castigated those who designed and imposed the Plan for Excellence for ignoring what was good about the curriculum and failing to invest the time necessary to do the "tinkering" it needed. Instead, she complained, they found it easier to capitulate to the demands of "a special-interest group" and force unwilling and nervous educators to throw "the baby out with the bath water." Was it censorship? These women suggested that, at a minimum, self-censorship followed the imposition of the Plan for Excellence. And, of course, the curriculum and its guiding vision as it once existed are gone.

The question remains: Were the events in River Haven and Rock Spring School an attempt at censorship? A curriculum was written hastily in the summer by a few members of the community, with minimal help from teachers and administrators. That curriculum was imposed on a nonsupportive principal and teaching staff. No evidence other than a contrived display of unidentified student work, which even one of the parent organizers admitted was biased, was offered as the curricular smoking gun. Teaching practices and content were changed and eliminated, and a more traditional pedagogy and materials were put into place. The board of education slapped injunctions on two parents and their attorney in an attempt to prevent them from meeting with other Community Partners and discussing the charges against Karen. The Concerned Parents circulated a request for specific complaints against Karen, and as formal charges were made, they escalated in number and severity. The voices of the teachers supporting the principal were silenced by their own union president. Whatever once existed at the Rock Spring School is no more. A vocal group of parents, with the expressed or implied endorsement of the acting superintendent of schools, some members of the board of education, the head of the union, and some veteran faculty, succeeded in attacking a vision for teaching and learning and shutting down a curriculum and the practices of an enthusiastic staff. A principal was removed. Policies were ignored. Two principals have served Rock Spring School since Karen's suspension and the settlement of her case.

To bring some closure to our case study, we called Cathy Young to get her reaction to the way things turned out in River Haven. Cathy, Ron Cluney, and their attorney found some satisfaction in winning more than $200,000 in a civil suit against the Waterview Board of Education filed in federal court for violation of civil rights and defamation of character. Cathy told us that parents seem to like the new principal, a woman who has a tendency to be pleasant and direct. She quickly attends to complaints and aims to settle disagreements and clear up misunderstandings immediately. Cathy remains closely connected with the school, and she believes the school is "OK," but she added that she does not see anyone at Rock Spring "taking any big risks." We were reminded of the aftermath of the Kanawha County textbook wars, a censorship battle that divided a county in West Virginia. When James Moffett (1988), the editor of the challenged textbook series, returned to visit 8 years later, he found that teachers taught "very prudently," sticking close to their grammar lessons and even fearing the impact of teaching gender as it related to grammar.

When we asked Karen herself if she felt that what happened at Rock Spring was censorship, she replied cautiously:

> It depends on how you define censorship. It certainly feels like censorship. Especially the event where the Plan for Excellence was imposed on a teaching staff, a principal, on an entire school without negotiation or dialogue or discussion about the ramifications of what that would be. It's not as narrow as a book banning, although it encompasses things like imposing textbooks back on teachers. So I say yes and no. It's not the classic sense of censorship cases that we know about nationally, but it certainly has many of the same elements and certainly has the same emotional tone as any book-banning situation has had in any community . . . cutting off of the professional's voice has certainly been part of this whole dilemma in that you have a group of noneducators in the community, on the

school board dictating terms to a group of professionals, and that I see as censorship, again in the loss of power and freedom . . . it definitely has the same emotional effect. It's chilling. It cuts off people's ability to talk about it. It feels like you've been stripped of your voice.

Zena, who had leveled charges of McCarthyism at the Concerned Parents, concluded, "If it looks like a duck . . ." Was it censorship? In some ways, we think it was; and it certainly remains as complex, troubling, and pernicious as many of the censorship attempts we have followed as we researched and wrote this case study. As we consider the total impact and aftermath of the conflict, we have begun to characterize what happened in River Haven as "The Big Chill."

"THE BIG CHILL"

In Lawrence Kasdan's 1983 film *The Big Chill*, a group of old college buddies congregate for the funeral of one of their friends, Alex, a man for whom everyone had had the highest expectations. Alex's failure to achieve what was expected and his untimely death by suicide force the other friends to reflect on their own past and present lives, casting "The Big Chill" on the group and helping them realize that they had both changed and remained the same. They would go on with their lives. At times when we were interviewing the Community Partners and Karen, we felt as if we were attending a wake with no visible body—yet everyone was talking "wake talk," telling us about what had been or could have been. Karen herself, referring to the dismantling of what she and the Rock Spring teachers had created, concluded, "But it was a death. It was a loss. It was a grieving process [for] what we had worked so hard to build." Whether or not one wants to label the events that transpired in Rock Spring School as censorship, "The Big Chill" in River Haven has silenced many voices; and while much has changed, much remains the same.

A principal and her cohort of teacher change agents were silenced as their convictions about teaching and learning were discredited and dismissed by a group of angry parents who found supporters on the board of education, in the administration, and among some of the faculty in the schools themselves. These teacher change agents had found their voices in progressive education classes, professional development workshops, classroom-based inquiry, and informal faculty room chats, where Karen was surprised to discover that lunches with conversations about Vygotsky were on the menu. From what we heard, these teachers were excited to work in a school where their principal and many colleagues shared their vision for teaching and learning. They, in turn, collaborated in the development of a curriculum that they believed would enable their students to find their own voices as writers, readers, and inquirers in ways that would not have been possible in a more conventional skills-and-drills curriculum. Many voices were silenced as the curriculum these educators created died with the birth of the Plan for Excellence.

The teachers' union played a significant role in the conflict by privileging the voices of some teachers, silencing others, and, ultimately, failing to protect the rights of both factions. Instead of recognizing the complexity of the problems that were unfolding and what was at stake, the union leadership opted to relegate the dispute to the old familiar teachers-versus-administrators category, overlooking the fact that the same forces in the district schools, on the board of education, and in the community that were empowering them at the moment could turn against them when it was convenient. It seemed to us that as long as the union's proverbial ox was not getting gored, and the inside circle of union stalwarts appeared to be protected, the union leaders found it easy to gloss over a disturbing series of actions and events that set some dangerous precedents with the ultimate potential to harm the very teachers the union was trying to protect. We suspect that if circumstances had been different and some of the privileged teachers had been victims of the Concerned Parents, there would have been a great hue and cry from the union. Still, the union leadership essentially ignored the request of a group of veteran teachers to file an academic freedom grievance against the principal. Furthermore, the union totally dismissed and trivialized the concerns of a group of mainly untenured teachers and silenced their complaints about their own academic freedom. The union leadership, in their haste to project the problems as simple teacher/administrator conflict, failed to address the complex academic freedom issues of both factions of teachers.

While mediation in a conflict of this nature may not be something a union typically does or even advocates, the union leadership nevertheless should have recognized what was at stake here as a special-interest group seized control of a curriculum and pulled the strings of a puppet superintendent of schools and a board of education that seemed more interested in litigation than education. Instead, the union leaders missed an opportunity to assume a new role and to encourage dialogue that could have made a difference to their own members and the climate of a school and district. As we will further explore in Chapter 7, national union leaders are recommending that local unions assume new professional roles in sharing with administrators responsibilities for decision making on issues related to curriculum and students (Greenhouse, 1999). Yet in River Haven, the union president himself informed us that he had "counseled" the teachers to remain quiet, because their jobs could be next.

Will the teachers who lived through this debacle be willing again to raise their voices as change agents or even as colleagues of equal stature within their own union? As Cathy said, "You know, it's hard to think that you would want to embrace something new or do something new when you know the community will probably jump you for it." In this case, the teachers apparently had to worry that they could be jumped by their own colleagues. As we said previously, no teacher currently working at Rock Spring agreed to be interviewed, and all but one were unwilling to complete anonymous questionnaires we mailed to them in plain envelopes. We understand their fear but regret their silence, since they have a right to speak out about what happened. This study would have been richer and fuller with their input, and what they learned from a traumatic series of events would have been so valuable to share with a wider network of educators. Once again, the voices of teachers were silenced, and, in this instance, by their own union, an organization charged with giving them a voice.

Some veteran teachers, like Marsha Bennett, believed that their knowledge and experience were overlooked and their perspectives on teaching and learning were undervalued in the march to change at the Rock Spring School. Our conversations with Marsha herself and the interviews with parents and with Karen helped us recognize that Marsha was a formidable person who was accustomed to having her voice heard. As much as Marsha disliked Karen, her leadership style, and the changes she was making, she nevertheless acknowledged that she and Karen "actually probably had more philosophical conversations than anybody else." Karen, in her enthusiasm to effect change, made a mistake when she alienated Marsha. It is every change agent's challenge to find ways of working with the Marshas in our schools, teachers whose position and reputation in classrooms and communities cannot be and should not be minimized, even though they may be resistant to questioning the status quo that appears to work for them. The change agents at Rock Spring could not disregard Marsha as one of those teachers who was resting on her lesson plans and waiting for retirement. Marsha, too, had something to share, and she was not a person a principal and her young teacher allies could afford to dismiss. There is no simple and easy formula for helping people like Marsha find their voice in a change process that seems alien to them. And, ultimately, it may be their right not to change. Nevertheless, it is important, as Mike Rose (1989) might say, to continue to invite them into the conversation. Where Marsha went wrong, in our estimation, was in using her privileged status to undermine for her own personal reasons what clearly was vital to many of her colleagues; and, as she was silenced, she silenced them.

In some ways, both the Concerned Parents and the Community Partners were silenced. Both groups concurred that better communication between the Rock Spring School and families was necessary. We and many of the Community Partners we interviewed suspect that even the best efforts at communicating would not have satisfied many of the Concerned Parents, who wanted nothing short of Karen's dismissal from her job and even, as David demanded, from the profession. Still, everyone who was a party to this dispute called for improved communication with families. What the parents were seeing at Rock Spring School challenged the unexamined, commonsense assumptions about teaching and learning they had developed during their own years in school (Mayher, 1990). It was evident to us that Karen did make many formal and informal attempts to explain her philosophy and practices to the community, but her efforts and those of her staff were viewed as inadequate. We believe that even the best of efforts would have been insufficient for her most vocal detractors. We think that some of Karen's struggles to reassure parents that their children were doing fine backfired on her. The Concerned Parents, especially the ones who were worried and angry about problems they perceived with their children's progress, needed more than a pat on the back and the reassurance that everything would be fine. Karen's invitation to "trust me" was an empty entreaty to them. By attempting to pacify these parents and earn their trust, Karen unintentionally silenced their concerns and increased the tension.

Parents in both factions told us that the teachers who tried to articulate their core beliefs about teaching and learning and the practices that emerged from these beliefs often wanted for words to explain what they were doing and why. Terry, a Community Partner and a teacher herself, recognized the problem when she used her own knowledge and experience to rescue a floundering novice teacher who was trying to explain her practices to an agitated parent during a meeting. We remain convinced that there was more than one new teacher at Rock Spring who was silenced by her own lack of words to explain the choices she was making in her classroom, and this inability to articulate a vision for learning and teaching certainly is an issue that presents substantial challenges for teachers, teacher educators, and administrators.

In River Haven, neighbors were silenced by neighbors as people took sides in the battle, refused to speak to each other, and sometimes even prevented their children from playing together. The Waterview Board of Education ultimately slapped a gag order on Cathy Young and Ron Cluney to prevent them from holding meetings and discussing the charges against Karen, who, with her attorney, was also served with an injunction to force her not to discuss the charges. These injunctions were kicked out of court after court, yet the board continued to appeal them. Cathy and Ron finally sued the board in federal court for violation of their civil rights and defamation of character, a suit that was settled in their favor in February 1997. In our opinion, these gag orders represented one of the most egregious forms of silencing that occurred during the dispute, and we admire the courage of the parents who used their own money and risked their homes and financial security to fight and win a First Amendment battle.

As we analyzed the unfolding of events in the Rock Spring controversy, we concluded that children were silenced, too. As mentioned previously, parents told us that children of warring families were forbidden to play with each other. Children were also silenced in their school. All the Community Partners told us Karen was popular with the children. She was a visible presence in classrooms, and she invited children into her office to listen to stories and to read to her. When Karen was suspended, these children wondered what had happened to the principal they saw in the halls and classrooms every day, a friendly figure who knew all their names. The acting superintendent of schools appeared at Rock Spring one day and offered the children a sugar-coated semitruth to explain the messy reality of the suspension, telling them that they had a special job for Dr. Hunter in the central office. This prevarication pandered to the children, kids who knew better based on what they had been hearing in their own homes. Dorothy Stout's explanation for Karen's sudden departure and continued absence trivialized their concerns and silenced their inquiries.

As we looked closely at the events that transpired in River Haven, we came to believe that children were silenced in even more subtle ways. It seemed to us that students and their work were used and misused to make a contrived point about their failure to achieve when there was no hard evidence of failure—only rumors that their performance lagged behind students in the other district elementary schools and that they were singled out as less competent when they reached middle school. Parents displayed children's work in public, with their names excised and with no explanation of what their work represented or what their own intentions for their writing might have been. Children's work was exploited by adults to convey a misleading message that the adults, not the children, wanted to communicate. Even some of the Concerned Parents who organized the display of work admitted that it was neither unbiased nor fair but that they went ahead with it to make a point. However, in making their point, they obscured any meaning children were attempting to make for themselves in their writing. They removed the children's work from the context in which it was written and divorced it from the personal meanings and intentions of the authors. These actions seem disingenuous and unethical to us.

Although many of the Community Partners assured us that the teachers at Rock Spring continued to love children and teaching and did their best to create a lively community of learning in their school and classrooms, we cannot help but wonder what long-term impact the dismantling of a Best Practice curriculum, one that privileged children's voices and inquiry, will have on children's ability to find and use their voices (Zemelman, Daniels, & Hyde, 1998). When children are still in elementary school, we teach them about their towns, states, and nation. We try to show them how government works. What kind of implicit message about democracy did the Rock Spring conflict convey to children?

Herman Bailey characterized the actions of the Concerned Parents as "the process of consensus, democracy." However, we see nothing particularly democratic or consensual in the way the Concerned Parents went about overthrowing the curriculum and suspending the principal. They prevailed on a weak, vulnerable superintendent and a litigious board of education to get their way. Dorothy Stout, perhaps fearing the same powers who fired her predecessor and propelled her into her position only to use her, seemed to shirk her responsibilities as a chief school administrator and to allow the board of education and a vocal group of parents to sidestep established school policies and avoid more reasonable procedures for settling grievances. Instead, she assisted them or, at minimum, stood by as they advanced their agenda through a basic skills curriculum hastily written with little or no genuine support or assistance from teachers, gag orders against parents with opposing views, a quasi-public display of out-of-context children's work, and what we see as more than 100 concocted charges against a principal. All these actions appear to us highly irregular and unethical, and perhaps even bordering on illegal, although we acknowledge that we are not attorneys and are in no position to determine legality. It seems to us that if the central administration and the board of education in River Haven had wanted to settle this conflict with fewer casualties, they would have sought a means to allow the various factions to air their grievances in constructive ways. Many of the Community Partners called for mediation, a rational, democratic, and even more cost-conscious option that was ignored. Once again, an opportunity to hear the voices of people on all sides was lost. Was this democracy? What we see looks more like anarchy.

As we conclude this long case study of power, politics, and public schools, we, too, feel caught in the draft of "The Big Chill" at a wake without a body. We are left with the impression that the Concerned Parents and the Community Partners, if they even use those terms anymore, will go on with their lives, although Cathy, in our telephone conversation with her, hinted at occasional awkward encounters in public places. Cathy and Ron will not lose their homes to lawsuits and legal fees. Karen has reached a settlement that will give her a substantial annual salary for 6 years, enable her to pay more than $200,000 in legal bills, and allow her to seek new full-time employment while she continues to receive her settlement money. Dorothy and Marsha have retired. Herman Bailey lost his seat on the board of education. Many of the children who were named in the charges are now in high school. The district is out $1,000,000, money that could have been spent far more wisely on teaching and learning. The teachers at Rock Spring School, whoever is left after 6 years, continue to teach. Commenting on the waste of monetary and human resources, Emily agonized, "We all are paying for it." Much has changed, but much remains the same. Still, we remain troubled by a nagging feeling that the citizens of River Haven and the educators and kids at Rock Spring School have witnessed many deaths, not the least of which is the death of possibility.

REFERENCES

Cuban, L. (1984). *How teachers taught: Constancy and change in American classrooms, 1890–1980.* New York & London: Longman.

Giroux, H. (1983). *Theory and resistance in education: A pedagogy for the opposition.* South Hadley, MA: Bergin & Garvey.

Greenhouse, S. (1999, July 10). Teachers' union head urges more flexibility in contract talks. *The New York Times,* p. 14.

Jones, J. (1993–1994, Winter/Spring). Countering the 'far right.' *The Principal News, 21*(3), 8, 16, 21.

Kasdan, L. (Director). (1983). *The Big Chill* (Film). Los Angeles: Columbia/Tristar Studios.

Lears, T. J. (1985). The concept of cultural hegemony: Problems and possibilities. *The American Historical Review, 90*(3), 567–593.

Mayher, J. S. (1990). *Uncommon sense: Theoretical practice in language education.* Portsmouth, NH: Boynton/Cook, Heinemann.

Moffett, J. (1988). *Storm in the mountains: A case study of censorship, conflict, and consciousness.* Carbondale: Southern Illinois University Press.

Patterson, L. (1995). A quiet resistance: Critiquing gender issues in public schools. In B. J. Irby & G. Brown (Eds.), *Women as school executives: Voice and visions* (pp. 194–199). Austin, TX: Texas Council of Women School Executives, Texas Association of School Administrators.

Rose, M. (1989). *Lives on the boundary.* New York: Penguin.

Rose, M. (1995). *Possible lives: The promise of public education in America.* New York: Penguin.

Skrla, L. (1995). Dealing with informal power structures: Effective strategies for female administrators. In B. J. Irby & G. Brown (Eds.), *Women as school executives: Voice and visions* (pp. 118–120). Austin, TX: Texas Council of Women School Executives, Texas Association of School Administrators.

Tozer, S. E., Viola, P. C., & Senese, G. B. (1995). *School and society, historical and contemporary perspectives.* New York: McGraw-Hill.

Zemelman, S., Daniels, H., & Hyde, A. (1998). *Best practice: New standards for teaching and learning in America's schools.* Portsmouth, NH: Heinemann.

With Liberty and Justice for All? The Ambiguities of Academic Freedom in the Public School

ACADEMIC FREEDOM is an essential aspect of education in a democratic society. In Chapter 4, Jack Nelson and William Stanley suggest that teachers often do not perceive the need to protect their rights as teachers or those of their students to explore local and national issues of importance for the society. The evidence supports the conclusion that teachers in the Rock Spring School, and their union leadership, did not see the controversy that engulfed them as one whose nature involved academic freedom. Nelson and Stanley cite curriculum development, instructional practices, and the hiring, promotion, and retention of faculty as related to academic freedom and, more generally, to the purpose of schooling—the development of knowledge. In the Rock Spring study we see a curriculum attacked and a new one designed and imposed with no claim that the freedom of the teachers at the school to teach and of the students at the school to learn was being infringed.

The teachers at the Rock Spring School were ill prepared to enlist public support, cited by Nelson and Stanley as the most important element in maintaining academic freedom. The failure to win over the community to the approaches and changes being implemented left teachers at the school and those in the community who supported them unprepared and unorganized when faced with a challenge. They were silenced by their own union and removed from curricular and methodological discussions by a small group of active and assertive parents. This is unfortunate, for consideration of the issues in the context of academic freedom would have permitted a response more protective of the rights of teachers and of students as the conflict evolved.

Examining the case study, one cannot help but speculate that if the Rock Spring school personnel had known of the essential need for building community support, the learning possibilities that seemed so promising might have flourished. One can only wonder what the consequences might have been had the teachers' union advocated academic freedom above local politics. How might things have been different had the professional community in the Rock Spring School and throughout the River Haven District remained current in their understanding of the legal parameters influencing their work? Much pain might have been avoided.

In Chapter 5, we read of how approaching challenges from a context of academic freedom with an understanding of legal rights and important court cases can provide results different from those in River Haven. Gretchen Klopfer Wing was not daunted by the criticism that her teaching drew, and she was supported by an administrator who also believed in the right of teachers to teach and students to learn. Janet Cooper persisted for years in asserting that the actions for which she was criticized were appropriate and within her rights as a teacher. Her effort involved great personal cost, but as with Gretchen Klopfer Wing, resistance to the challenges met with success. Frustrated by the attacks on "filthy little books," Gloria Pipkin felt that she no longer had a future teaching in public schools. Jan Cole refused to back down when her teaching methods were attacked. The struggle for her academic freedom in the courts resulted in her legal vindication. Cissy Lacks also believed in academic freedom not only for herself but also for her students. Her case has been a convoluted one, but her defense of academic freedom has been significant. The record we present is mixed.

As Nelson and Stanley assert, an understanding of and a devotion to academic freedom are essential to protect the essential freedoms needed for education in a democracy. They are not, however, a guarantee of success. While Cole, Cooper, and Klopfer Wing emerged from their efforts successfully, the others became victims of challenges and censorship. The need for vigilance is ongoing.

Protecting the Right to Teach and Learn

JACK L. NELSON & WILLIAM B. STANLEY

Since freedom of mind and freedom of expression are the root of all freedom, to deny freedom in education is a crime against democracy.
—John Dewey, "The Social Significance of Academic Freedom"

THE PRIMARY PURPOSE for education in a democratic society is the preparation of an educated populace. That stark statement seems obvious,
since democracy is defined as self-governance and adequate self-
governance requires an educated public. We generally accept the idea
that an educated populace in the contemporary world needs a basic understanding of language usage, computation skills, and scientific reasoning, in addition to the necessary political, economic, and social knowledge for making civic decisions. However, many significant threats to
that basic premise continue in American society. There are many current
constrictions of teacher and student freedom, reflecting themselves in
limits on curriculum, teaching materials, and the process of teaching
itself.

TEACHERS, DEMOCRACY, AND ACADEMIC FREEDOM

Some people believe that the only civic knowledge needed is contained in
nationalistically slanted historical interpretations or narrowly constricted
views of free enterprise and traditional social mores. Their concept of
democracy is one of general conformity, where others share their views
of the world. Translated into schooling, this idea often leads to curricula
that are dominated by a single view of history, economics, and politics—

a view that does not value critical judgment and does not want competing ideas represented. This restrictive form of education is a serious threat to democracy and to education, in addition to demeaning the profession of teaching. Democracy is a dynamic concept in which continuing social progress is an expectation and critical thinking is necessary. Education in a democracy is always in tension between the forces that resist change and those that press for change. Helping students sort out the elements, logic, and quality of evidence presented by these competing forces is the role of schooling in a democracy. Critical civic education is an essential for an educated populace. Of course, critical civic education demands competent teachers who have the freedom to provide students with the freedom to examine controversial issues. Unfortunately, American schools do not have a sterling record in protecting teacher and student freedom.

TEACHER VULNERABILITY OVER TIME

There have been some pretty dismal times for academic freedom in American educational history, when teachers and their students were officially censored and restricted, when the classroom was limited to selected political views, and when teachers were in jeopardy and fearful of losing their positions merely for challenging popular conceptions. Colonial American schoolmasters were sometimes expected not only to teach but also to be church leaders—performing baptisms, issuing funeral invitations, and even digging graves. If they did not attend to these and other duties, they could be fired. Schoolmasters who committed minor transgressions against local religious and political customs were also threatened and dismissed. In many American cities in the early twentieth century, teaching was a patronage occupation. The teacher's job depended on who got elected; loss of that job was expected when different political parties won an election. Clearly, teachers in this setting could not be expected to discuss controversial political or economic matters. In several states in the early twentieth century, a teacher could be fired for dancing or for going to a poolhall or pub. During the 1950s, McCarthy-era investigations of teachers often led to dismissal, censorship, and teacher fear of discussing controversial topics such as communism or socialism. These sanctions against academic freedom were even incorporated into state laws binding teachers to obedience to certain political views; loyalty oaths were commonplace for teachers, but not for all citizens. In all of these instances, over a long period of American history, the restriction of teachers' freedom to teach imposed a similar restriction on students' freedom to learn. Where censorship of teachers occurs, students and democracy suffer. That, unfortunately, is a lesson that has not yet been fully learned.

We enter the twenty-first century with increased sophistication and the global spread of democracy. Since democracy and education are not served by restricting the freedom of competent teachers and their students, we must go beyond the narrow and biased blinders that limit what teachers can teach and what students can study. Teachers need and deserve to have full protection for their right to teach, and students need assurance of the right to learn. Sadly, however, there are still many gaps between a generalized acceptance of the idea of academic freedom for teachers and students, and the actual practices in the schools and communities.

Recent events illustrate these gaps. In 1995, a Colorado school district tried to fire a veteran, tenured high school teacher for showing the Bertolucci film *1900* to illustrate the negative consequences of fascism. This teacher had a very fine record as a stimulating teacher first in Vermont and then, for at least 10 years, in Colorado. As a good teacher, he had sometimes argued with the school administration in Colorado, and he had apparently gotten on the wrong side of the school principal. The teacher's social studies class, an honors course with a focus on debate, had been studying anarchy. Bertolucci's film, rated R and widely shown in public theaters several years earlier, was used as a springboard for discussion of the perils and pitfalls of anarchy, and it was an effective device. One issue for the school administration was that the teacher had failed to get administrative permission to show the film—a somewhat ironic twist that illustrates a concept of government opposite to anarchy, but not exactly consistent with democracy. That level of administrative oversight, of course, is also counter to academic freedom for teachers. The teacher was summarily dismissed, but the case went to a hearing at which Bertolucci personally testified, the Colorado Education Association provided legal support, and the American Association of University Professors (AAUP) offered assistance; the teacher won—a victory at that point for academic freedom. The principal subsequently tried to fire him on grounds that he was "late for faculty meetings" and had "missed classes." Fortunately, that case was also won by the teacher after considerable effort. Without the strong intervention of the teacher association and other offices, the essential academic freedom of a good teacher to use effective teaching material would have been denied. As it was, the dismissal action and resulting media publicity on the matter provided a chilling effect that could have caused many other teachers in Colorado schools to avoid controversy. So the threat to academic freedom remains; this teacher survived, but we don't know the fate of others who will not chance it.

In the past few years, parental complaints about young adult literature have produced censorious limits on what students can read in many communities. Judy Blume's books, for example, are widely read by adolescents and are considered to be good-quality literature, but they are also among the most common targets of censorship in schools and libraries. Vocal critics, school boards, and school administrators continue to censor and restrict such notable literary achievements as Richard Wright's *Native Son,* John Steinbeck's *Of Mice and Men,* Mark Twain's *Huckleberry Finn,* J. D. Salinger's *The Catcher in the Rye,* Maya Angelou's *I Know Why the Caged Bird Sings,* Chaucer's *Canterbury Tales,* and hundreds of other classic and widely respected books. Virtually every year school administrators and school boards cancel play productions, stop art exhibits, threaten teachers about dealing with sexual subjects, prohibit publication of student newspapers, and ban legitimate but controversial student organizations. Administrators have a mixed and often negative record in their support for academic freedom; it is not usually in the administrator's interest to have teachers and students deal with critical thinking or controversy (Daly, 1991).

OVERT AND SELF-CENSORSHIP

The *Intellectual Freedom Newsletter* of the American Library Association identifies current efforts to censor librarians, teachers, and young people; this monthly list of attacks on schools and libraries is sobering evidence of current restrictions on democracy and education. The national organization People for the American Way keeps track of censorship and monitors attempts to censor teachers and students across the United States. Its annual reports over the past 15 years have shown significant numbers of overt attempts to censor teachers and schools; for example, researchers confirmed 475 censoring incidents in 44 states during 1995–1996 (People for the American Way, 1996). These incidents are only the most obvious and more newsworthy events about which information on censorship is available. Even assuming that some of the reportage of censorship is subject to criticism because it may represent an overreaction to minor complaints, there has been a significant and continuing flow of censoring activity across the United States over a long period of time. This does not bode well for critical civic education.

Overt censorship and restrictions on teachers by school boards and administrators are only the tip of the iceberg. Many forms of censorship and other restrictions occur without publicity, without cries of outrage, without the knowledge of many people. These covert restraints occur when superintendents, school boards, principals, and teachers themselves decide that certain topics will not be open to inquiry in schools and this becomes a part of the ambience of the school. Teachers simply recognize that some topics are not permitted in this school. The threat of censorship and the vulnerability of teachers to administrative pressure create a chilling effect in schools that limits teacher and student freedoms. Teachers simply decide not to take the risk of dealing with controversy; they engage in self-censorship that restricts what their students can examine. Overt and covert restraints on the academic freedom of teachers and students are not merely inconveniences for education; they are fundamentally corrosive to the progress of society. Such restrictions constitute an elemental challenge to pedagogy.

ACADEMIC FREEDOM, TENURE, AND DEMOCRACY

Academic freedom should be a central concern for educators, because it is an essential component of our democratic culture. Dewey (1936) clearly stated this relationship: "Since freedom of mind and freedom of expression are the root of all freedom, to deny freedom in education is a crime against democracy" (p. 136). Phrased this way, the protection of teaching and learning is fundamental to democracy; it is the key professional concern for teachers. The public also has a stake in and strong reasons to provide that protection. The point is simply expressed: Education for citizenship in a democratic society requires academic freedom for teachers and students.

Historically, the major protection of academic freedom for teachers and students has been the tenure system. Without tenure, teachers can be fired for political or personal reasons, and a controversial teacher is most vulnerable when no rights to due process exist. Most states enacted tenure laws in the early part of the twentieth century partly to eliminate patronage hiring in the schools, partly to increase staff stability by providing teacher security, and partly to protect teachers from political influence and restriction. To gain tenure, teachers are normally required to complete two or three years of successful teaching, demonstrating that they are competent. A tenured teacher can still be fired, but only for just cause and with access to a hearing and due process. Tenure protection is necessary to academic freedom, since the legally prescribed causes for dismissal, the hearing, and due process requirements mitigate against summary dismissal for dealing with controversial topics.

Tenure is under threat because some consider it merely a device that enhances seniority and shields incompetent teachers. The link between tenure and academic freedom is often misunderstood because the public and even some teachers do not recognize the value of tenure as academic freedom's protection; they see it simply as job security. They think teachers need no more than First Amendment protection of speech. Yet the First Amendment does not protect teachers' job of educating for a democracy, only the right to speak. Therefore, the risk of being dismissed for performing their professional task of good education is always there. Teachers need more than freedom of speech to fulfill the obligations of critical civic education in a democracy. This point was made eloquently in a Supreme Court decision (*Keyishian v. Board of Regents*, 1967) that noted the necessity of a free marketplace of ideas in classrooms.

The primary role of teachers—to provide critical civic education for a democracy—is supported by tenure. Although the public usually understands why some job security is desirable, they seldom see why strong tenure laws are important, nor do they often see academic freedom as essential to education and democracy. Some members of the public believe that tenure allows incompetent teachers to keep their jobs and permits cunning teachers to brainwash their children. Too often teachers reflect this uninformed view that tenure is no more than a seniority-based employment benefit available to educators, not the basic protection for academic freedom as a right and responsibility of the profession. Some educators think that academic freedom and tenure are cosmetic terms for keeping a job or excuses for doing whatever comes to mind. Such educators do not think academic freedom is worth fighting over if the administration or board of education wants to exert control, but these teachers still want the security of their tenure. This is an internal threat to academic freedom, because these teachers have no professional commitment to education in a democracy. They want tenure but would not fight for academic freedom.

In contrast, we argue that academic freedom is the key legitimating concept for education in a democratic society and that the protection of academic freedom should be the foremost principle in teaching (Nelson, 1996). While academic freedom is a concept commonly associated with faculty in higher education, it is also an essential component of educational practice for teachers in K–12 schooling. Indeed, there is no serious educational activity that is not related to academic freedom for teachers and students. Funding, curriculum development, instructional practices, and the hiring, promotion, and retention of faculty are all directly related to the primary purposes of schooling—the development of knowledge. And that primary purpose depends on the freedom to teach and to learn. Consequently, the prospects for academic freedom are directly bound up with the fate of our democratic culture, and the survival of a democratic society is dependent on a certain level of public agreement regarding democratic values and institutions. The success and maintenance of academic freedom rely to a large extent on an informal social contract between educational institutions and the public.

Freedom to teach, to study, and otherwise to express ideas is dependent on public recognition of the professional status of educators and the public interest served by the marketplace of ideas. This teacher freedom undergirds student freedom to learn, and the protection of that dual and necessary freedom makes academic decision making a primary responsibility of faculty members. Yet curricular decisions are often made by boards and administrators with only minimal advisement from teachers.

While there is some recognition of the importance of academic freedom and tenure for precollege teachers, it is often circumscribed by traditional ideas of the school as an extension of the state and the family, and the teacher as a servant of both. State agencies and local community officials, acting *in loco parentis,* have always exerted far more control over curriculum and instruction in elementary and secondary schools than have teachers in those schools. Of course, academic freedom and academic autonomy have never been absolute in higher education either, since state governments often act to approve programs and mandate requirements. Teacher education programs are good examples of areas in which state regulation of higher education has been significant and often stultifying. Still, far more autonomy has usually existed in higher education than in K–12 education in terms of academic freedom and self-regulation.

THREATS TO ACADEMIC FREEDOM

Today, threats to academic freedom at all levels of education seem at least as serious as they have been at any time since the concept of teacher freedom became established in the twentieth century. Educators tend to take academic freedom and the tenure protection that helps maintain it for granted, as given parts of the culture of educational institutions. Such assumptions ignore how recently academic freedom has become part of the educational landscape, and they underestimate the struggles that were necessary to establish and maintain this freedom throughout the twentieth century. This freedom is especially fragile; it needs constant monitoring and vigilance.

Embedded in this social, political, and historical amnesia is an assumption that academic freedom is a fixed substantive concept that is accepted and applicable to a wide variety of educational situations. However, a closer examination of academic freedom shows that there is far less consensus on the meaning and importance of the concept than is often imagined. A number of disturbing trends that pose serious threats to the survival of academic freedom and its system of institutional support can be detected. Among these trends are the standards movement that takes academic decisions away from educators and replaces them with political decisions; the effort to destroy teacher tenure in many states; the movement toward field-centered teacher education, which rests heavily on teacher practice and disdains theoretical principles such as academic freedom; curriculum control by school boards at the local and state levels; government-mandated content and even teacher methods; unthoughtful government and media attacks on schooling and teachers that make teachers vulnerable to McCarthy-like restrictions; vigilante special-interest groups that protest controversial material in schools; fundamentalist religious and patriotic groups that demand a particular form of content or method in classrooms; and censorship of free speech and the arts in the wider society, which has a chilling effect on teachers. This list does not exhaust the threats to academic freedom. It is provided to illustrate them.

The maintenance of academic freedom is directly dependent on public support and a widespread consensus regarding the nature of democratic culture. Any threats to that culture can pose serious problems for educators in a democratic society. Significant threats to our democratic social values and academic freedom that were posed by the Red Scare in the 1920s and McCarthyism in the 1950s appear obvious in hindsight, but such threats were not obvious to the public at the time. There was broad public support of efforts to clean out communists and communist sympathizers from our schools. Protection of freedoms and rights were not considered of high importance. Teachers were fired for the slightest provocation; some were fired for merely claiming constitutional rights to remain silent. Congressional and state legislative hearings, offering grants of immunity, heard and publicly reported unsubstantiated testimony against innocent teachers that led to dismissals and public ostracism. Looking backward, the inherent unfairness of these shocking actions against competent teachers and their students is evident—but the tenor of the times clouded public judgment. Current threats to the social fabric have stimulated increased attacks on schools and teachers, expanding censorship and restricting freedom, but the public and many educators seem oblivious to such current dangers. These threats include some of those identified earlier, especially the efforts to censor or restrict public art, a free press, free speech, and peaceful protest. They also include attacks on civil liberties by radio and TV commentators as well as restrictive speech codes on college and precollege campuses.

THE CHANGING POLITICAL CULTURE

Over the past several decades our political culture and institutions, including education and the press, have come to be viewed with increasing suspicion and even contempt by large numbers of our population. Voter participation continues to be peculiarly low for a practicing democracy. Levels of political corruption appear to be reaching new highs. The need to raise ever greater amounts of money to be elected has badly distorted and corrupted political life.

The technological capacity of political, corporate, media, and other groups to control the formation and dissemination of knowledge has reached levels of effectiveness that would have been difficult to imagine at mid-century. The distinction between news and entertainment has blurred to the point of vanishing on most radio and television news broadcasts, and the media are far more concerned with handicapping the "horse-race" dimension of campaigns than the serious analysis of campaign issues. When the new information technologies are coupled with the knowledge explosion of the twentieth century, problems associated with trying to function as a reflective citizen are greatly multiplied. Teachers and schools have not escaped the negative influences of such developments.

Exacerbating the loss of faith in our political culture is the persistent fragmentation of the social order. The disparity of wealth and income between the most and the least powerful groups in our society has worsened over the last two decades, undermining the gains of the War on Poverty and the civil rights movement. Racism, ethnic strife, sexism, and homophobia remain deep and unresolved problems of the society. African American intellectuals write about the growing nihilism and despair in Black communities, as well as the increasing tendency to assume that the United States is an intrinsically racist culture with little prospect for change. The growing sense of despair among minorities is matched and fueled by the conservative White backlash against affirmative action and multicultural education.

Recent conservative scholarship, such as *The Bell Curve* (Hernstein & Murray, 1994), has contributed to these tensions by reviving "scientific" rationalizations for poverty and poor school performance among minority groups, especially African Americans. This is not the sort of social climate in which democratic practices such as academic freedom are likely to flourish. Indeed, the abolition of affirmative action in admissions at the University of California was an action of the public governing board of the university, done in direct opposition to the decisions of the faculty and the administration. This is a threat to both academic freedom and school autonomy in academic decisions. It also suggests that, even at the best institutions, academic freedom is not always secure.

PUBLIC SUPPORT FOR EDUCATION AND THREATS TO ACADEMIC FREEDOM

Beyond the general decline in support for our political culture, we can point to some specific educational developments that pose direct threats to academic freedom. Probably the most troubling development is the general loss of confidence in our public school system and increasing attacks on higher education. Of course, public education has been a target of criticism since it was established. Those who assume that there was a "golden age" of American education when we did it right are indulging in uninformed nostalgia. But the more recent attacks on public education are qualitatively different in their effects. In the past, there was a general consensus regarding the importance of public education in a democratic society. Most of the educational debates were about how such education should be conducted. However, during the 1960s, public expectations regarding educational reforms were raised to new levels by an unprecedented infusion of federal money for reforms and innovations. This period also marked the intensification of state and federally mandated school desegregation plans.

There was little evidence of any significant short-term effects of the education reforms of the 1960s. Desegregation efforts produced White flight and the de facto resegregation of many urban schools. Scholars such as Coleman and colleagues (1966) and Jencks and colleagues (1972) offered evidence that cultural factors beyond the control of schools were far more important determinants of student progress than the increased amounts of money spent on teacher salaries, materials, buildings, and reforms. Public consensus regarding the value of our public school systems declined appreciably (Goodlad, 1984). In addition, the cultural changes associated with the 1960s came to be understood as a cause of a more general cultural decline and the erosion of educational standards. This was a time of attacks on many social institutions and threats to broad social values.

The public is notoriously impatient to see evidence that educational reforms are working. Often these expectations are unreasonable. As a consequence, there is a tendency to move from one reform to the next without adequate time to assess whether the previous reform has had the desired effects. Some reforms were, no doubt, not worth saving, but the constant shift from one reform to another has only served to maintain a sense of perpetual crisis and failure. Since the reforms of the 1960s, we have witnessed almost three decades of new reform initiatives. Recall, for example, career education, the accountability movement, management by objectives, back to basics, national standards (Goals 2000), total quality management, authentic assessment, character education, outcomes-based education, magnet schools, voucher systems, and charter schools, to name some of the most prominent.

Each reform was instigated, in part, by a new criticism of public schooling. This critique of public education reached new levels of intensity in 1982 with the publication of *A Nation at Risk*, followed by a series of other reports critical of education. Following the disillusionment with the 1960s, the past two decades of attacks have taken their toll on public perceptions of education, as witnessed in various polls taken over the past three decades. Interestingly, this change in perception largely occurred regarding schools other than the respondents' local schools; annual Gallup survey data collected for Phi Delta Kappa over 25 years show that local schools continue to be rated highly while respondents think less of schools in other locations ("31st Annual Phi Delta Kappa/Gallup Poll," 1999).

It is now common to see media reports in which public education is described as a dismal failure and our students' performance a national disgrace when compared with students in other industrialized nations. The evidence presented in the media and through government sources for the claim that American schools were in significant decline was often in the form of standardized test scores (e.g., the SAT, reading and math tests) as well as hyperbole (Hirsch, 1987; Ravitch & Finn, 1987). Such allegations are taken as given and rarely challenged by reporters, although there is ample evidence that American schools were not significantly worse than they have been in other historical periods and were actually doing a good job considering their circumstances, such as the fact that the United States spent a lower proportion of gross domestic product on education than other industrial democracies (Berliner & Biddle, 1995; Bracey, 1991, 1992, 1993). In fact, the Bush administration actually engaged in censorship to prevent publication of a study demonstrating that U.S. public schools were better than the Bush administration wanted the public to believe (Carson, Huelscamp, & Woodall, 1992; Sandia National Laboratories, 1993; Tanner, 1993).

THE NATIONAL STANDARDS MOVEMENT AS AN EXAMPLE

Beyond the loss of public confidence in our schools, the federal government's response to the perceived (some would say manufactured) crisis in education has had other effects as well. A movement to set national standards gained considerable momentum during the 1980s and early 1990s. The idea of academic standards against which students would be measured was part of the public debate over schooling during much of the twentieth century, but the recent movement was characterized by significant bipartisan political support at the federal and state levels as well as an agenda consistent with the national drift toward conservatism over the last two decades. It resulted not from a call by educators but from a meeting of state governors from which educators were excluded. This conservative political context combined with strong educational considerations raises important issues for academic freedom. These issues have rarely been addressed in the debates over national standards, but they may be more important to teachers over the long term than any other issues posed by the standards movement.

The deprofessionalization of teaching (Apple, 1993) is incorporated in many current proposals for school reform—often imposed on teachers without their consultation or consent—and in the national standards movement as well. These actions to denigrate, ignore, or destroy teacher participation in academic decision making deserve full attention from teachers and students, and opposition where needed. Such attention and opposition, however, require teachers to exercise academic freedom to challenge the government and local leaders, an effort that has not had much success so far. Meanwhile, the deskilling of teachers continues apace. If teachers are deprofessionalized, do they need or deserve academic freedom? This is a serious matter, basic to an understanding of democracy and education. An examination of the conservative context of the standards debate leads to serious concerns about the protection of academic freedom for teachers and students and about the threat that these standards might pose to the essential purposes of education in a democratic society.

Standards, a crucial aspect of the long-term effort to bring a more mechanical and corporate form of accountability to schooling, have become a politically popular device to placate conservative critics. The standards movement derives much of its support from the business ethos of efficiency and cost savings that has afflicted public education since the turn of the twentieth century (Callahan, 1962), as well as from the behavioral science and measurement mentality that presumes that all significant human activity is measurable and malleable. This combination of corporate assembly-line structure and an increasing precision in the test-ing and reportage of test results raises serious questions about individual, educational, and social consequences. Such questions relate to social con-formity, intellectual restriction, ethical backwardness, and the reproduc-tion of a social-class hierarchy. Further, there are questions of individual integrity and social ethics that arise in examining the potential impact of narrowly constructed standards on the public schools.

The recent conservative critique of the national history standards is a good example of the fragility of academic freedom today. In 1992, the National Endowment for the Humanities (NEH) provided funding to de-velop national history standards. The National Center for History in the Schools, under the direction of Gary Nash and Charlotte Crabtree, was contracted to do the work. In 1994, before the project was completed, the standards were subject to a vicious attack by Lynne Cheney (who had headed NEH when the project was funded), Rush Limbaugh, Ralph Reed, Pat Robertson, and others (Nash, Crabtree, & Dunn, 1997). It is interesting that, for the most part, the actual standards were not criticized. What the critics attacked were the sample lesson plans and activities provided to illustrate how the standards could be taught. The critics felt that too much attention was placed on women and minorities, criticism of U.S. policies and practices in the past, and the study of Asia, Africa, and Latin America. There was also a call to place more emphasis on heroes in U.S. history. As a result, the standards were significantly revised, largely for political as opposed to academic reasons (Nash, Crabtree, & Dunn, 1997).

IDEOLOGY, KNOWLEDGE, AND ACADEMIC FREEDOM

More recently, the attack on public education has included higher ed-ucation and the search for knowledge as well as the public schools. At-tacks on higher education are not new, but the nature of the attack has changed—and in ways that pose serious threats to academic freedom in higher education and in precollege schooling. Schools at all levels are influenced by attacks on ideas and by critics' efforts to limit academic freedom. What is taught and what is censored in higher education greatly affect which ideas are permitted, examined, and respected in precollege schools. And teachers often teach as they have been taught. Restrictions on thought in colleges are reflected in restrictions in precollege schools; similarly, restrictions in schools limit the critical thinking of students who go on to higher education and to research. Restrictions in colleges also give sustenance to those who want to restrict precollege schooling.

Current intellectual debates, often referred to as the "culture wars," raise questions about knowledge, education, and academic freedom. The debates are a valid and valuable exercise, suited to education in a democracy. The effort to unduly limit and censor the opposite view, however, is detrimental to the basic premise of education and is an important threat to academic freedom for teachers and students. Throughout this century, conservative critics have expressed concern regarding the influence of leftist ideologies on the academy (e.g., Buckley, 1951), but the focus of this critique has shifted since the 1980s. The publication of Bloom's (1987) *The Closing of the American Mind* is one important indication of a turning point. Bloom's critique has been followed by many others (e.g., Bennett, 1994; D'Souza, 1991; Hirsch, 1987; Kimball, 1990; Ravitch & Finn, 1987; Shaw, 1989; Smith, 1990; Sykes, 1988, 1990).

The new conservative critics have made two basic charges. (1) Leftist ideas have gained undue influence throughout education, with the most dangerous effect of such influence being the politicization of the curriculum, particularly in the humanities. (2) The new leftist scholarship promotes various forms of relativism that undermine or reject traditional standards of rationality and objectivism. The importance of the new conservative criticism is the implied or direct claim that the leftist influence should be purged from the curriculum and that many of the proponents of multiculturalism and postmodernism are not entitled to the protection of academic freedom. The reasoning employed is not too dissimilar to the earlier arguments posed by Sidney Hook (1953, 1970, 1974) to the effect that communists did not have the right to teach in our schools since they rejected and worked to undermine our democratic culture and values. There are times, Hook (1974) claimed, that "in the interest of preserving the entire structure of our desirable freedoms, we may be compelled to abridge one or another of our strategic freedoms" (p. 93). Because Hook was one of John Dewey's most prominent students, his ideas on academic freedom are especially troubling; it is noteworthy that Dewey rejected Hook's view.

In many respects, the new conservative critics make a similar case against ideas about multiculturalism and postmodernism. Multiculturalism includes contemporary attempts by the left to politicize the curriculum by a focus on examining which groups and interests are favored and which are ignored in school studies; postmodernism includes the promotion of relativism and skepticism about what we know and can know (Menand, 1996). Multiculturalism provides an interdisciplinary avenue for discourse about divergent groups in society; postmodernism offers an intellectual critique of knowledge, its nature, methods, and use. Many vocal right-wing conservatives argue that those who propagate leftist ideas have abandoned the very standards of scholarship upon which academic freedom is based (Hook, 1970; Menand, 1996). But the conservative critics pose a false choice in this instance. Lumping all proponents of multiculturalism and postmodernism into one category creates gross oversimplification and distortion. Also, it is clear that curricula at all levels of schooling have always been politicized; they follow social ideas and expectations of what should be taught—not some completely objective and unchallengeable truth. The leftist critique of schooling merely makes that an obvious point, a place of departure to examine why schools follow certain ideologies and who benefits from that. This critique is uncomfortable for those whose views are well established in schooling, and they do not want to be challenged.

The conservative critique of multiculturalism and postmodernism is often based on a static view of knowledge and a serious misunderstanding of academic freedom. The conservative call to limit academic freedom tends to restrict and distort knowledge as opposed to promoting and protecting it. Since both our knowledge and our ways of knowing are in constant flux, our conceptions of academic freedom must be continually examined and applied pragmatically to be relevant to the changing context. For example, our concept of academic freedom must be flexible enough to incorporate the sort of protections required during dramatic scientific paradigm shifts, as described by Thomas Kuhn (1996). We do not want our schools to be in the position of silencing some future Galileo. On the other hand, flexibility does not require that we treat "creation science" as if it held the same truth value as evolutionary theory (Kuhn, 1996).

DISCIPLINES AND ACADEMIC FREEDOM

There is another serious issue obscured by the ferocity of the conservative criticism. Historically, the compact between the public and institutions of higher education has involved entrusting the monitoring of scholarship to experts in the disciplines. The disciplines, in turn, have worked through the departmental structure that organizes most institutions of higher education. Multiculturalism and postmodernism, in contrast, have an interdisciplinary focus (e.g., women's studies, African American studies, cultural studies, science and technology studies). In addition, postmodernism questions the nature, the value, and the very possibility of imposed standards, objective truth, and precise boundaries claimed by the disciplines. By extension, postmodern thought questions exactly the kinds of standards contained in the national Goals 2000 project and in lists in various states of necessary information that all students must possess; similarly, the rigidity and class bias of standardized testing and student tracking is questioned in postmodernist thought. These ideas challenge much in the traditional views of knowledge and its organization and presentation.

There is nothing sacrosanct about the social constructions we call disciplines, most of which emerged in the late nineteenth century. Yet precollege and higher education institutions are often organized as though the disciplines are entirely separate and distinct, the only avenue to knowledge. And many teachers act as though the disciplines defined knowledge, with students coming to learn the separation between fields rather than the connections. Disciplines are but one way of categorizing our perceptions of reality; they are not that reality. It has become increasingly difficult for scholars in the various disciplines to maintain foundational bases for their various knowledge claims, and some of the most intriguing avenues of scholarship are derived from nondisciplinary or cross-disciplinary study. Human problems do not limit themselves to disciplinary structures and are not subject to singular disciplines for solutions. In some situations it is clear that the disciplines have functioned to suppress and distort knowledge to protect traditional practitioners, limiting intellectual inquiry; this raises questions about accepted disciplinary standards. Ironically, the very disciplinary structure entrusted with the power to protect scholarly inquiry has, on occasion, actually diluted it—and diminished academic freedom in the process.

Exclusionary effects of the departmental/disciplinary structure appear when the national standards movement is examined. The general thrust of the national standards has been to reassert the primacy of disciplinary knowledge and to diminish the significance of interdisciplinary studies. This shift in focus has significant consequences for school curricula by limiting interdisciplinary approaches and imposing traditional views. This was most evident when the national standards in history were introduced and conservative critics were able to get the standards withdrawn and then significantly changed because they considered the original standards to be too multicultural and not inclusive of enough pro-American or traditional views. This was not a question of truth or knowledge, but of political ideology.

We should add that the conservative critics are not the only threat to the survival of academic freedom in the debates over knowledge and culture(s). The misguided arguments of extremist proponents of multiculturalism or postmodernism do much to undermine public support and academic credibility. Public education cannot function in a climate of disrespect or denial of opposing views. This stance is as dogmatic as the conservative positions attacked by those on the left. There is not only a significant danger from the extreme right; there is an equal danger from the unprincipled and antirational left. Academic freedom is under attack by both.

There is nothing intrinsically wrong with standards or disciplines, as long as we understand them as examples of many ways of knowing. They are not everlasting or universal truths, although they may seem to have that aura. The problem lies not in the concept of standards or disciplines as such, but in how they are developed, implemented, and open to modification or elimination. It is logically impossible to construct disciplines and standards without excluding some forms of knowledge. This effect is unavoidable. The danger is that standards or disciplines will be presented or perceived as permanent and unchallengeable. That is a serious problem when those inflexible standards and disciplines become the only criteria for measuring student achievement. In the highly politicized climate of public schooling today, the ideas most likely to be excluded are those that are critical of dominant or traditional forms of knowledge.

In addition, the very basis for a disciplinary approach to knowledge is a social construction that can have negative consequences. Of course, the standards movement is part of a response by conservative scholars against just this sort of criticism of disciplines (Giroux, 1989; Presseisen, 1985; Nelson, Palonsky, & Carlson, 2000). Standards are used to permanently fix certain information and disciplines. Proponents of a narrow disciplinary approach are unlikely to suppress this debate in the long run; democracy should win out, and the debates will continue. However, one of the negative consequences of the effort to limit the debate by setting precise standards and restricting knowledge to select disciplines is a gradual erosion of public support for public education and for academic freedom. After all, if experts can't agree on truth claims or even on how such claims could be established, why should they be entrusted with the power to monitor the production of knowledge? This description oversimplifies the issue, but this is how things probably appear to many outside the academy and many who don't like the uncertainty of fundamental issues.

Political disputes often lack subtlety. There may be good reasons now to reexamine and reject the departmental/disciplinary structure that had served to monitor and enforce academic freedom for most of this century. Protectionists leading the charge toward rigid standards and traditional disciplinary information may have become a force against change and challenge. But the continued success of academic freedom cannot exist in a vacuum, without some legitimate structure(s). We need new structures and arguments to supplant and expand the traditional disciplinary model, as well as a way to persuade the public that we can be trusted to maintain academic quality. This is more than an academic squabble; academic freedom is basic to a democracy. When public support for diversity in academic ideas is restricted, all teachers and students suffer—and the society succumbs to hardening of the democratic arteries.

RIGHTS, FREEDOM, AND THE TEACHER

A discussion of rights depends upon an understanding of diverse views of the nature of individuals and their societies. Individual rights exist within a societal context; they are defined, limited, and changed within that context. Rights grant power, whether to large masses of people, elite groups, or certain individuals. This defines, in the broadest terms, a distinction among democracies, oligarchies, and dictatorships. Democracies require basic rights of individual citizens for self-governance, and that self-governance depends on freedom in education. Oligarchies grant dominant rights to a small group of leaders, and only that group requires freedom in education. Dictatorships are even more hierarchical regarding rights, with the most rights accrued by the dictator and less requirement for freedom in education for broad categories of people.

There is a clear and forthright relationship between the requirements of a society that intends to be a democracy and the necessity of freedom for teachers and students to investigate ideas. The United States has a checkered history of support for teacher and student freedom. Those freedoms cannot be assumed or left to chance. There are many current insidious threats. These circumstances provide excellent reasons to renew our commitment to academic freedom (Daly & Roach, 1990). To paraphrase Jefferson: Democracy and ignorance cannot coexist. Democracy is shackled when the populace is shackled by censorship and restraint of thought. Yet teachers and their students continue to be limited and restrained in the search for knowledge. Prior to modern civil and democratic society, teaching was essentially the passing on of accepted and acceptable dogma. Teachers were not expected to deviate from or question authority, and students were penalized for doing so. In modern society, in a United States committed to democratic principles, such teaching should be an anomaly. Teachers and students not only deserve the right to teach and learn, they require it.

REFERENCES

Apple, M. (1993). *Official knowledge: Democratic education in a conservative age*. New York: Routledge.

Bennett, W. J. (1994). *The devaluing of America: The fight for our culture and our children*. New York: Summit.

Berliner, D.C., & Biddle, B. J. (1995). *The manufactured crisis: Myths, fraud, and the attack on America's public schools*. New York: Addison-Wesley.

Bloom, A. (1987). *The closing of the American mind: How higher education has failed democracy and impoverished the souls of today's students*. New York: Simon & Schuster.

Bracey, G. W. (1991). Why can't they be like we were? *Phi Delta Kappan, 73*(2), 104–117.

Bracey, G. W. (1992). The second Bracey report on the condition of public education. *Phi Delta Kappan, 74*(2), 104–117.

Bracey, G. W. (1993). The third Bracey report on the condition of public education. *Phi Delta Kappan, 75*(2), 104–117.

Buckley, W. F., Jr. (1951). *God and man at Yale: The superstitions of academic freedom*. Chicago: Henry Regnery.

Callahan, R. E. (1962). *Education and the cult of efficiency: A study of the social forces that have shaped the administration of the public schools*. Chicago: University of Chicago Press.

Carson, C., Huelscamp, R., & Woodall, T. (1992). *Perspectives on education in America, final draft*. Albuquerque, NM: Sandia National Laboratories.

Coleman, J. S., Campbell, E. Q., Hobson, C. J., McPartland, J., Moody, A. M., Weinfield, F. D., & York, R. L. (1966). *Equality of educational opportunity*. Washington, DC: U.S. Government Printing Office.

Daly, J. K. (1991). The influence of administrators on the teaching of social studies. *Theory and Research in Social Education, 19*, 267–283.

Daly, J. K., & Roach, P. B. (1990). Reaffirming a commitment to academic freedom. *Social Education, 54*, 342–345.

Dewey, J. (1936). The social significance of academic freedom. *Social Frontier, 2*, 136.

D'Souza, D. (1991). *Illiberal education: The politics of race and sex on campus*. New York: Free Press.

Giroux, H. (1989). Rethinking educational reform in the age of George Bush. *Kappan 70*, 728–730.

Goodlad, J. J. (1984). *A place called school: Prospects for the future*. New York: McGraw-Hill.

Hernstein, R. J., & Murray, C. (1994). *The bell curve: The reshaping of American life by differences in intelligence*. New York: Free Press.

Hirsch, E. D. (1987). *Cultural literacy: What every American needs to know*. Boston: Houghton Mifflin.

Hook, S. (1953). *Heresy, yes. Conspiracy, no*. New York: John Day.

Hook, S. (1970). *Academic freedom and academic anarchy*. New York: Basic Books.

Hook, S. (1974). *Pragmatism and the tragic sense of life*. New York: Basic Books.

Jencks, C., Smith, M., Acland, H., Bane, M., Cohen, D., Gintis, H., Heyns, B., & Michaelson, S. (1972). *Inequality: A reassessment of the effect of family and schooling in America.* New York: Basic Books.

Keyishian v. Board of Regents of New York, 385 U.S. 589 (1967).

Kimball, R. (1990). *Tenured radicals: How politics has corrupted our higher education.* New York: Harper & Row.

Kuhn, T. (1996). *The structure of scientific revolutions* (3rd ed.). Chicago: University of Chicago Press.

Menand, L. (Ed.). (1996). *The future of academic freedom.* Chicago: University of Chicago Press.

Nash, G. B., Crabtree, C., & Dunn, R. E. (1997). *History on trial: Culture wars and the teaching of the past.* New York: Knopf.

Nelson, J. (1996). Academic freedom. In B. Massialas & R. Allen (Eds.), *Critical issues in teaching social studies K-12* (pp. 387–408). New York: Wadsworth.

Nelson, J., Palonsky, S., & Carlson, K. (2000). *Critical issues in education.* New York: McGraw-Hill.

People for the American Way (Eds.). (1996). *Attacks on the freedom to learn.* Washington, DC: Author.

Presseisen, B. (1985). *Unlearned lessons.* Philadelphia: Falmer.

Ravitch, D., & Finn, C. (1987). *What do our 17-year-olds know?* New York: Harper & Row.

Sandia National Laboratories. (1993). Perspectives on education in America: An annotated briefing. *Journal of Educational Research, 86*(5), 259–310.

Shaw, P. (1989). *The war against the intellect: Episodes in the decline of discourse.* Iowa City: University of Iowa Press.

Smith, P. (1990). *Killing the spirit: Higher education in America.* New York: Viking.

Sykes, C. J. (1988). *Profscam: Professors and the demise of higher education.* New York: Kampmann.

Sykes, C. J. (1990). *The hollow men: Politics and corruption in higher education.* Washington, DC: Regnery Gateway.

Tanner, D. (1993). A nation truly at risk. *Phi Delta Kappan, 75,* 288–297.

The 31st annual Phi Delta Kappa/Gallup poll of the public's attitude toward the public schools. (1999). *Phi Delta Kappan, 81*(1), 41–58.

Voices of the Challenged

JAMES K. DALY, PATRICIA L. SCHALL,
& ROSEMARY W. SKEELE

Censorship is never over for those who have experienced it. It is a brand
on the imagination that affects the individual who has suffered it, forever.
—Nadine Gordimer, *Censorship and Its Aftermath*

A BOOK ABOUT challenges to pedagogy would be incomplete without a
chapter devoted to the voices of the challenged, a forum in which teachers who lived or continue to live within conflict can tell their own stories
firsthand. In the first three chapters of this book, we described River Haven, a community in conflict. We heard the voices of many parents embroiled in the conflict, a principal under siege, an administrator associated with the district, and one retired teacher. Missing were the voices of
all the current teachers from the Rock Spring School. We continue to wonder how they felt about what happened and how our case study would
have been different and richer and fuller if we had heard from them. As
we talked to people in River Haven and wrote this book, we often speculated about the teachers' silence and wondered if it reflected an ongoing
fear of reprisals if they spoke. Contemplating the silence of the Rock
Spring teachers, we decided to give voice to other teachers who were
willing to share their stories. We hope that their stories will help teachers
become more aware of the nature and consequences of challenges to pedagogy.

In this chapter, we let five teachers who have faced or continue to
face challenges speak for themselves. Unlike the Rock Spring conflict,
most of the incidents the teachers describe here are more typical of the
kinds of overt censorship attempts that continue to erupt across the na-

tion. Moffett (1988) attributed the increase in censorship attempts to the rise of conservatism throughout the world, a force he described as more than "a mere political ideology . . . it is a direction in which very different types of people move when they become anxious" (p. 187). These five teachers will tell you about the human cost of censorship, the mental anxiety, physical stress, ethical confusion, self-doubt, financial burdens, and career reevaluation they experienced. They describe their post-challenge doubts, misgivings, and hesitations as they returned, or failed to return, to their classrooms. These teachers, who understand the trauma of challenges, might have some advice for some educators who believe that censorship can be avoided, without educational loss to children, and who are convinced that teachers who become embroiled in controversies are the kind who are looking for trouble (Whitson, 1994). The five women who share their stories here learned that teaching can be a risky business. We will let our readers decide if these women were, in the parlance of sexual assault, "asking for it."

THE ADAMS COUNTY WITCH

By Jan Cole

Throughout our district—Adams County School District 12, North-glenn/Thornton, Colorado—the 1996 school year began with an over-whelming number of parents questioning and attacking our teachers and administrators. A parent accused a female second-grade teacher of sexual abuse for giving her daughter a gift, a bottle of perfume matching her name. In a three-page letter, a mother accused me of insensitivity for "punishing [her] child for not bringing all his school supplies." In truth, he stayed in for recess with several other children to complete a project because he had forgot materials the previous day.

I have stepped out before to tell my story, but not in a long time. Many of the scars are healed, but not all. Telling the story doesn't neces-sarily anesthetize the pain. There are times when listening to someone else who has suffered attacks by the religious right causes my heart to ache and my eyes to fill with tears, as they did when I wrote this story. At other times the tears still come unexpectedly.

The school year began much the same as other years, the bulletin boards nearly finished, the first week's plans ready, and the desks neatly arranged to leave a large empty space in the middle of the room. I was ready for my new students—filled with fresh expectations for the sixth grade. For our first use of the empty space, we sat on pillows in a circle reviewing classroom rules, answering questions, learning about acceptable behavior, and discussing the time-out room (the school's disciplinary area). The students had many emotional and learning problems. They were unruly, disobedient, and uncooperative. Many students had been to the time-out room the year before for a variety of offenses. "The time-out room is my worst punishment. I don't like to use it," I told them. "I'd like you to be in charge of your own behavior."

Sometime during the first 2 days, I had the children do a relaxation technique. They created an imaginary room in which they could relax, manage stress, study their spelling words, learn their math facts, or engage in creative writing. It's a technique I'd learned in a university class and had used effectively for about 7 years, so I thought nothing special about it. Eventually, the students would draw a picture of "their room," including its design and layout, a place to rest, a wall or screen on which to practice their words and facts, and anything else they'd like in the room. While they worked, I played baroque music by Telemann, as suggested in a popular book for teachers.

We spent a few minutes talking about fears and how they could keep us from getting what we want and need. Earlier in the year, I had participated in a workshop in which we had walked on a 30-inch bed of hot coals. It had been an exhilarating experience, and I was proud to share what I had learned about myself and fear, cautioning that the experience needed guidance and wasn't something you went out to your backyard to do.

Thursday morning of that first week, several children informed me, "Pam's leaving." Puzzled, I spoke with Pam at recess. No, she wasn't moving. She started to cry. "It's about the rooms in our minds or something like that. I don't want to leave, Ms. Cole. I don't know what the matter is." I reassured her that I would speak to her parents that evening at Back-to-School Night, not understanding anymore than Pam did about her leaving.

While visiting with other parents, I watched Mrs. Arlene Lehman, Pam's mother, looking closely and suspiciously at everything in the room. She didn't speak, didn't approach me as other parents did. She moved to leave. "Can I help you?" I asked.

"No." She offered nothing.

I tried again. "Is there a problem? Is there something I can explain to you?"

Her cool response was, "No, we'll be meeting with the principal in the morning."

I spent the rest of the evening worrying about what I might have done wrong, reliving the hours the children and I had spent those first few days. I didn't sleep well that night. I didn't know it would be the first of many restless nights to come in the next 4 years. Next morning, I headed for the principal's office, my heart pounding loudly. I interrupted the casual conversation between Mr. Robert Huckins, my principal, and Mr. and Mrs. Lehman. When they were ready to include me, Mrs. Lehman arrogantly began with, "We're Christians." List in hand, she proceeded with her accusations:

- Ms. Cole made the children sit in a circle on the floor and confess all their sins, all things they'd done wrong.
- Ms. Cole walked on fire, and it says in the Bible not to associate with people who have passed through the flames.
- Ms. Cole played flute music, which was related to Pan and the devil.
- Ms. Cole hypnotized the children, made them focus on a light; therefore, that is yoga; therefore, that is Hinduism; therefore, that is not separation of church and state.

I was stunned and interrupted to ask if I could respond to her list. First, I let them know that Pam didn't have to do the relaxation technique. Second, she could go to the library during that time. Third, the principal offered to put her in the class next to mine. Fourth, he could place her at a district school a few blocks away. Nothing dissuaded them; they believed that I hypnotized children and that that was evil. They removed Pam from my classroom, and I didn't see her again for several years.

Other than sporadic remarks about why Pam left, our class went on and the incident was forgotten—until October, when Mrs. Sandy Montoya requested a conference. She had many questions and comments similar to those of the Lehmans. She also inquired about Orville, a little clay figure I had made many years before as part of our behavior modification point system. Later, I discovered Orville had earned the title of the "demon on my desk." Mrs. Montoya apparently left satisfied with my explanations and later, during parent–teacher conferences, expressed no further concerns. According to her daughter, she was happy the children were learning how to relax.

One December afternoon a few days before Christmas vacation, Mr. Huckins called me to his office. Letter in hand, he briefly mentioned its contents before giving it to me. It was addressed to our superintendent and signed by the Lehmans. As I read the letter the second time, I experienced my first—and, indeed, not my last—feelings of shame and embarrassment. This letter had been sent to my superintendent!

It is our firm conviction that some of her methods are spiritistic in nature and qualify as religious instruction and not as purely educational. While we are concerned over admitted use of occult methods to find personal guidance, we recognize her right to practice her own faith. However, when she introduces eastern mediational techniques into the classroom we feel we must draw the line. Though Ms. Cole is personable and popular, we have seen adverse effects on our children due to this occult material.

"You don't have to do anything. Just relax and have a great vacation." The principal didn't seem as concerned as I was, but then he wasn't the accused.

Rumors began circulating the following March. Orville was a demon. I had a demon in me. Children needed to be protected from me. I learned that parents were meeting with a fundamentalist minister and the media to discuss "foreign religions in schools." A film condemning New Age beliefs and Eastern religions was shown at local churches.

My principal agreed when Mrs. Montoya requested another meeting, assuming it would be just the three of us. Five parents appeared with a representative from a Chicago group whose mission is to return Christianity to the public schools. Unprepared for this confrontation, I did my best to defend my position and support my teaching ideas. They came with new accusations: I didn't eat red meat, didn't use drugs, didn't go to a Christian church, used color therapy, taught meditation, used hypnotic techniques, used mind projection, initiated guided imagery, led children to the "inner rooms" of their minds, and promoted "altered states of consciousness." Mrs. Montoya requested that Jessica be transferred to another classroom.

My stomach was knotted; I felt numb, immobile as I packed that night for our 4-day Outdoor Education Program trip beginning the next morning. The next evening at camp I learned that Mrs. Lehman had called to warn the camp personnel that I practiced witchcraft and was going to make all the children meditate. Mrs. Lehman suggested that the camp director could help in "ferreting out the work of the devil" by encouraging the children to walk out if I said certain things. The week went smoothly despite obvious tensions and whispers.

More letters were sent to administrators, the principal, and myself. Rumors, whispers, and remarks from my students escalated. Some students told me they had been invited to meetings to see a movie about the awful things I did. Dealing with the issues and remarks frequently interfered with teaching time and the children's learning. Obviously the children's loyalties were torn between their parents and myself.

A special policy council subcommittee was set up to investigate the accusations. Members met with parents, ministers, and other members of the community. The list of accusations grew from 4 to 36 and included not using the time-out room enough, not having pierced ears, being emotionally unstable for having had tears in my eyes when two teachers delivered a rose and a card signed by all the faculty, teaching automatic writing, making children focus on a light bulb, requiring students to attend parent–teacher conferences, arranging students in a circle for problem solving, and hugging my sixth-graders.

Without preparation, without counsel, and without knowing all the accusations, I endured 4 hours of questioning from the 10-member subcommittee. Two weeks later my students were individually interrogated—a very stressful experience for them. I would have to wait until the August board meeting for their findings to be presented and until September to hear any decisions regarding my career.

After much deliberation and coaxing from school administrators, friends, ministers, and my brother (an attorney), and with the help of Bill Bethke, attorney for the Colorado Education Association (CEA), I filed a libel and slander suit against the three main instigating parents, Mr. and Mrs. Lehman and Mrs. Montoya. I had no idea how difficult this would become, but nothing else seemed to stop the vicious lies and attacks by a group of parents who, we eventually learned, were supported and coached by the Concerned Women of America, a religious right organization.

The story soon hit the local and religious newspapers and continued for months. Some of the headlines read "District 12 Teacher Accused of Occult Teachings," "Teacher Sues Parents Who Accused Her of Satanism," "School District 12 Owes Parents an Answer," "Teachers Have Rights Too," and "Teaching Parents a Lesson." Numerous letters to the editor also appeared in local newspapers.

Several parents monitored my classroom to gather evidence of my "inappropriate" behavior and supposed incompetence. The day my students and I used pantomime to explore nonverbal communication was followed by accusations of "mind controlling the whole sixth grade." Two long pieces of masking tape in the shape of a plus sign on the carpet—clearly marked N, S, E, and W to help my children learn coordinates on the globe—were rumored to be "the devil's cross." Collectively the rumors produced self-doubt and feelings of powerlessness, and adding to my paranoia about doing anything right or creative.

For years to come the stress took its toll with physical problems, sleepless nights, anxiety, tears, self-doubt, a waning sense of security, feelings of worthlessness and shame, and a desire to give up—to quit teaching. As a small-town girl from Minnesota, this "thing" was "too big" for me. During my 17-year teaching career I had never been taught how to deal with the public criticism and politics involved in this conflict. Sometimes I thought, "Perhaps they're right, maybe I am evil, maybe I am doing demonic things." I was overwhelmed by the negative public pressure and for about a month contemplated suicide.

Preparing for the trial was exhausting. In spite of the wonderful support I had from faculty, friends, family, my local association—particularly our president, Jay Rust—the CEA, and others, I felt a profound sense of isolation, finding no one, no group that could truly identify with my story, my pain. I was devastated when I heard the words "You're going to trial Monday, Jan."

The civil trial lasted 5 long and intense days. The jury ruled unanimously in my favor! I was awarded monetary damages for libel and slander from each of the three parents. The feeling of having this massive weight removed from my mind and body was indescribable. It was over, I thought, and they ruled in my favor.

But it wasn't over. There were more letters to the editor and articles in magazines and newspapers. Pat Robertson showed my picture on *The 700 Club,* a Christian television program, stating that my trial judge had erred and the case should be appealed. He continued:

> Ladies and gentlemen, here's the secret of education. Education has traditionally been the way that we transmit the values of a culture, our culture to our children. It's also the way that a totalitarian state indoctrinates its children contrary to whatever they believed before. The public education system can be used and has been used under the communist influence, under the Nazis in Germany, the Fascists in Italy, to move children's perception into a new realm of thinking and that very same thing seems to be rearing its head today. We get a feeling that there's someone or a group that are deliberately trying to move our children away from the traditions of their nation and indoctrinate them in a different set of values. (Robertson, 1989)

The Lehmans filed for retrial. Beverly LaHaye's Concerned Women for America, a conservative right-wing group, sent a three-page letter about my "occultic practices" to Christians across the United States requesting donations to continue the fight. This attempt by the right to regroup continued for almost 2 years. Finally, a check was delivered to my attorney, retrial efforts stopped, and the legal battles were over.

I've stayed at the same school all these years, but not without consequences. Some parents still don't want their children in my room. The witch-hunt, name-calling, and lies have stopped. I continue to do relaxation techniques, play flute music, rarely use the time-out room, don't eat red meat or have pierced ears. I still look for new and innovative ideas, but I am more cautious and think twice before I act. I've never regained the enthusiasm I once had for teaching. These battles do leave lasting impressions.

THE SAGA OF SUNSHINE CITY

By Janet Cooper

I began my teaching career in 1967, at age 44, with the Kingsville (Texas) Independent School District (KISD), and was assigned to teach U.S. history to high school juniors. From day one, I loved teaching! I was full of enthusiasm and constantly looked for ways to counteract the "I hate history" syndrome. I used various methods, including simulations. Simulations personally involve students in social and political issues through role playing and decision making. One year I used a simulation called *Division* (DeKock & Yount, n.d.), dealing with pre–Civil War political problems. Another year I used *Mission* (DeKock & Yount, n.d.), which covered issues arising from the Vietnam conflict. The students responded enthusiastically to role playing and the challenges inherent in the technique. Later, in evaluations, the students suggested that the simulations be used early in the school year because they felt they motivated them to learn more.

Following the students' advice, I began the 1971 school year with the simulation called *Sunshine* (DeKock & Yount, 1964), an activity correlated with the study of the Reconstruction Era following the Civil War. The purpose of *Sunshine* was to study the role of African Americans in U.S. history and subsequently to try to solve racial conflicts in the mythical modern city of "Sunshine." Simulations are valuable because learning is carried over to real-life situations.

In *Sunshine*, students were "born" by selecting a slip of paper from a hat. Each student's economic status, educational level, occupation, race, and neighborhood were included in the "birth" descriptions. An attitude test was given to each student on the first day of the simulation and stored in a sealed folder. Students took the same test on the final day of the simulation and could privately observe whether the simulation had altered any racial attitudes. The simulation included numerous student activities that involved the entire class in problems and social situations they might encounter in life. The students responded enthusiastically to all aspects of the simulation and conducted discussions seriously and in a mature manner.

One girl left the class after the first day of the simulation, telling me she thought the workload would be too difficult for her, since she was only a sophomore. It was typical for students to add and drop classes during the first weeks of the semester. This particular girl was White, but in the *Sunshine* simulation she had been "born" Black. About 2 weeks after she had left my class, her parents, Mr. and Mrs. X, made an unannounced visit to my conference room. They had many questions concerning the activities in the simulation, and their general attitude was rather hostile. I showed them all the materials from the *Sunshine* simulation and explained the program and the goals. When they left, I thought they were satisfied with my explanations. Days later, I was called to a conference with my principal, curriculum director, and personnel officer. They wanted information about *Sunshine.* Again, I explained the simulation and its relevance to post–Civil War Reconstruction. I was allowed to complete the project, but they advised me to ask their permission if I wanted to do another simulation. They said "nothing controversial should be discussed in the classroom." I had to bite my tongue at that statement, but I did agree to get clearance from them before initiating another simulation with my students.

Once the simulation was finished (20 days), the classes went on to other aspects of U.S. history. The school year went along beautifully and happily until February 1972, when my principal informed me that my contract would not be renewed for the following year. In response to my stunned "Why?", he answered that although he was recommending me for renewal, those "upstairs" wanted me to leave and that they would have to tell me the reason for this action. He implied that he was doing as he'd been instructed. He said that he would recommend renewal, but he would not make any other effort on my behalf. He suggested that to avoid any problems or controversy, I should resign. If I did, the school board would give me a good recommendation and I could seek employment in another town.

I was appalled at the hypocrisy of this suggestion and could hardly believe that this was happening to me. I was devastated. I had done nothing wrong, and I had worked very hard to inspire my students. I tearfully discussed the situation with my husband, and we decided I should not resign. With the principal's permission, we met with the school's personnel director, who told us the school district did not have to give me any reasons for nonrenewal. We then met with the superintendent, who said that he was recommending me for a new contract but that the school board made the final decision. I could not, in my wildest imaginings, figure out why they so desperately wanted me to leave my teaching position. It never occurred to me that the nonrenewal involved the *Sunshine* simulation, which had occurred months before.

The local and regional representatives of the Texas State Teachers Association (TSTA) and the local Texas Classroom Teachers Association (TCTA) declined to intervene in the matter. Later, the state TCTA offered monetary and legal assistance. Desperate to solve my dilemma, I called the National Education Association (NEA) office in Washington, D.C. After extensive interviews, NEA lawyers represented me at a school board hearing, which I had requested. At that hearing, in early June, school board members refused to answer any questions concerning their reasons for nonrenewal of my contract. Their attorney insisted no reasons were needed for their vote of nonrenewal. Through the grapevine, a hearty growth in small towns, I was informed that the *Sunshine* simulation had caused my problems. I learned that Mrs. X had been very loud and very insistent in her demands for my removal, saying that I was "inciting the students to revolution."

In midsummer I was quite surprised to read in the local newspaper that the Kingsville Independent School Board had petitioned the federal district court asking for a declaratory judgment that the school board had not violated my civil rights by not renewing my contract. My attorneys then filed a countersuit based on First and Fourteenth Amendment questions, asking for reinstatement, damages, and fees. After lengthy depositions from board members and district administrators, it became clear that racial attitudes were the cause of the problem. Much effort was made by the board members to hide that fact. They insisted that while they did not like the subject matter in the simulation, particularly the attitude test, it definitely was not the reason for my nonrenewal. One did mention that citizens thought I was teaching racial attitudes contrary to those of the community. They said there were too many complaints about the grading system, the attitude test, the time spent on this project, and the lack of relevance of the subject matter to American history. They stated that the number of complaints was so great that my effectiveness had been diminished. When questioned as to the details or nature of these complaints, they either couldn't remember or stated that they had heard that someone had complained. They also testified that they had never verified any of the complaints. I had never been advised of any complaints in the 5 years that I had been teaching. Even the earlier questions about *Sunshine* had not been described as a complaint. I was very distressed by this experience. They were talking about a total stranger, not me.

We finally went to court in April 1973. Many students and teachers testified on my behalf. The federal district court handed down a decision in my favor in September 1973. After initial acceptance by KISD, they voted not to honor the court's decision! Although I had won the court case, I still had no job. My attorneys then had to file another suit to force payment of fees and reinstatement. Again, the next decision was in my favor. Again the KISD board appealed. This process of decision, appeal, decision, appeal went on for 8 years. All the decisions and appeals, at all levels of the court system, were decided in my favor. At last, in 1980, the final decision, handed down from the Fifth Circuit Court to the federal district court, ruled that I be reinstated in my job and paid all wages for the 8 years. Further, the court ruled that the 8 years spent fighting the KISD would be applied to my retirement and my lawyers could collect fees and expenses. I could hardly believe it! I was so happy! By that time, I had just about given up the idea that I'd ever teach again. But the school board had all new members and there was a new superintendent and a new high school principal; the climate had definitely changed.

My colleagues greeted me with warmth and kudos when I returned to the classroom in the fall of 1980 and was assigned to teach U.S. history again. Relieved that the agony was over, I was delighted to be back in school and continued teaching until I retired in 1988. The 8 long years of litigation had stolen the best years of my life, but I was vindicated and reaffirmed in my conviction that defending myself had been the right thing to do. The process renewed my faith in the Constitution of the United States. It does protect our rights, even though the wheels of justice grind exceedingly slowly. I'm happy to say that this case has set a precedent for teachers in similar cases. The decision was instrumental in the passage of a Texas law that outlined due process for teachers. I'm grateful to the NEA DuShane Fund, the wonderful attorneys, and the support from parents and former students that gladdened my heart. The back wages and reinstatement were great, but when former students say "Mrs. Cooper, your class was the best class I ever had in high school!", their memories are my real reward.

THE TEACHER'S NIGHTMARE: GETTING FIRED FOR GOOD TEACHING

By Cissy Lacks

I almost didn't check my answering machine when I got home late that night. I pushed the play button more out of habit than curiosity.

Hello, Cissy. This is Mr. Mitchell, and the time now is 7:53. I would like to talk with you regarding the tape that was done about 2 or 3 weeks ago involving your class, and I have viewed it. I intended to talk with you earlier with regard to who has the tape. It's pretty shocking, and I would like for you to meet me at the administration building tomorrow morning at 8:30. There is no need for you to report to the school.

I didn't know what he was talking about, even after I thought about it all night, almost every minute of all night. The tape, it turned out, was one my students had worked on 3 months earlier. At that 8:30 meeting, I was suspended—a decision they had made before I arrived. Two months after that phone message, I was fired.

For the 25 years I taught creative writing, I followed the same practice. When students were serious about communicating what they or their characters were thinking, they needed to choose the words without someone else telling them what words to choose. This teaching method— allowing students their voices and then teaching them how to be most effective with those voices—was practiced in classrooms all over the United States. In my case, I had no directives to teach otherwise and, in fact, had been acknowledged as a successful and talented creative writing teacher using the very same methods for which I was fired. The issue, as I saw it, was not really about words. It was about whether a teacher should censor students' creative thoughts and expressions and about whether a teacher could be fired without notice because someone took offense at what students produced in a classroom assignment.

In a later meeting with the three administrators initiating the termination charges, I offered an example to show how censorship hurt student learning and to illustrate the potential of words for students' intellectual growth. I had a student at Berkeley High School who walked into my class everyday, went to the back of the room, and put his head on his desk. He was disconnected from me, from school, from learning, and probably from himself. But inside him was a poet he hadn't yet met, and when we started writing poetry in class, that poet inside him couldn't resist joining in. The first two exercises he read aloud came out like an unaimed shotgun exploding with street language, gang slang, and anger. Less than 3 weeks later he wrote a poem that won a district award and had his fellow students and me in tears:

ALONE

By Reginald McNeary

I'm all alone in the world today.
No one to laugh with no one to play.
It's been like that since the age of three.
No one to love, care or hold me.

I guess that's why I'm the way I am.
No one loved me so I don't give a damn.
No one to pick me up when I fall.
No one to measure growth or how tall.
Alone how it hurts inside.
If I were to die, no one would cry.
I never gave a damn about any other.
I love my shoes
More than I love my mother.
You might think I'm the Devil or call me Satan.
I have no love I'm so full of haten.
I guess that's why I have low self esteem.
The only time I show love
Is in my dreams.

Two days after the meeting, these administrators added a charge of profanity in poetry and submitted as evidence the first two poems. They had ignored Reginald's final poem, which had been published and had won awards. They didn't remember having seen it, they said. I would never be able to understand how or why people supposedly committed to education could do such a thing to me or anyone else.

Reginald's first two poems and the drama exercises my students taped were the evidence submitted by the Ferguson-Florissant District at my dismissal hearing. The drama exercises were first attempts by students who took themselves seriously and produced nothing provocative even though the students did use street language, and sometimes lots of it, in the dialogues for the characters they created.

That the concerns of the principal were more about race than about words was reflected in a comment he made to one student about the drama exercises: "And what offended me when I looked at that tape, I see Black students acting a fool, OK? And I see White folks videotaping it, OK? Did you think about that?"

Most people were stunned when I explained that I was fired for disobeying an appendix to the student discipline code, the only school board regulation mentioning profanity—along with tardiness, unexcused absence, littering, and the like. Several school employees testified that no teacher would expect that the student discipline code would or should apply to instructional activities or be construed in any way as the basis for disciplining a teacher.

The curriculum directives for teaching writing in the Ferguson-Florissant School District instructed teachers: "Don't tell writers what should be in their writing . . . don't bemoan what's wrong . . . and resist judgments." I have had to figure out how I could make sense of such a crazy misinterpretation of a district policy. Did some group of lawyers get together and make a sick joke of what teachers and school board members had negotiated in good faith? But then why did board members go along with it? Some people speculate that this group really wanted to get me. Perhaps, but I have come to another sad conclusion as well: Helping students was most important to me, but not to them.

We began the school board hearing knowing the odds we faced. The lawyer who represented the administrators and argued their case was also the lawyer for the school board. Still, we prepared for the hearing with the belief that the good of the students, the telling of the truth, the integrity of the classroom, and everyone's commitment to public education were most important to a school board. If abuses had taken place, the school board would do something to remedy the situation. My attorney began the hearing by saying:

> We will prove to you tonight that these charges have absolutely no merit whatsoever. Rather, they are part of a reckless, deliberate, and malicious scheme by several administrators in this district to fire a master teacher, whose teaching methods have been proven to work . . . we will prove to you that the actions . . . were taken in utter disregard not only of this teacher's rights but of the rights of her students to learn.

They called one witness—the assistant superintendent of personnel, who said he couldn't interpret curriculum directives and that we'd have to ask the assistant superintendent of curriculum. They showed the tapes of my drama students—with the TV screen facing the audience of more than 400 and numerous TV cameras from local stations, not the school board. And they submitted Reginald's first poems.

We tried to show how the process of learning takes place in a classroom. We brought in respected educators from both the district and the St. Louis community to testify. Students involved in the writing of the drama exercises testified on my behalf, as did my students from past years. Parents came forward, and even other administrators from the district testified that they had never heard that or thought that the student discipline code could be used in the way it was in my case. I testified, talking about the teaching techniques I had used successfully for 25 years.

Perhaps we should have known better than to even try. That same legal counsel who represented the administrators wrote the findings that the school board president later signed in my official dismissal. Later, one school board member, in deposition and under oath, testified that the school board had never discussed the student discipline code as it applied to my case and had discussed only 1 or 2 of the 23 findings listed in my dismissal.

Before my suit against the district was heard, I won the prestigious PEN Award for one person who had defended the First Amendment at some risk to herself. Actor Paul Newman introduced me. I closed with words I hadn't planned—words that came from being ABC's person of the week, from being on stage at Lincoln Center, and from hearing Paul Newman talk about me, the teacher: "I understand my obligations to speak about teaching and writing . . . and I will not let you or myself down."

Before the jury trial, the federal district judge, Catherine Perry, ruled on count one of my case, reversing the board's dismissal and ordering my reinstatement. She wrote: "The evidence presented to the board was overwhelming that many administrators and teachers in the district allowed class-related profanity depending on the context and degree of profanity." She went on to state: "Defendant submitted no evidence indicating that the district in fact enforced policy 3043 to prohibit students from reading aloud or otherwise using profanity in creative works."

In the courtroom, before the jury, my attorney put the legal issues of First Amendment and race discrimination in lay terms.

> You're here to decide a case about how a teacher of high school English in a troubled school where many kids are not interested in education, how she motivates the kids to write, how she turns them on to the value of poetry, how she gets them to engage in poetry contests, short story writing contests, work on a high school newspaper and sign up for journalism class. We're asking you to decide whether the district can summarily terminate a teacher who uses a time-honored teaching technique called the student-centered learning technique, which is the technique recommended by the Ferguson-Florissant School District, and we're also asking you to decide whether the illegally, racially motivated fears of two administrators, Vernon Wright and John Mitchell, was a consideration in the firing of Cissy Lacks.

The witnesses who had been at the hearing testified again, but at the jury trial a new witness testified—Reginald McNeary. He told the jurors:

> I was not going to try, and Ms. Lacks explained to us that writing was just what's inside of you, what you feel, and what's on your

mind. . . . I mean, it's really hard to write what somebody else wants you to write, because you have to have their standards, and you have, it's like they might not like it. . . . It was like I woke up, or whatever, because I never knew that I had the potential or ability that I had, and so now, it was like easy . . . within a month, I had about eight poems, I was writing songs, and I started a book, a book . . . when this month was over, it was like this is powerful.

He told what would have happened if I had censored those first poems:

I probably wouldn't have wrote again. I probably would have told her something . . . I mean, it's just like, to come out of, I don't think you understand where I was at, and I was not really participating, so to write anything, if I was just to write my name would be like a big or valiant effort, and if I was to come out of my shadow and write something and somebody was to criticize me, I would be mad. It would hurt my feelings, too. I probably wouldn't have came to the class again.

Reginald and the other students who testified on my behalf made me so proud to be a teacher. After 3½ years of waiting and preparing, 2 weeks of trial, and 7 hours of jury deliberation, we had a verdict.

On First Amendment claim, number one, did plaintiff have reasonable notice that allowing students to use profanity in their creative writing was prohibited? "No." I looked at the jurors. Each one of them was looking directly at me. For the first time in all those years since I had been fired, my body relaxed.

Number two, did defendant school district have a legitimate academic interest in prohibiting profanity by students in their creative writing, regardless of any other competing interest? "No."

On the claim of plaintiff Cecilia Lacks against defendant Ferguson Reorganized School District R-2 for race discrimination, we find in favor of plaintiff Cecilia Lacks. Has it been proven by a preponderance of the evidence that defendant would have discharged plaintiff regardless of her race? Answer: No.

When my attorney and I opened the door to the courthouse entrance, we saw a row of cameras on the courthouse stairs. I announced: "We won. Teachers and students won."

As we expected, the district appealed the decision, but so many people in the legal field said my case couldn't be overturned. The facts were too strong; the jury verdict was too firm. And I believed then what my attorneys told me about the legal system: "Juries decide fact. Judges decide law." I could never have predicted what was going to happen during oral argument in the Eighth Circuit Court of Appeals, but I predicted what was going to happen afterwards.

In the oral argument, Richard Arnold, who was chief presiding judge of the Eighth Circuit Court of Appeals, asked my attorney why Mitchell's statement about being bothered by "Black folks acting a fool and White folks videotaping it," was part of our race claim. At first, I thought he was joking.

Then he began to ask questions as if the findings from the school board were true, even though they had been disproved at trial and even though, supposedly, he had to take as true the facts from the jury trial. When my appellate attorney protested, Arnold asked him if now he was telling school boards whom they should believe and not believe. It was as if the jury trial had never taken place.

In rebuttal my attorney tried to bring in the testimony of the expert witnesses. Arnold interrupted, telling him not to do it because in another case, experts said students should use rap to learn how to write. It wasn't going to happen again.

I didn't understand what was happening. I had been told these judges couldn't retry the case; clearly, they had decided they could. I left the courtroom discouraged and disheartened. Even though these men didn't have any idea of how to teach, how to reach students, or what was going on in the real world of schools, they decided they did and, even more frightening, they were ready to make judgments based on their attitudes about learning and culture, not about their responsibilities to interpret law or respect a legal record. I was in deep trouble; teachers were in deep trouble; and it wasn't hard to see why schools were going to be in more and more trouble, too.

Their written opinion 5 months later was a sickening shock. They overturned every jury verdict and Judge Perry's reinstatement. To them, it was all about profanity and nothing else. Reinstatement was gone. Fair warning was gone. Legitimate academic purpose was gone. Title VII, race discrimination, was gone. For the sake of ruling on profanity and their view of civility, three judges dismissed the law.

They overturned the factual decisions of the case regarding fair warning and the First Amendment by saying the jurors had the wrong answers: "We reverse and hold, as a matter of law, that the answer to both of those questions was 'yes.'"

The race claim was the same:

We reverse . . . the idea that the board "had race on its mind" when it fired Lacks. . . . The idea . . . is questionable, especially given that the president of the school board, who signed the statement, testified that she did not believe that Lacks's case involved racial issues.

Now, school board members decided not only the credibility of the witnesses at the hearing but also the credibility of their own testimony at the trial.

We asked for the entire Eighth Circuit to reconsider the case. They refused. One of the judges, Justice Theodore McMillian, wrote an opinion in dissent, requesting them to reconsider. In it, he said, "When good educators are scared away or driven from our schools because they cannot trust the system to treat them honestly and fairly, we are all affected, most especially our children."

We asked for my case to be heard before the Supreme Court. Fifteen national education organizations signed an *amici* brief on behalf of my case and on behalf of public education. In it, they said: "This Court should review the obviously flawed decision of the Eighth Circuit because it raises issues of great import to the governance of the public education system." My case was not taken. The appeal decision was the final one.

When my legal battles began, I spoke to new teachers and I wished them the same joy, frustration, and pleasure in being with students that I had experienced. I wished them the same long-term relationships I had formed with many of my students. I hoped that they would have dialogues with students that allowed them to establish a sacred classroom space in which respect, trust, and joy permeated the learning activities. I wished them the opportunity to see their students become productive adults.

Also, I told them that for every lesson planned, for every assignment made, I didn't want any person to teach in fear of losing a job. I didn't want any classroom teacher or any class of students to fall prey to such a chilling effect on learning. I didn't want my name to be associated with the case that struck fear in the hearts and minds of teachers. And I certainly didn't want self-censorship to take place because teachers were afraid. I wanted a strong statement to be made for academic freedom and teachers' rights to teach because those practices were critical for good education.

What I wanted did not happen. Still, I plan to keep the pledge I made to talk about teaching and writing. Some scary and dangerous circumstances created the atmosphere for my firing, and situations like mine are appearing in schools across the country. Public education has become a cultural battleground instead of a learning field. I am convinced that teachers afraid to teach produce students afraid to learn, and that combination makes for a society in turmoil because its citizens are afraid and unable to deal honestly and effectively with the realities confronting them.

Further information can be obtained on the Cissy Lacks website: http://home.stlnet.com/~clacks/

FILTHY LITTLE BOOKS

By Gloria T. Pipkin

As a junior high English teacher in northwest Florida, I have lived a teacher's worst nightmare: prolonged attacks on instructional methods and materials. Shortly after my department was named by the National Council of Teachers of English as one of 150 Centers of Excellence, I sat among the audience at a school board meeting and heard a prominent member of the community—a former school board member for 16 years—urge that I be fired for exposing kids to what he had called on other public occasions "filthy little books." This time he called them "a form of pornography."

Earlier, in an open letter mailed to parents of our students, the same critic had warned of the content of books we were reading in our school, noting that some of these books "read like *Playboy* and *Penthouse*." A few days after sending the letter, he ran a half-page ad in our local newspaper, with excerpts from three books. The headline of the ad was "Your Child's Textbooks/Have You Read Them?" A coupon at the bottom of the ad invited readers to write in and protest "the obscene language and explicit sexual descriptions being used in the Bay County Classrooms."

Several petitioners appended comments to the coupons. "From the description I heard of Ms. Pipkin's attire at a recent school board meeting, I can only assume that this type of reading material stimulates her in some manner," one respondent noted.

Others wrote: "I strongly recommend that Gloria Pipkin be fired from the school system for contributing to the delinquency and moral decay"; "We are opposed to the libertinish behavior and beliefs of Pitkin [*sic*] and other teachers who would degrade our young people"; and "These teachers are fortunate they are living in this era. Sixty years ago they would have left town on a rail."

What kinds of books were we using that provoked such a reaction? What was the nature of the "pornography" we were accused of purveying? The book that came to symbolize the entire conflict was Robert Cormier's *I Am the Cheese,* a challenging and complex novel about a family betrayed by the government. After a few informal complaints about the book, the principal required written parental permission for its study. Nearly all of the affected parents responded, and 91 of 95 granted permission for their seventh-graders to read this highly acclaimed young adult novel. For those who opted out, our longstanding department policy allowed parents and teachers to choose a mutually acceptable alternative.

Despite the overwhelming support for *I Am the Cheese,* one parent filed a formal complaint. A review committee recommended that it remain in the curriculum, but the superintendent removed it anyway.

Although contemporary literature became the primary focus of the public debate in our community, our pedagogy was also at issue. In a letter (Shumaker, 1986) to the editor of our local paper, the parent who filed the formal challenge warned:

> The problem is much larger than a mere three objectionable books at Lakeland Junior High. Some proponents of this low caliber of reading have chosen to focus attention on two or three books in order to bring our attention away from the entire circumference of the situation (p. 4C).

The letter writer went on to say that the books were "just the tip of the iceberg (or inferno)." She asked rhetorically:

> What happened to the teaching of English in English class? While I certainly appreciate the effort made by some teachers to inspire more creative writing in our children, I see a definite need for more instruction in grammar, spelling, punctuation, and sentence and paragraph structure on the junior high level. (p. 4C)

When I first joined the department, the curriculum was ultratraditional, and textbooks were the order of the day. Most classes spent the majority of their time marching lockstep through various levels of *Warriner's English Grammar and Composition* and *Basic Goals in Spelling.* Workbooks such as that hoary classic, *Keys to Good English,* supplemented the grammar text. If the teacher felt that time could be spared from the basic skills, students read stories and poems from the same edition of a literature series that was popular when I attended junior high in the late 1950s. Most teachers never got to the "Composition" section of the grammar book, and students wrote very little. Only advanced classes (part of a rigidly stratified tracking system) read real books, and even then the teacher's choices were confined to titles such as Hawthorne's *The House of the Seven Gables* and Dickens's *Great Expectations*.

When I became head of the department, I wanted to lead by example rather than through coercion. I began to use our department meetings as staff development sessions in which we explored the research on language learning and the best of current teaching practices. Individually and as a group, we also began to read and study young adult literature. Although there was definitely a climate that favored innovation and creativity, no teachers were compelled to use books they didn't like or to adopt methods that didn't suit their style. No one was forbidden to use textbooks or workbooks. Although we had very different philosophies and teaching approaches, over time we came to share some crucial understandings about teaching and learning the language arts. At one point we put those in writing as follows:

> Although the members of our department have diverse teaching styles, we share a commitment to establishing a literate environment, one in which students and teachers work as partners, moving together inside the processes of reading and writing. Our classroom practices are continually modified as we learn more about our students' needs and interests, yet the following assumptions undergird all our teaching:
>
> 1. Growth in reading and writing, our primary goal, can be achieved only through practice.
>
> 2. Students read more when high interest books and other reading material are readily available.
>
> 3. Students write more when they control the material, write for real audiences, and compose in a workshop atmosphere.
>
> 4. Students must be given frequent opportunities to talk and write about what they read.
>
> 5. Students should be introduced to a variety of contemporary as well as classic literature.
>
> 6. Students should be given frequent opportunities to publish their work.
>
> 7. Teachers must understand, respect, and build upon the level of experience that students bring to reading.
>
> 8. Teachers should work in an environment which promotes flexibility and creativity.
>
> 9. Teachers and students accomplish more when parents are fully informed about our program and involved in it.
>
> 10. The program should ensure that our students' achievements equal or surpass those of others in the district.

Many parents welcomed the changes in our department, but a few objected to what they viewed as a resurgence of John Dewey's progressivism and of secular humanism. Although the school board took no overt action against the teachers involved, the pressure to censure us and to remove a host of books continued. During the next few months, two other teachers and I received threatening phone calls and even a sinister message fashioned from words cut out of magazines and newspapers. I recognized the beginning of the death threat as a verse from the Old Testament book of Isaiah: "Woe unto you who call evil good and good evil, who put darkness for light, who put bitter for sweet, for they have revoked the law of the Lord." In addition to personal calls and letters, we were excoriated (and sometimes defended) on an almost daily basis in letters to the editor of our local newspaper.

When I applied to reinstate *I Am the Cheese*, the chairman of the school board demanded to know whether I was approaching the board as a citizen or as a teacher. I replied that I had difficulty separating those roles.

"No, ma'am!" he barked at me. "You have been told by the principal of your school that this reading material has been rejected. And you . . . are supposed to be following the edicts of the boss."

It seemed that the specter of defiant women (all 11 teachers in the English department were women) challenging the prerogatives of male administrators inflamed our critics as much as the challenged books did.

Not only did our critics object to specific books used for whole-class reading, they also attacked the existence of classroom libraries. The mother who challenged *I Am the Cheese* complained to a *Washington Post* reporter that our classrooms looked like "B. Dalton with desks." She went on to say that she didn't allow her children to go to the theater and choose what movies they wanted to see, and she didn't want the school giving them similar choices with books.

In response to the controversy surrounding *I Am the Cheese* and classroom libraries, the school board developed a policy governing the selection and review of instructional materials. One of the selection criteria introduced by the superintendent required that all materials be free of "vulgar, obscene, or sexually explicit" content, although the school board ultimately approved an amendment that allowed books whose literary merit outweighed their other attributes. Overall, the effect of the policy was to discourage teachers who wanted to bring new books into the system. On my second attempt to get approval of *I Am the Cheese*, the school board grilled me for nearly an hour before voting 4 to 1 to deny my request. The message went out loud and clear to teachers throughout the district: Advocate a controversial book, and this could be you.

As a result of the adoption of the new policy on book selection, the superintendent and school board were required to review hundreds of books, including many that had been studied for years. To facilitate this process, the superintendent instituted a bizarre system that required high school English teachers to categorize their selections. Category I books were pristine, that is, free of any vulgar language or sexually explicit material. Category II books were those that contained a "sprinkling" of such references, and Category III was reserved for materials with "a lot" of vulgarity or sexual references. Altogether 64 novels and plays were placed in Category III, which meant, according to the superintendent, that these works could not be studied by whole classes. Parents who wanted their children to read the books independently could apply to the teacher in writing, but the books could not be discussed in class. Titles restricted in this manner included *Hamlet, The Red Badge of Courage, The Scarlet Letter, The Autobiography of Benjamin Franklin,* and many other classics.

Shortly after this classification scheme was announced, 44 parents, students, and teachers (including me) filed suit in federal district court against the school board, superintendent, and principal of my school, on the grounds that they had acted to remove books from the system for constitutionally impermissible reasons. One day after the lawsuit was filed, the school board voted to overturn the superintendent's recommendations and approve the 64 classics, but more than two dozen young adult books remained restricted.

More than 5 years after the original challenge to *I Am the Cheese* was filed, plaintiffs in our lawsuit reached an out-of-court settlement with the school board that restored all books and secured many favorable amendments to the onerous materials selection and review policy. Long before the lawsuit was settled, however, our department was decimated. A little more than a year after the challenges were filed, seven Lakeland Junior High English teachers either transferred or resigned. The teachers who were hired to replace them received strong orders from the principal to "teach grammar," and they complied. Nearly all the classroom libraries disappeared, and once again hefty anthologies replaced class novels. In another year I was the only teacher left from the infamous Lakeland 11, and I became a professional pariah, isolated and consumed with self-doubt. What was once a professional Camelot had become for me a wasteland.

I lasted 3 years alone, before the physical and emotional toll of our lengthy battle overwhelmed me. I left the public school system in 1990 after more than 20 years as an English teacher. From this life-altering experience I learned that excellence is no defense against attacks on pedagogy—that, in fact, mediocre teaching is rarely challenged. I also learned that intellectual freedom is not a gift of the gods, that the fight is never over and the victories never final. As long as schools exist, there will be those who would impose rigid control over the ideas and images available to our students. Although the passage of time and a great deal of reflection have helped bring meaning and even coherence to seemingly incomprehensible professional tragedy and loss, I have come to the sad conclusion that I have no future as an English teacher within the public schools.

CURRICULUM ON TRIAL

By Gretchen Klopfer Wing

No one denies that experience is a teacher, but its lessons can often appear in a timed-release way, like cold capsules. An experience I had in my third year of public school teaching took this form. Although I laughed through it at the time, I now find myself contemplating it more seriously as the years go by. The main lesson I learned is that, while I was lucky, good fortune is no substitute for teacher empowerment. As a corollary, I also learned that, for teachers, political confidence is an indispensable tool in itself, the lack of which can invite a dangerous self-censorship.

In the early spring of 1990, I was teaching civics to five sections of ninth-graders at a high school in North Carolina. I liked my freshmen, and I tried to keep my classes as lively as possible with interactive and group activities and the occasional field trip. The high school, which serves most of the county, is a two-story, red-brick building in the shape of a large E sitting outside a small town, the historical county seat. The town was typical of many in the central Piedmont area.

Despite the small size of the town, the high school was bursting at the seams with 1,500 students, pulled from all over the county. North Carolina may still be predominantly rural, but it's a thickly settled kind of country life; tobacco farms are not traditionally large. Most of the high school kids were not college-bound, and the Future Farmers of America were by far the largest, most organized, and most popular club at the school. Today, I'm sure there are more kids there whose professional parents commute down the interstate to jobs, but in 1990 the character of the school was undeniably rural. The student body was almost evenly divided between African American and Caucasian students; perhaps a 2:3 ratio. Other minorities were almost nonexistent.

Taking my students' backgrounds and prospects into account, I approached the curriculum with the traditional notion that civics is simply "what every citizen needs to know"; that is, the workings of our economic, legal, and political systems. A principal who believed very firmly in allowing teachers full freedom to teach, as long as they "did their job," assisted me in this. Unfortunately, many of the high school teachers interpreted their job as being to model citizenship by doing what they were told, following the textbook curriculum, and creating as little fuss as possible. The local chapter of the National Education Association functioned mostly as a social club. The tiny, fledgling chapter of American Federation of Teachers to which I belonged was considered somewhat subversive. While I liked all my colleagues and respected them professionally, I was to become extremely dismayed by the lack of power they felt to do anything in their teaching that might be challenged by either the community or the administration. Only in hindsight have I come to analyze that powerlessness and to understand its social roots.

The South has a very hierarchical society, with great emphasis placed on respect for authority. Many of my students called me "ma'am." On the telephone, parents were nearly always deferential; even if uninvolved in their children's education, they at least assured me they would make their children "mind." For better or for worse, however, this same attitude toward authority carried over to the teachers, many of whom had been raised in the area. Our principal, who had a respect for academic freedom, had difficulty relating to teachers. The difference between me and some of my colleagues, however, was that I recognized that, while we might be chastised for coming late to a staff meeting, we were just as likely to be praised for taking risks in our teaching.

Risk taking requires confidence, however, and most of us have to have a reason to feel confident. I had two good ones, which were interrelated: my parents, Quakers who had both been active in the early days of the civil rights movement, and my education at Carolina Friends School (CFS), a Quaker school that my parents had helped to start. If not for CFS, I myself would have been a student at the high school. Instead of learning automatic respect for authority, however, I spent my formative years learning to respect the power and grace of the individual. This basic difference, along with the experience of watching my parents challenge state law, set me apart from most of my colleagues. While I feared the sarcasm of our principal, I never thought about his power as an agent of curricular control—or anyone else's power for that matter. Fortunately, this attitude was one he respected.

Because the students and I enjoyed the study of law, I devoted a major portion of my civics curriculum to civil and criminal justice. The culminating activity was a trip, with another teacher, to the courthouse at the county seat to observe an actual criminal trial. The lengths of trials vary, so it was impossible to learn more than 1 day in advance exactly what would be on the docket during our half-day visit. On a previous courtroom trip, the students had been intrigued to find themselves witnessing a rape case, which demonstrated how slowly the wheels of justice grind. The next year we had observed several cases that involved drunken driving. This year, we learned the trial would again be a rape case.

It's always wonderful to get out of the school building on a crisp and sunny day. My students had been well instructed about courtroom deportment, and they quietly filed into the stately old room as the prosecution's first witness gave testimony. The students were transfixed by the crime-scene descriptions, but after hearing a doctor and a nurse testify about the alleged victim's injuries, it was difficult to get them to leave for lunch.

We brought another group of students for the afternoon. Now the alleged victim was testifying, and my students heard graphic descriptions of the rape, as well as the language used by the defendant. We had discussed this possibility before the trip, and I was very proud that no one snickered or acted shocked. They discussed the case avidly, even weeks after the verdict was returned. During an afternoon break, as my students craned to get glimpses of the defendant and his accuser, a reporter for a local newspaper approached me. She was there to cover the trial, so I was surprised to find that her questions to me were all about why I had exposed my students to such a spectacle. As a mother, she said, she would have been shocked to have her daughter hear such testimony. I replied that this was real life and that I thought it far better for students to learn about crime in a courtroom than only on TV shows. Besides, I told her, my students and their parents, who had signed permission slips, had been given plenty of preparation for this and would now have plenty of debriefing. I also mentioned the obvious: that what they heard in the courtroom was nothing compared to what they heard in the school hallways every day. I knew I was being interviewed, but it never occurred to me that this would be anything other than positive publicity for my school.

The next day I was greeted by a headline in the local section of the newspaper that said something like "Students Get Courtroom Lesson in Rape." The article was devoted almost entirely to my classes' presence at the trial, rather than to the trial itself. The reporter had called my principal, superintendent, and school board chairperson for comments. Since local field trips need only the principal's approval, neither of the latter two had any knowledge of the field trip, of course; finding themselves in an uncomfortable position, they immediately called my principal to ask what was going on. He not only explained but also told them he would handle it.

Being a feisty soul, my principal was very much enjoying the conflict, and he invited me into his office to listen to him spar by telephone with the offending reporter. Using the same logic, but with a great deal more force than I had, he challenged the reporter to explain what she thought I had done wrong and to justify the obvious bias in her supposedly objective article. It was fun to hear. Afterwards, he assured me of his support and said everything would be fine. With that, I assumed the incident was over. Several other teachers voiced their concerns to me throughout the day: Since I did not yet have tenure, wasn't I scared? But at that time I was too cocky to feel scared. The students and I discussed the reporter's reaction and decided she was silly and biased.

But it wasn't over; from there the incident created some odd ripples. Over the next few days newspapers in a large city picked up the story. A local Baptist minister wrote a passionate letter to the editor, condemning the school administration that had allowed a poor, misguided teacher to take a field trip to a courtroom. They should have been safeguarding the morals of our children. Other letters followed, both in opposition and in support of the minister. The story appeared in newspapers more than 100 miles away. I continued to find it all rather amusing.

Finally, the story played itself out. My principal received the support of the superintendent, and the board chair called me personally to reassure me. My students, meanwhile, found the whole flap outrageous, and we had many good discussions about the value of real-life education and the hypocrisy of adults. One student, with approval from the rest of the class, wrote her own letter to the editor, which was published. That result alone would have made the whole episode worthwhile to me. We were also very much gratified that not one parent called to complain, although none called to express support either.

Years later, thinking back on the incident, I realize how cavalierly I had treated the situation. I was used to taking risks and facing the consequences. I had tried methods others considered daring. I used *Inherit the Wind*, a film portraying fundamentalist Christians in an extremely unflattering light, in a class full of Baptists. But I had never had to face serious consequences before. If just one or two variables in that particular equation had been changed—a weak principal, a more vocal parent, a politically sensitive superintendent—I, as an untenured teacher in a school with a very weak union, could have been in a lot of trouble.

Teaching now in the state of Washington, I very much carry the two lessons I mentioned at the outset of this story with me. I place high value on the institutional integrity of a school, the need of all its members to value academic freedom. This is especially important at the highest levels of administration, as school boards increasingly become curricular battlegrounds. At the same time, I have learned that teachers are all too often their own worst enemies when it comes to censorship, declining to expose their students to certain books, films, or experiences for the sole reason that someone might object or that getting permission is just not worth the trouble. This experience has taught me that teachers who submit to the fear of challenge are simply giving away their power as educators, the very thing that should make them a valuable resource to their students.

Challenge for its own sake is, of course, irresponsible, and I always operate by the simple rules of institutional responsibility. First, I maintain a good professional relationship with my principal, vice principal, superintendent, and at least one member of the school board. Second, when something controversial is used in my class, I give parents appropriate warning and provide alternatives for students whose parents might object to their participation. I have been very lucky; I know there are teachers whose experiences with challenges have led them to the opposite conclusion. They self-censor and never rock the boat, and students receive no lessons in the true meaning of integrity.

REFERENCES

DeKock, P., & Yount, D. (n.d.). *Division* [Simulation game]. Lakeside, CA: Interact Learning Through Involvement.

DeKock, P., & Yount, D. (n.d.). *Mission* [Simulation game]. Lakeside, CA: Interact Learning Through Involvement.

DeKock, P., & Yount, D. (1964). *Sunshine* [Simulation game]. Lakeside, CA: Interact Learning Through Involvement.

Gordimer, N. (1990, June). *Censorship and its aftermath*. Address to the International Writer's Day conference, London.

Moffett, J. (1988). *Storm in the mountains: A case study of censorship, conflict, and consciousness*. Carbondale: Southern Illinois University Press.

Robertson, P. (1989, April 20). *The 700 Club*. Denver, CO: Channel 2.

Shumaker, Mrs. R. M. (1986, June 8). Banning books [Letter to the editor]. (Panama City, FL) *News-Herald*, p. 4C.

Whitson, J. A. (1994). Critical literacy versus censorship across the curriculum. In J. S. Simmons (Ed.), *Censorship: A threat to reading, learning, thinking* (pp. 13–28). Newark, DE: International Reading Association.

The Politics of Change and Teacher Education

THE TWO CHAPTERS in this final section of the book address the politics of school reform and the implications of institutional change for teacher education. In the case study of River Haven, we witnessed the results of reform gone awry. In Chapter 6, Joan Naomi Steiner paints a different picture of change. She profiles three districts that attempted school reform. She focuses on the political nature of change itself and explores the roles played by administrators, students, parents, and teachers as they faced the realities of institutional transformation. In Chapter 7, we strive to place what happened in River Haven in the broader perspective of national school reform and teacher education. We conclude the book with a call to action for teachers, teacher educators, families, and all stakeholders in education. We consider the impact of change and reform on schools, the roles of those responsible for change, and the implications of reform for educators, teacher educators, and communities.

Institutional Challenges to Pedagogy

JOAN NAOMI STEINER

> Despite all the restrictions currently in place in many school districts, cur-
> ricula can be changed, tests can be deemphasized, teacher-proof materials
> no longer need to be bought, and so on. Teachers who fall back on *"They
> won't let me do it"* as an excuse to avoid change must be challenged to
> specify each "they" and then to see if it's really true either that "they" won't
> permit experimentation, or that "they" exist at all. Although any of this is
> hard for an individual teacher to do, groups of teachers within a building
> have enormous potential power to change their teaching strategies and
> approaches if they have a coherent plan for doing so and if they unite
> together to win administrative and parental support.
>
> —John Mayher, *Uncommon Sense*

WE AS EDUCATORS do not always think of ourselves as political. I sometimes hear teachers say that they chose teaching as a career because they
do not like politics. Critical theorists, such as Aronowitz and Giroux
(1985), have helped educators understand that teaching is never a neutral act:

> Education is seen as an important social and political force in the process of
> class reproduction. By appearing to be an impartial and neutral "transmit-
> ter" of the benefits of a valued culture, schools are able to promote inequality
> in the name of fairness and objectivity. (p. 80)

Schools and teachers in the United States have espoused autocratic
principles that constitute the old order of education (Hunter, 1986). To
maintain a democracy, education for all people is essential if they are
to participate in sociopolitical decision making. The public learns how to

act for itself through participation in democratic practices. Thus any school model that seeks to be apolitical threatens to thwart the historical tendency of widening the practice of democracy in our nation (Arono- witz & Giroux, 1985).

Recent school reform efforts (National Association of Secondary School Principals [NASSP], 1996; National Council of Teachers of En- glish & International Reading Association [NCTE/IRA], 1996) call for more democratic participation of all stakeholders along with interpre- tive teaching models and philosophies that value student-centered class- rooms (Zemelman, Daniels, & Hyde, 1993). These reform efforts are fac- ing tough resistance from traditional school cultures that promote process–product classrooms (Cochran-Smith & Lytle, 1990) in which stu- dents are sorted and tracked by IQ tests and teacher-perceived abilities. Schools in the past have determined and/or limited future options for students. Students have resisted authoritative practices as shown by high absenteeism, high dropout rates, and rebellious conduct.

Institutional reform for the twenty-first century calls for broad and sweeping changes within districts and schools (NASSP, 1996; National Board of Professional Teaching Standards [NBPTS], 1997; New Standards Project, 1997). As districts embark on change, all stakeholders—including students, colleagues, parents, and the community—need to become in- volved in the change process. We as teachers must build an understand- ing of how we are political and of how political issues relate to common institutional challenges to pedagogy. Only then can we act more con- sciously and deliberately as change agents in classrooms, schools, and districts.

This chapter examines how three districts attempt to institute school reform. The political nature of curriculum, administrative restrictions, student's reactions, and collegial relationships is found to constrain and limit pedagogical change in classrooms and buildings and throughout districts. With pseudonyms used for people and places, each district is profiled to illustrate how districts face change and how each handles the political implications of change itself in different ways.

SCHOOL DISTRICT OF PARKERTON

Curriculum

As a newly hired director of curriculum and instruction, I learned through my initial conversations with the administrative team that for many years the district had not written curriculum in any content area or at any grade level. The administrative team—comprised of superintendent, directors of curriculum and special services, and elementary, middle school, and high school principals—valued teachers' efforts. Parkerton teachers enthusiastically described their classrooms and students. The teachers seemed at ease when interacting with their administrators. After further discussion, both teachers and administrators told me that although the district did not have current curriculum documents written, they did indeed have curriculum. They concluded that the "real" curriculum in the district existed in teachers' hearts and minds and, as a result, in daily classroom practice (Apple, 1981).

When the English language arts teachers in Parkerton were ready to write curriculum documents, they wanted to honor Best Practice grounded in current thinking about language learning as shown by Britton (1982, 1985), Calkins (1994), and Graves (1983) and as rooted in their own classroom successes. Teachers wanted "living documents" that could be revised and rewritten as needed based on daily classroom use (Applebee, 1996). I discovered, however, that for some Parkerton teachers and administrators, writing curriculum represented an underlying threat. Several teachers admitted that they had never written curriculum and that they had no idea how to begin since the only examples of district curriculum guides were more than 20 years old. Although they wanted a written, living document, they confided that it would be easier to just keep doing what they had always done (Mayher, 1990).

I discussed teachers' reluctance to write curriculum with the superintendent who explained that until recently, the district had not had a director of curriculum to initiate curricular articulation and to oversee curriculum writing. What troubled me, however, was that many of the teachers were initially enthusiastic about curriculum writing. Many teachers were integrating current instructional strategies (Zemelman et al., 1993) as well as being current in their practice. Several teachers had rich professional experiences outside the district (Marzano, 1992), including leadership roles in state professional organizations. This led me to wonder whether embedded in the district's culture were unarticulated reasons for the absence of written curriculum. I began to ask more questions.

As I reflected on my own experience as a classroom teacher, I remembered the confidence I had felt knowing that my school board had approved the course I was teaching with its written curriculum and selected texts. Whenever parents would object to their child reading *Of Mice and Men* (Steinbeck, 1937), for example, I had a curriculum document with selected texts that had been board approved. I was, in fact, teaching the novel with the board's approval. Why wouldn't teachers want their school board's approval if for no other reason than their own protection when objections were filed?

As a result of further questioning, I learned that curriculum documents written under my direction in Parkerton would not be seen or approved by the school board. Administrators explained that if the board had an opportunity to see curriculum, they would be inclined to dictate curriculum to teachers. Several administrators told me that seeking board approval for curriculum would be a serious mistake since the board had a long history of micromanaging the school district. Administrators explained that the board would view curriculum approval as another opportunity to play the role of "boss." Both the superintendent of 10 years and the high school principal of 15 years cautioned me. Neither would consider or support seeking board approval for curricular matters. What at first seemed to be, from the superintendent's perspective, a lack of leadership in curricular areas was, in reality, a fear of school board micromanagement in curricular concerns. The administrative team believed that they were powerless to do anything to change the situation (Aronowitz & Giroux, 1991).

As a result, Parkerton teachers over the years had not been empowered through the curriculum-writing process (Mayher, 1990). Curriculum articulation, either pre-K–12 or across grade levels and disciplines, had not occurred. Although many teachers were current in theory and practice, incorporating the work of Avery (1993), Gardner (1983), Graves (1983), and Marzano (1992), opportunities to share with colleagues had been minimal. Teachers had had few opportunities to validate themselves through their work, share ideas about teaching strategies, and transform themselves collectively through working with students (Aronowitz & Giroux, 1985). The administrative team, on the other hand, continued to value the status quo and focused the school board's attention on matters involving policy. Since board members viewed themselves as the "boss" in all district matters, the superintendent believed that it was better to have no written curriculum than to have a board dictating curriculum to teachers.

Administrative Restrictions

The superintendent of Parkerton perceived herself as a grassroots leader who championed site-based management and team decision making. Other administrators and teachers, however, perceived her management style to be top-down as the school board dictated. Several veteran teachers revealed that board members viewed teachers as having very little, if any, status. According to Parkerton teachers, administrators were viewed by the board as having even less status than teachers. The differing perceptions of power and status among the superintendent, teachers, and school board created severe restrictions for any pedagogical change (Aronowitz & Giroux, 1985).

Change was difficult for this district, since only change mandated by the board was tolerated. One element especially frustrating to district administrators and teachers was the district's writing proficiency gateway test. The board wanted all students in the district to be proficient writers as defined in the state standards document and, to that end, initiated writing proficiency testing in the third and sixth grades. The board called for the formation of a committee composed of board members, parents, teachers, and administrators and charged with designing a high-stakes writing assessment. After meeting for 2 years, the committee chose a timed writing prompt scored by an external test company so that students' scores could be nationally normed (Comprehensive Test of Basic Skills, 1996). A score of 4 on a 6-point rubric was determined as passing by the board. The first year a large number of students failed to accomplish the board's high standard. Students who failed were given several options: after-school tutoring, summer school, and/or the opportunity to retake the test as many times as necessary. Since scoring was done externally, teachers did not understand the scoring system used by the test company. When the results were distributed to parents, neither teachers nor administrators knew how to explain the scores or how to design an individual plan for writing improvement.

How did this happen? First of all, the superintendent knew that she would be unable to convince the board to develop an internal writing assessment since teachers were so poorly regarded by the board. To speak against an external high-stakes test would be viewed by the board as a lack of accountability in the district. Her perceived unwillingness to hold teachers accountable, she believed, would lead the board to think that she was covering up teacher incompetence. Her own future would be at risk as a result. Although the other administrators knew the negative impact of high-stakes testing, they feared that the board would view their objections with suspicion. Parkerton teachers knew that they would be held accountable for their students' success or failure. They also knew how failure could adversely affect their students' self-esteem and undermine their efforts to encourage students to become risk takers. Since the board micromanaged the district, administrators and teachers perceived themselves as powerless. Board members, on the other hand, were reaffirmed in their belief that they know what is best for Parkerton's students.

Students' Reactions

Students in the school district of Parkerton, for the most part, followed a compliance model: They seldom questioned procedures and policies (Hampel, 1986). One reason students had not questioned matters concerning them was that they had not been asked to enter into any of the conversations regarding procedures and policies that may affect them. Although I observed compliance in classrooms throughout the district, kindergarten classrooms marked the beginning of learning "how to do" school well.

Kindergarten teachers believed that as classroom teachers they were offering children choices in their daily work and play; however, as I observed kindergarten classes, the overpowering message to students, implicitly and explicitly, centered on following established rules and accepting teachers' authority (Aronowitz & Giroux, 1991). I found that it was in kindergarten that students were learning lessons that they would use the rest of their years in school and perhaps throughout life.

The contradiction between teacher belief and perception became especially apparent when kindergarten teachers were learning how to use responsive teaching strategies (Bowers & Flinders, 1990), specifically readers'/writers' workshop approaches (Avery, 1993). After teachers had selected and read a book for our study group discussion during Friday lunches, I arranged for the author, a nationally known consultant, to work with kindergarten students and teachers in their classrooms. At first the teachers were very nervous about having an outsider work with them. They believed that they were already following the suggestions in the book that we had been discussing. As the time drew near, the anxiety among kindergarten teachers seemed to grow.

The consultant did demonstration teaching for 2 days in kindergarten and for 2 days in first grade with kindergarten, first-, and second-grade teachers observing her and the class in a fishbowl fashion. Before teachers observed classrooms, the consultant briefed them on how to observe, especially how to observe one student (Armstrong, 1980), and how to record those observations using a two-column journal (Avery, 1993). After the readers'/writers' workshop, teachers met to debrief and to share observations. Most of the discussions centered on student work generated from the workshop and how instruction influences student work.

In classrooms empowering students as authors, students wrote with more imagination and were more willing to take risks in their thinking and writing. Students were better able to talk about their work and to ask peers questions that helped everyone think more critically about writing.

In classrooms with teachers who did not see students as authors, students wrote very little and seemed to have difficulty even narrowing down a topic to talk or write about. In the debriefing sessions, teachers were able to make connections between genuine conversations with students about their writing and writing improvement. Teachers also experienced first-hand the importance of students' learning how to talk about their writing with peers in order to gain further insights about their work.

Collegial Relationships

Teachers also became empowered through their work together. One teacher was so excited about how much his students improved that he wrote a letter to the school board:

> Dear School Board Members,
>   I would like to thank you for allowing substitute teachers to take our classes while a national consultant did a workshop with us. It was very beneficial to watch her demonstration teaching and to conference with her and the other first-grade teachers. She gave me many useful ideas for writing in my classroom. It was helpful for the first-grade teachers to see what we are doing in kindergarten and for us to visit first-grade classrooms to find out what is being done with writing. The workshop was practiced, and I know the children will benefit from it. Since it was at the end of the year, I only had time to implement the program for 4 days. However, it made a difference in report card marks. Sixteen children went to higher marks in just 4 days.
>
> Sincerely,
Robert Watson

Through the process of learning how to empower students, the teachers themselves were moved from idea to action and transformed in the process, as *transformational intellectuals* (Aronowitz & Giroux, 1985). Teachers were beginning to develop their own voices as evidenced in what for this district was the bold act of writing a letter to the school board.

The elementary reading specialist, who was in his first year, was also a part of the workshops and became an advocate for students. He had thought that the elementary principal blocked student progress in writing. The principal, from the reading specialist's perspective, played favorites with staff members by giving some teachers special consideration in his decision making regarding resources and professional opportunities.

According to the reading specialist, resources were not distributed equitably; therefore, some of the students were advantaged over others (Kozol, 1991). Through the workshops, the reading specialist's initial suspicions were substantiated. He went to the superintendent to discuss his concern. For political reasons, the superintendent was reluctant to investigate his concern. As a result, the reading specialist resigned his position in the district. Since the reading specialist was highly regarded by the superintendent, she changed her mind and investigated his concerns by interviewing 14 elementary teachers to gain a broader perspective. As a result of the superintendent's findings, the principal was placed on probation and was given a plan for improvement. This occurred, in part, because the reading specialist's beliefs were validated through the curriculum articulation process.

One of the principals told me that the district was more like three districts: elementary, middle school, and high school. The superintendent had not built an infrastructure to support a pre-K–12 school culture; moreover, each building was allowed to operate in isolation. Ironically, site-based management, intended to validate teachers and administrators, enhanced the feeling of isolation.

As a result, teachers in the school district of Parkerton worked more as individual professionals than as teams. Since there was little pre-K–12 articulation, teachers in the district did not know each other even though there were only about 100 teachers in the district. Many teachers had been teaching in the district their whole careers. I was surprised to find how much the teachers appreciated the nametags that I had requested for our first pre-K–12 articulation meetings. The lack of articulation between and among buildings produced misunderstandings about building-level curriculum and about teachers themselves. The middle school teachers were viewed by the high school teachers as not teaching enough content. The middle school teachers viewed the high school teachers as not caring enough about students. Through the articulation process, teachers from both buildings began to uncover some misunderstandings. Through focus groups, teachers began to develop a pre-K–12 program perspective. They began to reconsider and reconstruct their role in the total program. Teachers' perspectives evolved from a single grade level or building to a broader program or district perspective. Their newly emerging perspective allowed them to understand more clearly how school is seen through the eyes of a student.

SCHOOL DISTRICT OF MILFORD

Curriculum

The following experience occurred when I applied for a position as director of curriculum in the school district of Milford. In an interview with a team of teachers and administrators, I was asked why I thought teachers in the district did not use district curriculum guides. The interview team explained that curriculum documents "just sat on shelves." As I thought about my own teaching experience, I sensed the formation of yet another question: How can we make teachers follow curriculum guides and hold teachers accountable? (Aronowitz & Giroux, 1985, 1991). I suggested that the audience for curriculum documents needed to be the classroom teachers who would use them. I also suggested that if teachers used the writing process in their curriculum work, they would probably take greater ownership for curriculum documents (Applebee, 1996).

Later, I learned that curriculum documents in Milford had been written more for the administration and/or the school board. Teachers were given a rather limiting format to follow, with specific directions on how to use the format. When the audience was changed to teachers and when teachers began to develop their own voices, teachers started to view curriculum as a living document. By using the writing process, teachers transformed themselves through their work together. The curriculum-writing process afforded teachers the opportunity to make curriculum useful in their daily work with students.

One way of making curriculum useful to teachers and students is to pilot "curricular events" in classrooms. When teachers were able to approach implementing a curricular unit as a pilot, they welcomed revision and change. When teachers were able to ask students for their input on how useful the unit was to them, another important dimension of understanding was gained. Both teachers and students became partners in the pilot, and avenues for articulation were cultivated and valued. Students and teachers negotiated the curriculum and, in the process, empowered each other and gave life to the curriculum document (Boomer, 1982).

One challenge that Milford teachers and administrators faced was having to think about curriculum in ways other than traditional scope and sequence, stated behavior objectives, and carefully planned units (Hunter, 1989). Veteran educators especially found it most difficult to think about curriculum in new ways, since their previous experience with curriculum was rooted in a more traditional paradigm (Hunter, 1989). After exploring how research—including that of Britton (1982, 1985), Gardner (1983), Graves (1983), and Vygotsky (1934/1978)—has given us new ways to think about teaching and learning, teachers had difficulty thinking about how curriculum would naturally take on new dimensions to reflect new understandings. Since the current teaching staff of the school district of Milford was a veteran group, one of the biggest challenges to changing pedagogy was helping experienced educators recognize and reenvision old "habits of the heart and mind."

Milford teachers were not alone in their struggle for change. Without a strong parent education component, Milford parents struggled, too. They objected because they believed that today's school should resemble the ones that they had attended when they were students some 25 or so years ago. If lasting change was to occur in Milford, parents and educators needed to form partnerships and become a community of learners (Zemelman & Daniels, 1988).

Milford teachers and administrators were taking a bold step toward pedagogical change. Schools and communities that engage in grassroots efforts and value process-centered approaches to learning find the process to be empowering and inviting. Shared decision making enhances personal and professional growth for all stakeholders.

Administrative Restrictions

Unlike the school board of Parkerton, Milford's board hired their superintendent to act as a change agent. For that reason, the whole administrative team believed that they, too, were part of an effort to create change in the district. Together they formed teams composed of community members, teachers, parents, board members, and administrators. Each team was charged with studying a critical issue identified through their strategic planning process, such as early reading intervention, building construction and renovation, technology needs for the future, and character-education curriculum. After 2 years of meetings, teams presented their recommendations for change to the school board. Then the unexpected happened: The superintendent hired to act as a change agent, who was indeed the impetus for the work up to that point, announced that he was taking a new position in another state. Shortly after that, other administrators resigned to join other districts. Within 10 months, five out of fourteen administrators had resigned and left the district. Speculation about why such a large number of administrators were leaving the district was widespread. The large turnover in administration severely restricted any hope for change as imagined by the community and school staff. In fact, several administrators who have remained in the district now say that in the future the community will probably not tolerate much change. They told me that they believed that the district in the future will be more interested in what has been proven to be "tried and true."

Students' Reactions

Milford itself was located in an isolated area in the northern part of the state. Students were generally not able to frequent cities, which are 100 to 200 miles away. Although students and their families felt fortunate to be protected from what they perceived as urban problems, students lacked firsthand experiences in multiculturalism and diversity. Some students, I was told by teachers, would eat in a restaurant for the first time on their senior class trip. With little outside influence, students complied with rules set down for them. In short, students generally accepted the expectations of their teachers and parents (Aronowitz & Giroux, 1985).

Milford students did not openly question curriculum and its relevance to their lives. Students who could not find themselves in the school curriculum became discipline problems for teachers and administrators, simply skipped classes, or dropped out of school at the legal age. A physical education teacher was quoted in the local paper highlighting his new middle school physical education program: "Students need new ideas or they get bored." Many Milford students, especially middle school and high school levels, described school as boring.

Milford students were all required to take physical education. The program's new emphasis was lifetime sports such as bicycling, golf, cross-country skiing, and tennis. Up until this time, the program had consisted only of traditional components such as tumbling, volleyball, and wrestling. The new program emphasized exploration rather than evaluation of skills. The teacher/program innovator stated: "The level of interest is high at the other schools that offer this type of program. Discipline is at a minimum, because kids want to go to class." The hope of this teacher was that in the future more Milford students would attend class, stay in school, and develop lifelong interests.

Collegial Relationships

With administrative turnover, Milford teachers through their local union had developed a strong and powerful hand in protecting themselves and their jobs. A strong local union, I learned, had grown out of a historically heavy-handed administrative management style. With more administrative change ahead, teachers continued to bond and to become an even stronger cohesive unit. Several middle school teachers told me that they really ran their school. They had worked for 11 different principals in the past 16 years. The staff had learned how to become self-sufficient out of necessity. When the current principal detailed changes that she wanted to make in curriculum and disciplinary procedures, she met highly resistant teachers. They suspected that she would not be in the district long enough to bring about any change. The principal knew this. She told me that even though she felt a need to leave after her first year, she decided to stay on another year just because so many of her predecessors had left after just 1 year.

Teachers in the school district of Milford experienced difficulty in their attempts to change curriculum. They became a threat to the teachers' union that had protected them from change over the years and, as a result, from any perceived possible losses. The physical education teacher, for example, wanted to offer an exploratory curriculum for physical education at the middle school level. As he tried to gain his colleagues' approval, he was shunned and verbally warned by colleagues to stop his efforts. Since this teacher truly believed in his plan and was committed to offering students a better middle school program, he continued. The principal was very supportive of the teacher. But this administrative support made it even harder for the teacher to interact with his peers. His efforts came to full bloom, however, when he was recognized for his program in the community newspaper. Although his persistence paid off for students, the professional alienation proved difficult for him to live with on a daily basis.

The school district of Milford spent much of its energy guarding against change. Although I never clearly understood the underlying political circumstances that supported this district's history, I sensed that the school board and the teachers' union ran the district because they were the real stakeholders in the district. The board president of 22 years was well liked by the teachers' union and community. The board president, not the superintendent, was perceived by teachers and administrators as the person who, in reality, ran the district.

BUFORD JOINT SCHOOL DISTRICT

Curriculum

As a Buford classroom teacher, I had been involved in developing a process for writing curriculum that aimed to put students at the center of curriculum writing. Twenty-two Buford High School teachers from all disciplines (including counselors and principal) worked together to develop a curriculum-writing process. We divided into two teams. We then brainstormed various portfolio pieces that we wanted our students to create. Next, we wrote as a group what used to be known as curriculum units. We called them "curricular events," which essentially were student activities that would generate identified portfolio pieces. As one teacher remarked, "We worked backwards. Instead of starting with curriculum, we started with what we wanted students to have created with the curriculum."

As our two teams worked collaboratively, one question guided our thinking: How does my subject area serve the students in their work? Teachers envisioned ways that would serve the students in creating identified portfolio pieces. We talked, listened carefully to each other, and engaged in the sort of conversations that we had never had before, although many of us had worked together for more than 20 years in the same building. As a group, we learned how each of our subject areas served the students in their work. We tried to write descriptions of curricular events or activities in a way that captured the richness of our conversations. We called these descriptions our curriculum document. Between the two groups during that 1-day workshop, we wrote more than 20 interdisciplinary curricular events.

As a follow-up, several of us met to choose one of the curricular events to pilot. Since we could not change our building schedule in order to plan as a team, we learned how to integrate curriculum at a workshop given by Robin Fogarty (1991). Based on that workshop, we agreed on one of Fogarty's integration methods. The curricular event we chose to develop was inquiry-based: Who are the disadvantaged in our community? At the onset we believed that people in our community were economically better off than most. We decided to invite speakers from the community to inform staff and students on the topic. As a result, both staff and students learned that our community had a growing population of disadvantaged people. This realization was our impetus for further inquiry.

The math teacher had her students gather research on economic conditions, demographics, and other statistical data and present the data on charts using the computer. The science teacher incorporated the project in a unit on nutrition. Students learned through computer research as well as laboratory experiments. The family and consumer education teacher and her students volunteered to make a nutritious meal and to serve the meal at the food kitchens in the community. My writing students joined them as volunteers and upon their return wrote about their experiences. The art teacher and his students worked with the writing students to illustrate their poetry, short stories, and reflective writing.

For the Buford teachers involved in this collaborative project, one of the most rewarding times was when the students themselves were interviewed about the project by local newspapers. The students articulated their connections between/among subject areas. They found excitement in inquiry-based learning. They, like the teachers, had not thought that the community had many disadvantaged people. Instead, students found that they knew some of the people who regularly ate at the food kitchens. One person was identified as a formed classmate who had dropped out of school. Students' stories were powerful. We as teachers knew that we were involved in a process that allowed us to work in exciting new ways and, at the same time, offer students a qualitatively different learning experience.

The Buford district faced several challenges as the integrated project unfolded. The teachers who worked collaboratively on the integrated unit needed to meet an hour before school on a regular basis because the schoolday as it existed did not support collaborative work styles or team planning. Changing time schedules on any day would interfere with bus schedules; students' job responsibilities, including special programs such as co-op classes; and traveling teachers' schedules, to name a few. Until high school schedules became more flexible for Buford teachers and students, any integrated work would probably be voluntary and piecemeal. Adjusting schedules to accommodate change is one reason change is so difficult at the secondary level.

Collegial Relationships

One challenge facing Buford teachers who took part in this project was collegial jealousy. Teachers who volunteered to work in nontraditional ways were labeled as "brownnoses" and were often scorned by colleagues who feared that they would look bad if someone else was more innovative. Innovations that allow for individual differences ran against the grain of the teachers' union culture. Although the teachers' union was in the process of rethinking its role in the district, contract negotiations, working conditions, and benefits all reflected a "one size fits all" model of thinking. The attitude of the teachers' union made any change very difficult.

Other challenges of collegial jealousy involved the director of curriculum. Although she was invited to attend the 1-day workshop on integrated curriculum writing, she chose not to attend or even to respond to the invitation. The high school teachers noticed her absence but did not openly discuss it at the workshop. After the workshop, teachers told me that they thought that she was not very current in her field and was probably intimidated by the secondary teachers and the new process of curriculum writing. I learned later from a neighboring district administrator that he had asked Buford's director of curriculum if one of the secondary teachers involved in the integrated curriculum workshop could conduct a similar workshop in his district. The director of curriculum told the neighboring district administrator that, in her opinion, none of the teachers involved would be capable of leading his workshop. This information validated, in my mind, what Buford secondary teachers told me.

Administrative Restrictions

Over the years, the school district of Buford had very little administrative turnover, which provided stability; but inherent in this stability was a low tolerance for change. Except for pockets of change instigated by a few innovative teachers, the district remained as it had been for years. In managing the status quo, the administration—perhaps inadvertently—along with the board became a roadblock to change. Teachers worked for change quietly and without recognition. They learned how to carry the extra workloads that any change requires because they knew that they would not be supported with extra resources—and they knew that they would not be valued for creating the extra workload.

Sometimes, teachers were reluctant to become involved in change because they had little trust in the administration. The director of curriculum had requested curriculum documents from surrounding districts so that teachers could compare what they were teaching to that which was being taught in neighboring schools. This initiative was presented as a means to update curriculum; however, teachers could see that in many curricular areas, Buford was far more consistent with current thinking about integrated curriculum (Fogarty, 1991) than the neighboring schools. Teachers soon began to understand that the goal in the "reform" was to look like other districts, no matter how outdated. They discovered that the initiative was an attempt by the administration to argue that the district was comparable in offerings and opportunities to other districts. This became clear in light of the pending threat of school vouchers. Change from the director of curriculum's perspective involved looking more like other schools, not aligning curriculum with new research on teaching and learning.

Students' Reactions

Buford students were fairly receptive to change when they could see relevance of school work to their daily lives. Students enthusiastically described what they had learned about the disadvantaged who lived in their town in an interview with a local newspaper. Students said that most of the people at the Salvation Army were eager to talk with them and that they were able to talk with people about a variety of subjects. In the newspaper article, a student reflected on the experience: "These were people with big dreams, good intentions, and a little bad luck." In a debriefing afterwards, another student was astonished that some of the people at the soup kitchens had college educations: "We talked to people who are too educated. They're overqualified. One lady had a job and lost it. Now I know that just because you go to college doesn't mean you'll get a job."

Buford students and teachers benefited from the project. Both teachers and students worked in new and different ways. Both were empowered and trusted to explore new possibilities for learning through integrating curriculum and setting the stage for new conversations (Applebee, 1996).

CONCLUSION

Each of these districts is a living entity and, like anything living, struggles to maintain itself. In each district there are small pockets of educators working to make schools more democratic for students, despite limitations and resistance offered by traditional school culture. I observed a high degree of frustration among teachers, administrators, boards, and community members in all three districts because they found it difficult to sustain the high degree of energy needed to sustain change. One common challenge to all three districts was not having time to reflect on past practice in order to inform future decision making (Schön, 1983). Until school districts integrate time for reflection and dialogue into their regular schoolday, little lasting change can be accomplished.

In each district I found administrators who valued the work of teachers and students. Administration itself presents restrictions to pedagogical change. Since administrators report to school boards and the larger community, they are not always willing to take risks and jeopardize their jobs for innovative projects and teaching techniques. As a result, administrators sometimes seem to teachers not to care about or even notice innovative work with students. Since each district's culture is created over time by a multitude of factors, a single administrator who wants to create change is up against the cultural grain of each school, the entire district, and the community.

In each district there are concerns that school curriculum is not meeting the needs of students. Today's buzzwords in educational circles revolve around standards and standards-based curriculum as well as applied learning. Public discussions have brought to light the need to rethink not only what we teach but also how we teach. Since parents generally expect schools to remain as they remember them, any curricular and pedagogical change becomes highly political in each community. Curricular and pedagogical change, for that reason, must involve all stakeholders, or it is doomed to fail.

In each district these are collegial relationships that also restrict change. From a small core of teachers in one building to a districtwide teachers' organization, change is closely monitored so that ground won in the past is not lost in the future. This watchdog approach alienates teachers who are willing to take risks. Peer pressure is usually strong enough to force teachers back into the ranks of the status quo.

Change is slow and difficult for all districts because school is a political entity (Aronowitz & Giroux, 1985). One important step in speeding up the institutional change process is for all involved to gain a better understanding of the forces that resist change in both schools and the larger community. Teachers, administrators, parents, and community members who realize that any change will be a political undertaking will have a much better chance of bringing to light their shared vision for the future.

REFERENCES

Apple, M. (1981). *Ideology and curriculum*. Boston: Routledge & Kegan Paul.

Applebee, A. (1996). *Curriculum as conversation*. Chicago: University of Chicago Press.

Armstrong, M. (1980). *Closely observed children*. Oxford: Oxford University Press.

Aronowitz, S., & Giroux, H. A. (1985). *Education under siege*. South Hadley, MA: Bergin & Garvey.

Aronowitz, S., & Giroux, H. A. (1991). *Postmodern education*. Minneapolis: University of Minnesota Press.

Avery, C. (1993). *And with a light touch*. Portsmouth, NH: Heinemann.

Boomer, G. (Ed.). (1982). *Negotiating the curriculum: A teacher-student partnership*. Sydney: Ashton-Scholastic.

Bowers, C. A., & Flinders, D. J. (1990). *Responsive teaching*. New York: Teachers College Press.

Britton, J. (1982). *Prospect and retrospect*. Montclair, NJ: Boynton/Cook.

Britton, J. (1985). *Language and learning*. Bungay, UK: Chaucer Press.

Calkins, L. M. (1994). *The art of teaching writing*. Portsmouth, NH: Heinemann.

Cochran-Smith, M., & Lytle, S. (1990). Research on teaching and teacher research: The issues that divide. *Educational Researcher, 19*(2), 2–11.

Comprehensive Test of Basic Skills (CTBS). (1996). Monterey, CA: CTB/McGraw-Hill.

Fogarty, R. (1991). *Integrate the curricula*. Palatine, IL: IRI Skylight.

Gardner, H. (1983). *Frames of mind: The theory of multiple intelligences*. New York: Basic Books.

Graves, D. (1983). *Writing: Teachers and children at work*. Portsmouth, NH: Heinemann.

Hampel, R. L. (1986). *The last little citadel*. Boston: Houghton Mifflin.

Hunter, M. (1989). *Improved instruction*. El Segundo, CA: TIP Publications.

Kozol, J. (1991). *Savage inequalities*. New York: Crown.

Marzano, R. (1992). *A different kind of classroom: Teaching the dimensions of learning*. Alexandria, VA: Association for Supervision and Curriculum Development.

Mayher, J. (1990). *Uncommon sense: Theoretical practice in language education*. Portsmouth, NH: Heinemann.

National Association of Secondary School Principals (NASSP). (1996). *Breaking ranks: Changing an American institution*. Reston, VA: National Association of Secondary School Principals.

National Board of Professional Teaching Standards (NBPTS). (1997). *An invitation to national board certification*. Sothfield, MI: National Board of Professional Teaching Standards.

National Council of Teachers of English & International Reading Association (NCTE/IRA). (1996). *Standards for the English language arts*. Urbana, IL: National Council of Teachers of English.

New Standards Project (1997). *Performance standards*. Pittsburgh: National Center on Education and the Economy and University of Pittsburgh.

Schön, D. (1983). *The reflective practitioner*. New York: Basic Books.

Steinbeck, J. (1937). *Of mice and men*. New York: Viking Penguin.

Vygotsky, L. S. (1978). *Mind in society*. Cambridge, MA: Harvard University Press. (Original work published 1934)

Zemelman, S., & Daniels, H. (1988). *A community of learners*. Portsmouth, NH: Heinemann.

Zemelman, S., Daniels, H., & Hyde, A. (1993). *Best practice: New standards for teaching and learning in America's schools*. Portsmouth, NH: Heinemann.

The Distant Drum: A Call to Action

JAMES K. DALY, PATRICIA L. SCHALL, & ROSEMARY W. SKEELE

If a man does not keep pace with his companions, perhaps it is because he hears a different drummer. Let him step to the music which he hears, however measured or far away.

—Thoreau, *Walden*

WE HAVE REACHED a moment in history when change in schools is inevitable. The nature, process, and outcomes of this change are yet to be determined. While all the stakeholders in education should have a role in this transformation, teachers are uniquely positioned to lead the efforts as the process unfolds. By reexamining the roles they play in schools, teachers will help to redefine teaching and learning for the new millennium. If the predictions for anticipated retirements and record enrollments hold true, as many as 2 million teachers will be hired in the next decade (Pollak, 1999; Tell, 1999). If the inevitable change we expect is to make a positive, long-term impact on schools, it will be critical to fill classrooms with teachers who are well-prepared, reflective, and committed to "serious, thoughtful, informed, responsible, state-of-the-art teaching" (Zemelman, Daniels, & Hyde, 1998, p. viii).

As teacher educators, we are well aware of the widespread and significant criticism of colleges of education and teacher preparation programs that echoes from diatribes in the halls of Congress to conversations at the kitchen table. The dissatisfaction with traditional teacher education is reflected in the growth of alternative routes to certification (Pollak, 1999) and the proliferation of boards addressing standards for certification and professional development (Soler, 1999). We would be naive to ignore the criticism and to absolve ourselves of any responsibility for the perceived failures of teachers and teaching. Mayher (1990) chastises teacher educators for espousing "different approaches to instruction or a different theoretical framework underlying it, but failing to embody these approaches in their practice" (p. 272). As a result, he argues, "our students have easily learned to discount them; to do as we do, not as we say" (p. 272).

Furthermore, even as the better-educated and deeply committed new teachers find jobs, they frequently become mired in the seductive and resilient cultures of schools, abandoning their shiny goals and ideals at the faculty room door. To better prepare teachers for the responsibilities and challenges they will face in collaborative endeavors at revitalizing schools, we will make specific recommendations about what we think they will need to know about the history of educational reform, the reaction of teachers to such reforms, the role of communicating change to the public, the current state of teachers' unions, and ways to build community. In Chapter 4, Nelson and Stanley explained that education in a democracy is always in tension between the forces that resist change and those that press for change. Teachers, who are well aware of the role of intellectual and academic freedom in the classroom, should be prepared to live in the tension that will inevitably arise as the comfort of the status quo is challenged.

CHANGE AND REFORM IN TEACHING

Educators who understand the widespread disillusionment with public education are better equipped to offer a more informed perspective on change and reform in schools. Articles in newspapers and magazines have contributed to the popular perception that public schooling has failed. This impression of failure has generated a long history of reform efforts, which often break down because the culture of the school is powerful and seductive. Larry Cuban (1988) tells us that in the last 100 years of school reform, changing teacher behavior is cited as the most common objective. Yet during that long history, little actual change occurred in classroom practices. Teachers, in their traditional role, have acted as providers of information, typically lecturing to large groups and following rules, policies, and procedures determined by others. Even teachers who enter the profession with a knowledge of and experience with Best Practice (Zemelman et al., 1998, p. viii) and motivated to be change agents can be absorbed into the culture of schools. These schools may or may not be environments that support quality teaching and learning. Too often, teachers have been expected to adapt to and adopt what "experts" cite as essential, ignoring the knowledge they've acquired from their own classroom experiences.

A better approach to reform is needed, one that involves educators in regularly assessing their practice with active and ongoing institutional support. Teachers who reflect on what they do in their classrooms, assess their successes and failures, and make refinements to the belief system that shapes their practice will create an environment conducive to change. In a review of Kate Rousmaniere's *City Teachers: Teaching and School Reform in Historical Perspective* (1997), Murphey (1999) writes, "Rousmaniere implies that to ignore teachers and their work culture is to ignore the engine that drives the machine" (p. 208). Reform should flow from the teacher, and the environment should encourage change. When teachers participate and define their own profession, change is more likely. The current status of educational reform is problematic, because reform movements do not typically start with teachers. Reform movements generally do not even involve teachers.

Reforms that seek to change teacher behavior too often fail to address the institutional structure of the school where reform is sought. Years ago Apple (1982) revealed that in the United States, teachers and administrators were confined to work environments that were more arduous, complicated, and unpredictable than those encountered in most other professions. In addition, teachers are blamed for student failure while decisions that control curriculum and pedagogy typically are made by others. Teachers themselves need to analyze and change the roles and expectations of the schools in which they are employed.

Apple (1982) and others have gone so far as to suggest that those with the power to change schools have effectively deskilled teachers. The failure of schools and of teachers as a group to seek out and implement Best Practice is a failure more of the system and the institution than of the individual or the group. Many times teachers have been excluded from reform movements that have an impact on what they do in their classrooms. Too frequently teachers have not been encouraged to critique their own practice or that of their peers. They have not been invited to evaluate the structure of their schools because they are not expected to do so.

Any reform that addresses roles and relationships of people in schools carries implications not only for teachers but also for all the groups with vested interests in education. School board members, politicians, administrators, parents, and community members have power to influence how teaching and learning take place in the local public schools. If these stakeholders in education use that power to maintain the status quo, reformers may well see unusual alliances that work against change, as at the Rock Spring School. The teachers at the school and their principal were a threat to the power of several groups. Their efforts to examine their own assumptions about teaching and learning, to change curriculum, and to reflect on and modify practice were seen as threats by veteran teachers, parents, and the union leadership. The changes these teachers enacted challenged long-held assumptions of what school should be for many parents—parents willing to confront a vision for education that threatened their perception of schooling.

We hear from the community, politicians, the media, and school administrators in reports, studies, and research, but rarely do we hear the voices of teachers. Reform should be built on the knowledge, experience, and leadership of teachers. What little control they have over content and pedagogy vanishes as teachers accommodate the imposition of state and national standards, mandatory curriculum, standardized tests, nonteaching responsibilities, large classes, and naive expectations that social ills will be cured in the classroom (Goodlad, 1994). If we expect teachers to assume new roles, we must support them with improved working conditions, adequate facilities and teaching materials, and less stressful working environments. Teachers who have the freedom to make decisions and collaboratively develop goals for their classrooms and schools must understand that with increased professional autonomy comes accountability. If teaching is to become a profession like other professions, then teachers must take responsibility for their actions.

FAILED ATTEMPTS AT REFORM

History demonstrates that initiating pedagogical reform in the classroom is usually unsuccessful if the change does not flow from teachers. During the 1970s, federally mandated science reforms were touted in the media and encouraged by universities but never used in the classroom (Ravitch, 1983; Welch, 1979). States mandated numerous reforms for teaching math during the 1980s, but the methods that they promoted were rarely used. Collaboration, writing through math, and use of instructional manipulatives were practices largely ignored by teachers (U.S. Department of Education, 1993). Finally, in the 1990s, when scores on standardized tests declined in California, the state was castigated by many groups for encouraging teachers to use "unproven" teaching methods. As ridiculous as it might seem, the criticisms leveled against the state were proven baseless when researchers determined that for more than 10 years teachers had rarely adopted the state-recommended instructional reforms (California State Department of Education, 1995). While we do not necessarily endorse all aspects of these curricular reforms, we cite them to illustrate the problems with trying to mandate reform.

Before teachers are willing to participate in change, many complex issues need to be addressed. The possibility for change depends on social, political, economic, cultural, psychological, and philosophical issues that mold the teachers' practices. Teachers reflect on a broad range of questions that focus on their own needs and those of their students. Should they scrap the tried-and-true, traditional ways of doing things? What's in it for them or their students? Have they been doing the wrong thing all these years? Will there be support from colleagues, administrators, students, and families? Will their students succeed? Change is risky.

Educators face a dilemma because they have a limited ability to make and defend choices regarding content, materials, and methods. Teachers are cynical about reforms because many fads pass as reforms. A skeptical teacher lamented that every 3 years, change occurs, whether it works or not (Miller, 1999). Teacher skepticism may be justifiable, since some academics criticize educational inquiry because it is not demanding and lacks precise standards for measuring student achievement (Miller, 1999). This research "black hole" has a profound effect on teachers' outlooks on the value of educational inquiry in their day-to-day world of classroom practice. Teacher-driven action research holds much promise, but too many teachers look outside their classrooms for answers to the essential questions they pose about learning. Teachers and others concerned with teaching and learning must recognize and value what teachers know.

UNREALISTIC EXPECTATIONS

A Place Called School (Goodlad, 1984) and *High School* (Boyer, 1983) both include chapters entitled "We Want It All." Each author writes about the unrealistic expectations we have for our schools. Recently, in an interview with Sandra Tell (1999), Goodlad stated that parents want "academic development, social development, civic development, vocational development, [and] character development. They want it all" (p. 15). These were familiar words—words that echoed throughout our interviews in River Haven. Goodlad believes that parents consider their children to be an investment—"ensuring the future economic value of the family" (p. 15). To protect their investments, parents define the mission of the public school based on their children's personal needs. When schools or teachers can't meet what are often exaggerated expectations, parents are disappointed and at times seek ways to shift the blame, vilifying teachers and

administrators. "Whether a principal is considered to be a hero or a vil-
lain, it seems, is a function of the theory that is used to define and describe appropriate practice" (Sergiovanni, 1996, p. 47).

Much of the outrage and despair directed at public education has
been based on the assumption that schools are already enclaves of change
and innovation. This often is not the case. Many, if not most, schools have
remained relatively stable and traditional. Correctly or not, the traditional
model embodies for many a sense of structure and stability associated
with an educational past often perceived as more positive than reality
suggests (Bracey, 1997). However, as Nelson and Stanley reminded us in
Chapter 4, the public has unreasonable expectations for educational reforms, often pushing for new reforms before there is time to implement
and assess the last change. Educators find themselves caught in between
the public's simultaneous yearning for the good old days and demand for
schools to meet current social, political, and economic objectives. This
leads to confusion, disagreement, and conflict.

THE UNION CONNECTION

The hierarchical model of institutional decision making has been comple-
mented by the growth of strong teachers' unions engaged for years in
seeking to improve the teacher's job in narrowly constrained areas. With
little legal authority to address working conditions, the union is engaged
in an adversarial relationship with administrators and school boards. The
growth of strong unions, engaged in an "us versus them" culture, has
preempted efforts by many to raise teaching to the status of a profession.
Hogan (1979) suggests that teachers may have sacrificed some of the respect and individual authority they enjoyed in communities before the
advent of collective bargaining. While Harries-Jenkins (1970) asserts that
professionals have autonomy, teachers are treated like assembly-line
workers, who are told what to do and when to do it (Besag & Nelson,
1984). The Report of the Task Force on Teaching as a Profession (Carnegie
Forum on Education and the Economy, 1986) relates that the best teachers
are frustrated to the point of cynicism by the institutional arrangements
that characterize schooling. Citing the components of professionalism
that help make work challenging and fulfilling, the report concludes that
such characteristics are rarely found in schools. Teachers are suffocating
in bureaucratic environments where their behavior is governed at every
turn by those who do not teach. In this context the actions taken and not
taken by the union leadership in River Haven seem understandable.

Over the years, the union has sometimes been an impediment to

innovation. Teachers who operate outside of union-negotiated boundaries become social outcasts at their schools. New teachers soon discover
that it can be risky to be different, to be creative, or to promote new ideas.
Unions became another force molding the teacher's classroom practice.
Teachers' unions recently have begun to recognize that the industrial
model superimposed on schools never allowed teachers to attain the status granted professionals in other occupations. The American Federation
of Teachers (AFT) has initiated dialogue that would allow school administrators to make educational decisions in consultation with teachers. The
new policies would give individual teachers and administrators the
power to make decisions based on curricular and student needs, even if
they involve issues such as seniority, length of classes, and teaching load.
Sandra Feldman, the AFT president, said, "The proposal seeks to treat
teachers as professionals who would share major instructional decisions with principals at individual schools" (quoted in Greenhouse, 1999,
p. 14).

This proposal is a radical step for teachers' unions. The changes Feldman suggests are welcome improvements that, if continued, should have
a remarkable effect on teacher autonomy and academic freedom. According to Feldman, the AFT supports these initiatives. In response, the
National Education Association (NEA) announced that it is advocating "a
new unionism" that would be less confrontational and more involved
with quality teaching—a.k.a., professionalism (Greenhouse, 1999). These
dramatic reforms by both major unions reinforce the concept that teaching should be reconceptualized as a profession in order to accomplish its
mission successfully in the new century.

Teachers often have limited impact on curriculum and working conditions, yet they can use the power of the union to engage in a new dialogue that includes them in decision making at all levels. This dialogue
can address professional issues that in many ways go beyond the traditional boundaries of collective bargaining. Teachers will recognize that
this is a major paradigm shift from the culture in which they currently
practice. Political and sociological consequences will follow these
changes, and we predict that resistance will be significant.

A CONTENTIOUS ARENA

Any major change in schools has a far-reaching impact on communities.
Just as teachers will have to make a paradigm shift as they assume new
roles in decision making, the public will also have to adapt to change and
assume new roles. Most people would recognize that public education is

a contentious arena. An increasingly empowered citizenry has become actively involved in virtually every aspect of education. This seems desirable in a democratic republic, and yet it poses challenges for schools. If educators are honest about wanting democratic schools, they must be willing to invite open dialogue, really listen to the many voices of the public, and live within the tension created by a more democratic approach to decision making. This is an inevitable and desirable outcome of public involvement.

As educators listen to this chorus of voices, what happens when the voices of some drown out those of others? When does accommodating some become censorship of others? Teachers need to be sensitive to these conflicting demands. They must learn to recognize that the attempts of those who seek to restrict schools from using materials or methods that they perceive as antithetical to their beliefs can often lead to censorship.

CENSORSHIP

Although the causes of censorship may be debatable, the results often are predictable. Communities become polarized, and the morale of educators, students, and families suffers. Carol Hagan (telephone interview, 11 September 1993), a Missouri English teacher, described the despondency she and her colleagues experienced during an organized right-wing attack by Phyllis Schlafly and the Eagle Forum because of her decision to use journals in her seventh-grade class: "It divided the community. There were strict lines—those who were for the teachers and those who were against them. You got the feeling you were trash." The incident Hagan described precipitated others, in a pattern familiar to those who track these cases. One successful attempt at censorship generally leads to more, and schools in other locations become targets as well (Jenkinson, 1979). School boards, nervous about challenges, adopt stricter policies; and publishers, motivated by profit and loss, engage in prepublication censorship (Glatthorn, 1979).

Powers outside the classroom constrain teachers' abilities to make professional decisions. External accountability systems, such as statewide testing and curriculum standards, atomistic performance objectives, and state-adopted curricula and texts, further reduce teachers' autonomy (Nelson, 1990). Commenting on these external constraints, Mayher (1990) chides teacher educators for not helping teachers develop the "confidence and competence needed to resist the onslaught" (p. 254). In such situations teachers appear to be relatively nonreflective and cautious.

This hesitation contributes to teacher self-censorship. Teachers self-censor for a number of reasons. They fear challenges. They are unwilling or unable to deal with controversy. They anticipate the lack of administrative support. They are proponents of censorship. They are intimidated by some of the vocal elements in the community. They fear being isolated from their peers. They fear job loss. They are constrained by the chilling effect of overt censorship attempts. They are unaware of the relevant legal decisions that impact on the choices they make in the classroom. What can be done to help teachers who find themselves struggling in this contentious arena? A commitment to academic and intellectual freedom is essential.

IMPLICATIONS FOR TEACHING

We've made a claim that teachers and preservice teachers for the most part are unaware of the concepts of intellectual and academic freedom in the precollege setting. We believe that these ideas must be developed in both undergraduate and graduate programs. Therefore we make recommendations that flow from our own research in River Haven, our experience as teachers, and the other voices we have heard throughout this book.

New Knowledge, New Skills

Teachers should be prepared to address controversy and community conflict. They need to know about the nature of challenges to teaching controversial topics both past and present and successful strategies for responding to them should they occur. Student teachers need to examine policy documents concerned with such issues in their field experiences and professional development courses. Preservice teachers need an opportunity to explore with their mentors the dimensions of intellectual and academic freedom in real classrooms and school settings.

As teacher educators, we prepare students for an educational climate where challenges exist and appear to be growing. In Chapter 5, we presented real-life situations that overwhelmingly confirm that teachers are vulnerable to the widespread attacks that arise in public schools today. The question that seems unavoidable is: How can we prepare students to innovate if the serious study of academic and intellectual freedom is not integrated into their professional development? Not only is legal knowledge of relevant court rulings essential, but so is a working knowledge of the real nature of intellectual freedom in the schools in which they observe and teach. We would encourage preservice teachers, as part of their field experiences, to examine and analyze actual curricula and school district procedures and policies for addressing challenges. They could interview library/media specialists, teachers, and administrators to learn how they address conflicts over books and teaching methods. Examining the role of intellectual freedom in the professional culture of schools should be a critical component of the education of preservice teachers (Katz, 1985). In a historical environment of imposed restraint on teachers and students, Nelson (1990) argues that academic freedom is the most significant concept that teachers can embrace because it shapes their belief system and practice. We contend it is the responsibility of teacher educators and the leaders of teachers' unions and professional organizations to make teachers aware of the support many of these organizations provide for teachers facing challenges.

Communication

Honest, open dialogue among teachers, administrators, families, students, and the wider public has the potential to strengthen the curriculum and improve schools. Dialogue provides educators with meaningful information about the needs and expectations of the multiple communities within communities they serve and simultaneously educates the public about schools (Apple, 1982). Misinformation circulates and confusion prevails when educators fail to respond to questions, misunderstandings, and challenges in a timely, responsible way, using jargon-free language the general public can understand. Written school policies provide an important formal process for airing concerns about school issues. These policies, of course, are good only if they are recognized and followed. Many problems can be resolved through these policy-prescribed channels, but others will continually resurface even after an initial crisis is settled. It is important to continue serious dialogue to better understand the nature and cause of these ongoing concerns and to offer a rationale for the school's decisions. Still, since we are educators in a pluralistic culture, we may find that some cases will never be closed, as we respectfully agree to disagree with the complainants.

Educational conflicts arise at many levels. Government bureaucracies impose requirements and regulations. National standards and standardized testing dictate curriculum. Superintendents and local school boards generate new programs, policies, and procedures. In addition to the formally established centers of power, numerous informal organizations and networks effectively promote and effect change in schools. These organizations are as diverse as professional organizations for educators, the PTA, the National Organization for Women, and the Eagle Forum. On the home front there are state and local activists whose influence exceeds their numbers. Many teachers can recount stories about school board meetings that were held hostage by the local crank with an ax to grind. At times, despite safeguards, one individual has the ability to bring school practices and even curriculum into alignment with his or her personal educational or political perspectives.

Before conflicts arise in schools, teachers need to be prepared to address the issues, taking a proactive stance. While many educators naively shun political activism, the forces that initiate attacks on schools are politically savvy, well prepared, well funded, and well organized to take action. As teacher educators, we would serve our students well to call their attention to these facts of political life and help them develop the insights and skills they will need if they find themselves facing a challenge. Prevention is always the preferred strategy. Even when your side wins, before the victory party is over, the opposition is often regrouping for its next attack. The cases involving Jan Cole and Cissy Lacks demonstrate the energy and persistence certain groups exhibit when pursuing an educational target. "Education—for democracy and for critical citizenship—is a constant struggle" (Edelsky, 1998, p. 53).

Educators should take the initiative at the local, state, and national levels to communicate more effectively with the public about teaching and learning. Brinkley and Weaver (1998) tell us that in Michigan a small group of citizens, some teachers, weary of attacks on public schools, conceived Michigan for Public Education (MPE). MPE is a grassroots, nonprofit organization representing public education, whose members want to articulate educational issues in an open forum. The group has been actively "advocating educational equity and excellence" on local, state, and national levels since 1994. MPE has noteworthy advice for starting up similar organizations. They suggest that, to be effective, groups should provide information, an open environment for discussions, and different viewpoints on educational topics. Members produce a newsletter, occasional papers on critical topics, and fact sheets; they also maintain a Website. They speak about important issues at meetings, testify at public hearings, network with other organizations, and advise policy makers. The MPE is a model for democratic action for public education. Colleges of education or student education associations need to consider initiating similar programs.

Building Bridges

We subscribe to a constructivist view of teaching and learning. Constructivist philosophies embrace the concept of schools as communities and acknowledge the social nature of learning. This approach offers the learner powerful opportunities to construct knowledge by building a context for learning based on past knowledge, the social culture, and links to the real world. Sergiovanni (1996) helps us to understand that communities support student learning in various ways. He defines communities as people freely sharing "a tightly knit web of meaningful relationships" (p. 48) and a "common commitment to a set of ideas and ideals" (p. 50). He explains that providing the conditions for learning is an important objective of teaching. The knowledge that students produce is shaped by their values and past experiences. To bring personal and culturally defined meaning to learning, teachers can expand the school community to include many groups outside the classroom. Steiner's rich descriptions of the Parkerton and Milford districts in Chapter 6 paint vivid pictures of the kinds of relationships that evolve within schools and districts. She brings to life the institutional challenges that support and impede the development of school communities. Teachers and teachers, teachers and administrators, and teachers and families are important groups that support the school community and improve the climate for learning. Teachers who close the classroom door fail to recognize the intricate relationships that can promote or hinder learning. If we expect to improve schools, change must become a collaborative endeavor. "Change is a journey . . . local implementation by everyday teachers, principals, parents, and students is the only way that change happens" (Fullan & Miles, 1992, p. 752).

Teachers and Teachers. While we acknowledge that this is easier said than done, teachers within a school need to establish open dialogue with their colleagues. Developing a professional community based on Sergiovanni's model means that the community's driving force and goals exclude self-serving rewards. In this ideal situation, everyone would be striving to support the mission of the school and these schools would represent what Tonnies (1887/1957) first called communities of relationships, place, and mind. These communities create ties resembling those found in families, coexist in a location for a certain period of time, and share common objectives and purposes. Establishing professional communities of teachers would lead to improved learning and the development of teaching as a profession.

The traditional roles of teacher and administrator require drastic change in order to develop educational communities. In these communities, teachers and administrators would articulate goals, values, and perceptions. Administrators would relinquish hierarchical roles that work against teachers becoming leaders. Teachers would do their jobs based on personal responsibility for commitments without top-down control and the attendant rewards and punishments. We are proposing a noble enterprise here.

Educators who have been recognized as great teachers usually build support webs throughout their teaching community. Each school and district has distinct features that can be addressed with different strategies to promote teacher involvement. Currently, in many schools, teachers are relegated to token advisory committees that have no real authority or power. When California changed from basal readers to a literature-based curriculum, teachers were not involved in the decision. They were given new books selected without teacher input (Webster, 1994). There is no one definition, one correct model, or one to-do list that will produce empowered teachers; but teacher involvement in curricular reform is always necessary.

A study by Webster (1994) revealed that in schools diagnosed with serious problems of any type, a new administration was less apt to share leadership with faculty. Teacher involvement in decision making was minimal and principals were more autocratic, reporting that their problems were so overwhelming that only top-down control would work. This is unfortunate, since Webster later relates several cases that illustrate that students are better educated in schools where teachers are empowered to make decisions about facilities, curriculum, practice, and students. Another educational irony: Teacher input is least requested in schools where it is most needed.

Within a school, certain groups of teachers have more influence than others. Seniority has an important role in determining power and status. Our years of experience in classrooms have convinced us that through either support or resistance, senior faculty control change and reform to a surprising degree. According to Tanck (1994), approval from long-tenured faculty frequently is the key to the successful implementation of change. The River Haven experience, in which senior teachers opposed changes, illustrates the effect that a small group of influential teachers, well known among parents, can have on a school. The principal, who was the center of the conflict, believed that the power of these teachers had considerable consequences.

We've often heard teachers describe themselves as professionals, yet for a number of reasons we believe that teaching has not yet reached the status of a profession. Tanck (1994) states that making teaching a profession "is the only true hope for reform of education" (p. 88). In other professions, members govern entry to the profession through licensure. They control, assess, and discipline members. Like members of other professions, teachers receive specialized training and possess certain competencies. Until teachers routinely participate in hiring practices, sit on tenure review committees, identify their own professional development needs, and establish and monitor the criteria by which they will be judged, they are prevented from defining and shaping their own profession. In some locations, legitimate attempts to involve teachers in decision making are being made at the local level; however, much remains to be done at the state and national levels. We believe that teachers need to help set the criteria and expectations that evolve into certification standards. Without ongoing participation in all these areas, teachers cannot be expected to ensure the quality of the profession by the regular review of their own performance and that of their colleagues. One could imagine the outrage that would occur if nonmembers intruded into these processes in other professions.

As in other professions, acquiring content knowledge and keeping abreast of current practice are indicators of professional competence for teachers. Professional development programs, typically initiated by schools, don't always meet teachers' expectations or interests. Many times administrators determine the nature of these programs based on fads, availability of speakers, or so-called reforms—things that others believe are necessary for teachers—but rarely on teacher-identified needs. As teachers, we remember colleagues who snoozed through these one-size-fits-all sessions. As presenters on the other side of the professional development desk, we couldn't help empathizing with the teachers we've spotted in the back of the room reading newspapers, doing crossword puzzles, and grading papers. Devoid of teacher ownership, these programs are usually scattered, spotty attempts to implement change. It is no wonder that would-be reforms stop at the classroom door.

What struck us as unique at the Rock Spring School was the evolution of a professional development process that flowed from classroom practice. Teachers were inquirers in their own classrooms, asking essential questions about teaching and learning. We spoke to a professor who worked with some of these teachers in graduate classes. She was impressed that the teacher-driven initiatives taking place at Rock Spring and nurtured in their graduate classes created a synergy that helped teachers redefine their practice. These teachers, in the spirit of true professional development, sought more than just graduate credits and a step up on the pay scale. This professor confirmed Karen Hunter's observation that there was an excitement at Rock Spring about working together to create change seldom found in schools.

Teachers should be involved in determining meaningful professional development that will equip them with the knowledge and skills to initiate needed reform. Teachers know and understand their students, their school, and their community much better than many who are advocating reforms. Professional development can be reconfigured in many ways to meet diverse needs, both inside and outside the school, involving teachers collaborating with other teachers. Teachers know what they need to create change. Many opportunities to promote change exist at all levels, from kindergarten through college. Colleges of education are becoming more involved with K–12 schools and teachers. Many government grants require K–college partnerships and professional development schools where classroom teachers are becoming mentors for new teachers and members of teams that collaborate to prepare teachers. New teachers and experienced teachers complement each other while sharing knowledge and practice. New technologies are helping teachers gather information, communicate with other teachers, establish links with colleges and universities, and share materials, methods, and classroom experiences. Many opportunities for transformation are possible. These developments require the active participation of teachers in order to ensure their success and to contribute to the evolution of teaching as a profession.

Teachers and Administrators. Involvement in whole language generated controversy for some of the teachers at Rock Spring School, but much more radical was their evolution into a school culture in conflict with the culture of schooling. Those teachers brought their excitement about the possibilities of a new way of teaching and learning into their daily conversations in the teachers' lounge and engaged the interest of their principal. Acting as colleagues rather than as adversaries, they read, discussed, and sought to implement activities and projects on which they agreed. The college professor we previously mentioned recalled the action research projects the Rock Spring teachers carried out in their classrooms. Together, with the support and involvement of their principal, they enthusiastically created a learning environment that was student-centered.

This collaboration between teachers and administrators seems not only reasonable but desirable. Sergiovanni (1996) points out that administrators and teachers share a collective practice that involves stewardship of the young. It is, however, contrary to the norms of schooling. The degree to which it is atypical may well be seen in the actions of the union leadership in River Haven. For years the leadership saw the principal as someone needing to be taught the rules. New curricula, new assessment, and working collegially within the school were not objectives for the union. The "script" for schools requires that teachers not get cozy with administrators, who cannot be trusted because of their role as evaluators.

The River Haven teachers were a threat. They were a threat to the power of the union and to the various other holders of power in the community. Teachers and administrators working together to fashion a school that was student-centered, always in the process of becoming, and unconstrained by the bureaucratic realities of the modern public school struck at the very reason for existence of some power holders. From the superintendent to the school board and the board attorney, such a situation was a threat to their own legitimacy. The River Haven staff wasn't playing by the rules. Besag and Nelson (1984) point out that institutions change people through norms and roles. The actors in the institution quickly learn and accommodate the expectations that their positions require. Teachers and administrators have different roles, and the actions at River Haven challenged that contention. Their actions did not go unpunished.

Sergiovanni (1996) suggests that as the modern school has grown, it has borrowed extensively from the world of business. Management theories that were successful in the world of commerce and economics have been transplanted into the world of schools. All these theories and the bureaucratic practices they generate are hierarchical, and Sergiovanni points out how by their nature they serve schools poorly, suggesting that in their place a management system needs to emerge that has evolved from the history and nature of the schools. He makes the case that schools are not businesses. They seek to meet different purposes, serve different people, and embrace working conditions that are not typical elsewhere. Needed is the creation of a unique leadership suited for schools, one that endeavors to create learning communities actively making social and intellectual connections between both those in the school and those in the larger community.

We should aim to create an environment that permits those in schools to begin to entertain the possibility that these new systems can emerge. History and tradition act in opposition to such thinking. Often, even administrators who endorse reform efforts and the right of teachers to deal with change and controversial issues and methods are resistant to classroom and school changes that challenge the status quo. If any complaints about these changes surface, administrative support tends to evaporate (Daly, 1991). Teachers quickly learn from such behavior that administrative support for change must be cultivated and cannot be taken for granted.

Those in schools who see both the necessity and the potential for change need to do what they do best, and that is to educate teachers, administrators, parents, school boards, community leaders, and politicians. Change agents should anticipate hesitation and resistance on all fronts. Compelling evidence must be provided to demonstrate the benefits of reform. How does this happen? Everyone needs a vision of what these new learning communities could look like. Teachers and administrators can work within their unions and professional organizations to make the vision become a reality. Dialogue and reflection are needed to build a foundation that is theoretically sound and intuitively practical. Reform-minded educators should see that professional and popular literature on these new possibilities is readily available for anyone interested in reading it. Community-based media can be used effectively to get the word out and initiate and maintain dialogue about the changes that are occurring in the schools.

For schools to become learning communities, the school culture must change. Learning communities cannot be legislated or mandated. They require a culture in which the actors within the institution are committed to the process of creating and maintaining new institutions that are different from any others in our society. School culture is what people believe (Sergiovanni, 1996), and we need to make the school community believers in the desirability of school reform that builds on democratic national impulses and the unique nature of schools as places where adults and children teach and learn from one another.

Teachers and Families. Families and teachers working together can help develop common goals for learning. Current federally sponsored initiatives encourage parental involvement because research repeatedly indicates that student achievement is greater when families are involved with and support their children's education. Establishing productive relationships with families is critical in most communities.

The "classroom connection" is often cited today as the meaningful link between families and the school. Usually, teachers are not formally trained to work with families (Harvard Family Research Project, 1997). A study by Veenman (1984) revealed that new teachers perceived interactions with parents as one of their principal problems. Professional development in this area is critical today. Anderson and Smith (1999) identified four practices that contribute to successful teacher–family involvement and help to meet the diverse needs of family groups:

> Communicate effectively—both formally and informally; plan for special needs—childcare or work schedules; make parents feel welcome—identify factors that cause discomfort; and establish a community feeling—involve parents in planning, implementing, and evaluating school activities (p. 160).

Meaningful partnerships among schools, teachers, and parents are essential at a time when families and community members believe that they not only have a right to be heard but also a right to be heeded. Teachers and school administrators, who share professional training and experience, believe that parents should respect their decisions. There is a better chance that extended conflicts in schools could be resolved between teachers and families if more collaboration existed between these two groups who passionately affirm the same goal—"Caring for the children we share" (Epstein, 1995, p. 701).

Many families like to be invited into schools. They appreciate teachers who provide information, suggestions for involvement, and leadership (Davies, 1993; Epstein, 1995; Leitch & Tangri, 1988). A study (Phelps, 1999) of teachers identified as outstanding revealed that "most teachers perceived parental involvement as synonymous with teamwork based on frequent interactions, positive communication, and openness in sharing information and feelings" (p. 155). It is important to note that teachers in this study believed that dialogue between families and individual teachers was more important than communications from school administrators. Boyer (1995) confirms that parents identify parental involvement as a characteristic of good teaching. Families are a child's most important teachers. It is reassuring for a teacher to receive feedback about a child from the family, removing the uncertainties of being a "single parent" in the classroom (Carr & Allen, 1989). Teachers and families can affirm each other's decisions, share success stories, and close the gaps that occur when teachers are forced to design an educational plan without a home–school connection. Schockley, Michalove, and Allen (1995) believe that learning is significantly affected by the relationships among parents, curriculum, teachers, and children. They report that the involvement of families significantly changed classroom communities and the members of those communities. When families and schools work together, schools and families were most often characterized as "caring" (p. 5).

We're convinced that the people in River Haven missed an opportunity for dialogue. All the parents we met were earnest people who cared deeply about their children and education. At a certain point it was clear that all involved in the controversy were boarding trains on a collision course. No one acted responsibly or well to halt the impending disaster. Many people stoked the fire, instead of pulling the emergency brake. Those who flashed the warning lights were too late. The administration and the board of education failed to meet the responsibilities inherent in their positions in the school system. Everyone was a victim of the structure of public schooling that concentrates power in the hands of a select few. As we suggested at the conclusion of Chapter 3, the story could have had a different ending, but we will never know.

CONCLUSION—DO YOU HEAR THE DRUM?

We've made many recommendations in this chapter that focus on possibilities for teaching, learning, and the communities concerned with schools. Making recommendations is easy when we are safe and secure in the academic freedom of the university system. But making recommendations a reality is another story. What we encounter in actual schools is typically a far cry from our perceived mission for education. The gulf between recommendations and reality creates the kind of cognitive dissonance that heightens the awareness of teachers and presents the opportunity to recognize that something could be wrong. This recognition is essential to becoming, in the words of Aronowitz and Giroux (1985), a transformative intellectual. We have not been out of public school classrooms so long that we don't recall in our own teaching careers the stinging rejection and isolation we experienced when we marched to a different drummer. Jim, concerned about professional rights, was told by a colleague to forget about that stuff and plan the Christmas party, while Pat was advised that her problem was that she took her job too seriously. Once, when Rosemary applied for a position, she was told that her ideas were a poor match for public schools. We all recall particular administrators who made continuing in public education a daily challenge. Years later, our current students report similar reactions when they question the institutional arrangements of schools.

The status quo resembles that inviting old easy chair we can't throw out. It's comfortable and secure and constantly beckons us to curl up and fall asleep. If we choose to remain awake, our recommendations will be a call to action. Both teachers and students need "the skills . . . to locate themselves in history, find their own voices, and establish the convictions and compassion necessary for exercising civic courage, taking risks, and furthering the habits, customs, and social relations essential to democratic public forms" (Freire & Giroux, 1989, p. ix). Our recommendations are an invitation not only to dialogue but also to discord. Both must be welcomed. If we are unwilling to live within the resulting creative tension, democratic reform is not possible. Teachers will have to live and thrive "with more uncertainty than some of us find comfortable" (Mayher, 1990, p. 285).

The resulting uncertainty will create levels of discomfort far beyond the classroom door. We do need change, and that change can't consist of gimmicks and ill-conceived, top-down, simplistic recommendations and initiatives. We cannot afford to bypass teachers, educators, families, and communities on the journey to change. Who knows more about schools than teachers? Who knows more about children than families? We are all in this together, and it is our hope that we will begin the work that will show the nation just how good teachers and schools can be. Do you hear the drum?

REFERENCES

Anderson, A. L., & Smith, A. B. (1999). Community building with parents. *Kappa Delta Pi Record, 35*(4), 159–161.

Apple, M. W. (1982). *Education and power.* Boston: Routledge & Kegan Paul.

Aronowitz, S., & Giroux, H. A. (1985). *Education under siege: The conservative, liberal and radical debate over schooling.* South Hadley, MA: Bergin & Garvey.

Besag, F. P., & Nelson, J. L. (1984). *The foundations of education: Stasis and change.* New York: Random House.

Boyer, E. L. (1983). *High school: A report on secondary education in America* (Report to The Carnegie Foundation for the Advancement of Teaching). New York: Harper & Row.

Boyer, E. L. (1995). *The basic school: A community for learning.* Princeton, NJ: Carnegie Foundation for the Advancement of Teaching.

Bracey, G. W. (1997). A nation of learners: Nostalgia and amnesia. *Educational Leadership, 54*(5), 53–57.

Brinkley, E., & Weaver, C. (1998). Organizing for political action: Suggestions from experience. In K. S. Goodman (Ed.), *In defense of good teaching: What teachers need to know about the reading wars* (pp. 183–190). York, ME: Stenhouse.

California State Department of Education. (1995). *Improving mathematics achievement for all California students.* Sacramento: Author.

Carnegie Forum on Education and the Economy. (1986). *A nation prepared: Teachers for the 21st century* (Report of the Task Force on Teaching as a Profession). New York: Carnegie Corporation of New York.

Carr, E., & Allen, J. (1989). University/classroom teacher collaboration: Costs, benefits, and mutual respect. In J. Goetz & J. Allen (Eds.), *Qualitative research in education: Substance, methods, experience* (pp. 123–131). Athens, GA: College of Education, University of Georgia.

Cuban, L. (1988). Constancy and change in schools (1880s to the present). In P. W. Jackson (Ed.), *Contributing to educational change* (pp. 85–105). Berkeley, CA: McCutchan.

Daly, J. K. (1991). The influence of administrators on the teaching of social studies. *Theory and Research in Social Education, 19*(3), 267–282.

Davies, D. (1993). Benefits and barriers to parent involvement: From Portugal to Boston to Liverpool. In N. F. Chavkin (Ed.), *Families and schools in a pluralistic society* (pp. 205–216). Albany: State University of New York Press.

Edelsky, C. (1998). It's a long story—And it's not done yet. In K. S. Goodman (Ed.), *In defense of good teaching: What teachers need to know about the reading wars* (pp. 39–55). York, ME: Stenhouse.

Epstein, J. L. (1995). School/family/community partnerships: Caring for the children we share. *Phi Delta Kappan, 76*(9), 701–712.

Freire, P., & Giroux, H. A. (1989). Pedagogy, popular culture and public life: An introduction. In H. A. Giroux & R. I. Simon (Eds.), *Popular culture: Schooling and everyday life* (pp. vii-xii). New York: Bergin & Garvey.

Fullan, M. G., & Miles, M. B. (1992). Getting reform right: What works and what doesn't. *Phi Delta Kappan, 73*(6), 744–752.

Glatthorn, A. (1979). Censorship and the classroom teacher. In J. E. Davis (Ed.), *Dealing with censorship* (pp. 48–53). Urbana, IL: National Council of Teachers of English.

Goodlad, J. (1984). *A place called school: Prospects for the future.* New York: McGraw-Hill.

Goodlad, J. (1994). *Educational renewal.* San Francisco: Jossey-Bass.

Greenhouse, S. (1999, July 10). Teachers' union head urges more flexibility in contract talks. *New York Times,* p. 14.

Harries-Jenkins, G. (1970). Professionals in organizations. In J. H. Jackson (Ed.), *Professions and professionalization* (pp. 51–107). Cambridge, UK: Cambridge University Press.

Harvard Family Research Project. (1997). *New skills for new schools: Preparing teachers in family involvement.* Cambridge, MA: U.S. Department of Education.

Hogan, R. F. (1979). Some thoughts on censorship in the schools. In J. E. Davis (Ed.), *Dealing with censorship* (pp. 86–95). Urbana, IL: National Council of Teachers of English.

Jenkinson, E. B. (1979). Dirty dictionaries, obscene nursery rhymes, and burned books. In J. E. Davis (Ed.), *Dealing with censorship* (pp. 2–13). Urbana, IL: National Council of Teachers of English.

Katz, L. (1985). Facets. *English Journal, 74,* 23.

Leitch, M. L., & Tangri, S. S. (1988). Barriers to home–school collaboration. *Educational Horizons, 66*(2), 70–74.

Mayher, J. M. (1990). *Uncommon sense: Theoretical practice in language education.* Portsmouth, NH: Boynton/Cook, Heinemann.

Miller, D. W. (1999, August 6). The black hole of educational research. *Chronicle of Higher Education, 45*(48), A17–A18.

Murphey, K. (1999). [Review of the book *City teachers: Teaching and school reform in historical perspective*]. *Harvard Educational Review, 69*(2), 205–211.

Nelson, J. L. (1990). The significance of and rationale for academic freedom. In A. C. Ochoa (Ed.), *Academic freedom to teach and to learn: Every teacher's issue* (pp. 21–30). Washington, DC: National Education Association.

Phelps, P. H. (1999). The power of partnerships. *Kappa Delta Pi Record, 35*(4), 154–157.

Pollak, M. (1999, July 21). Faulting plans to raise bar on teachers. *New York Times,* p. 8.

Ravitch, D. (1983). *The troubled crusade: American education, 1945–1980.* New York: Basic Books.

Rousmaniere, K. (1997). *City teachers: Teaching and school reform in historical perspective.* New York: Teachers College Press.

Schockley, B., Michalove, B., & Allen, J. (1995). *Engaging families: Connecting home and school literacy communities.* Portsmouth, NH: Heinemann.

Sergiovanni, T. J. (1996). *Leadership for the schoolhouse: How is it different? Why is it important?* San Francisco: Jossey-Bass.

Soler, S. (1999). Teacher quality is job one: Why states need to revamp teacher certification. *Spectrum, 72*(2), 14–19.

Tanck, M. L. (1994). *Celebrating education as a profession.* In D. R. Walling (Ed.), *Teachers as leaders: Perspectives on the professional development of teachers* (pp. 83–117). Bloomington, IN: Phi Delta Kappa Educational Foundation.

Tell, C. (1999). Renewing the profession: A conversation with John Goodlad. *Educational Leadership, 56*(8), 14–19.

Tonnies, F. (1957). *Gemeinschaft und Gesellschaft* [*Community and society*] (C. P. Loomis, Ed. & Trans.). New York: HarperCollins. (Original work published 1887)

U.S. Department of Education. (1993). *Digest of educational statistics.* Washington, DC: Author.

Veenman, S. (1984). Perceived problems of beginning teachers. *Review of Educational Research, 54*(2), 143–178.

Webster, W. E. (1994). Teacher empowerment in a time of change. In D. R. Walling (Ed.), *Teachers as leaders: Perspectives on the professional development of teachers* (pp. 103–117). Bloomington, IN: Phi Delta Kappa Educational Foundation.

Welch, W. W. (1979). Twenty years of science curriculum development: A look back. *Review of Research in Education, 7,* 282–306.

Zemelman, S., Daniels, H., & Hyde, A. (1998). *Best practice: New standards for teaching and learning in America's schools.* Portsmouth, NH: Heinemann.

Rock Spring Elementary School Controversy Timeline

1970–84	Ralph Valle is principal of the Rock Spring School.
9/84	Karen Hunter hired as principal.
1986	Hunter and teachers attend whole-language workshop.
1985–86	Rock Spring Elementary School enrollment growing; additional teachers hired.
1986–87	Whole language initiated at Rock Spring School.
Sum/88	Hunter travels to New Zealand to study whole language.
Fall/88	Hunter receives tenure.
Spr/89	Hunter informs teachers by memo that the fifth grade would be self-contained in fall 1989.
Spr/89	Fifth-grade teachers (including Bennett) apply for transfers to other schools.
Fall/90	Morgan and O'Brien work to change PTO to PTA.
Spr/91	PTA initiated. Cathy Young runs for PTA president against David Morgan. Young wins.
Spr/91	Fred Pacifico retires as superintendent and is replaced by John Paulsen.
Fall/91	On first day of school, fifth-grade parents had concerns about curriculum and practices. Meeting held with Hunter, Paulsen, and parents. Problems appeared to be resolved by 12/91.

4/28/92   At PTA meeting, vice president of PTA reads letter from Concerned Parents criticizing teaching methods used at Rock Spring Elementary School.

5/20/92   Hunter delivers her response to the letter from Concerned Parents.

5/27/92   Concerned Parents write letter to Waterview Board of Education demanding changes in teaching practices at Rock Spring School.

6/24/92   Concerned Parents gathered 500 signatures from parents on a petition calling for changes in materials and methods.

6/30/92   Union contract with the district expired.

7/92   Paulsen takes sudden vacation after closed meeting with Waterview Board of Education.

7/8/92   Students' work from three schools compared at board of education meeting. At same meeting, Herman Bailey, parent and consultant to Concerned Parents, reads his evaluation of the methods employed at the Rock Spring School. Dorothy Stout, assistant superintendent, announces that major changes will be implemented at Rock Spring School before the start of fall classes.

8/4/92   John Paulsen officially resigns as superintendent with a buyout of $110,000 plus benefits for one year.

8/92   Dorothy Stout appointed acting superintendent.

8/8/92   Plan for Excellence 1992–93 presented.

9/92   Plan for Excellence 1992–93 implemented and monitored.

10/6/93   Hunter suspended after 59 separate tenure charges filed by board of education.

10/9/93   Rock Spring School teacher reads statement at board of education meeting that more than 80% of Rock Spring teachers support Hunter.

10/93   Union president (Lodge) warns teachers not to demonstrate support for Hunter.

10/27/93 Restraining order against Hunter, Young, and Cluney handed down.

4/4/94   61 additional charges lodged against Hunter by board of
          education.

1994–99   Hearings held in case of *Waterview Board of Education* v.
          Hunter.

6/99   Hunter and Waterview Board of Education settle suit.
          Charges against principal dropped. Hunter receives
          $600,000 to leave district.

Case Study Cast

Anita Bailey   An active member of the Concerned Parents who believed that Karen Hunter's practices at Rock Spring School caused many problems for her children.

Herman Bailey   A school administrator in another district who was a leader of the Concerned Parents. He believed that Karen Hunter's influence at the Rock Spring School was harmful to many children, including his own. He actively sought her removal as principal.

Marsha Bennett   Rock Spring teacher who disagreed with Karen Hunter's educational philosophy. She transferred to another district school when Hunter announced that all classrooms would be self-contained.

Zena Brant   Outspoken parent who supported Karen Hunter and the educational philosophy at the Rock Spring School.

Martina Canon   Member of Concerned Parents who believed her child was not reaching his potential at Rock Spring School because of teaching practices.

Ron Cluney   Parent who supported principal and was served with gag order by the board of education.

Cynthia Fields   Rock Spring parent who supported Hunter and sought to resolve the problems.

Robin Fisher   Teacher in another school district who was pleased with the education her child was receiving at Rock Spring School.

Karen Hunter   Principal of the Rock Spring Elementary School who was challenged by parents because of her philosophy of education. Later, serious accusations made by parents led to charges filed by the board of education.

Terry Kosc   Parent who supported Karen Hunter. She believed that the Rock Spring School was a good place for her children. She was employed as a teacher in another school district.

Ken Lodge   Middle school teacher who was president of the teachers' union. He disagreed with Hunter and advised teachers not to demonstrate support for her.

Veronica Manley   Rock Spring teacher who was not recommended for tenure by Hunter. Many parents supported her, but the superintendent and board of education followed the advice of the principal and refused to renew her contract.

Emily Mason   Hunter supporter who felt that her child, who had a learning problem, thrived under Hunter's direction at the Rock Spring School.

Andy Monroe   School administrator in another district who was Karen Hunter's mentor and long-time partner. Often referred to as "Andy Baby" by Hunter's detractors.

David Morgan   Parent who was friend and supporter of Hunter for years. He was instrumental in writing the Plan for Excellence. He later had difficulties with Hunter, joined the Concerned Parents, and became one of her most outspoken critics.

Geri O'Brien   Member of the Waterview Board of Education who perceived that her children received a fine education at Rock Spring School. She was a staunch supporter of Karen Hunter. She was shunned by other members of the board who she felt excluded her from school board business.

Fred Pacifico   Superintendent of Waterview schools for 14 years. He was well liked by everyone and retired from the district just as major problems were surfacing at Rock Spring School. He left before the conflict erupted.

John Paulsen   Superintendent for 1 year in the Waterview School District. He had difficulties with parents, teachers, and the board of education. His contract was not renewed and he received a buyout of $110,000.

Hillary Roland   Very active Concerned Parent whose child had learning difficulties she believed were caused by the teaching practices at Rock Spring School.

Dorothy Stout   Assistant superintendent of Waterview schools for many years. She was appointed acting superintendent and later superintendent after Paulsen resigned in the midst of the conflict.

Ralph Valle   Principal of the Rock Spring School from 1970 to 1984. He transferred to another school in the district when he reportedly was having difficulties with parents at the Rock Spring School.

Cathy Young   President of the PTA and parent with children at Rock Spring School. She was pleased with the practices at Rock Spring and supported the principal. She was served with a gag order by the board of education.

Slide Presentation About the Plan for Excellence to Parents and Waterview Board of Education

WATERVIEW PLAN FOR EXCELLENCE, 1992

Areas of Focus

Language Arts
Mathematics
Assessment
Communication

Implementation Plan

Goals
Methods and Resources
Timeline
Assessment

LANGUAGE ARTS

Language Arts Goals

Reading

"To expand teaching of phonics and decoding skills and enhance vocabulary."
"To identify each student's reading instructional level and to support
student's use of challenging reading materials."

Writing

"To strengthen grammar, spelling, editing and handwriting skills."
"To emphasize pride in the proper presentation of one's work."

Language Arts—Methods and Resources

K–2 Reading

Increased emphasis on phonics and decoding skills.
Reading materials at instructional level.

3–5 Reading

Increased focus on vocabulary development.
Reading materials at instructional level.

K–2 Writing

Individual and group writing conferences.
Spelling words from common word lists and student writing (except K).
Editing skills lessons including grammar, punctuation, parts of speech, and organization of thought.
Handwriting lessons.

3–5 Writing

Individual and group writing conferences.
Spelling words from common word lists and student writing.
Editing skills lessons including grammar, punctuation, parts of speech, and organization of thought.
Handwriting lessons.

Language Arts Assessment

Reading Assessments
Writing Portfolio
Tests
Handwriting Samples

MATHEMATICS

Mathematics Goal

The major focus of our mathematics program is the understanding of math and the use of math skills in problem solving.

Enhancement Objective

"To strengthen computational skills for the achievement of speed and accuracy."

Mathematics—Methods and Resources

K: To enhance computational skills with speed and accuracy

Worksheets
Math Standards Activities
Computer Software

1–2: To enhance computational skills with speed and accuracy

Worksheets
Math Standards Activities
Homework
Computer Software

3–4: To enhance computational skills with speed and accuracy

Worksheets
Math Standards Activities
Homework
Speed is applicable

Mathematics Assessment

Computation Assessments
Quizzes and Teacher-Made Tests
Standardized Tests

ASSESSMENT

Assessment Goal

"To increase the frequency and type of assessment measures and strengthen the reporting to parents."

Assessment—Methods and Resources

Assessment Results Shared with Parents
Homework Corrected with Explanations
Tests/Quizzes
Standardized Tests
Increased Reporting of Individual and Building Results
Identification and Evaluation of at-Risk Students

COMMUNICATION

Communication Goal

"To improve communication from school to parents and parents to school."

Communication—Methods and Resources

Curriculum Statements
Communication and Coordination between Grade Levels
Monthly Grade-Level Classroom Newsletters
School Newsletter
School Visitations
Parent Surveys

Key Points/Actions

Monitoring and Feedback
Increased Consistency
Improved Communication
Increased Assessment and Testing

Organizations Against Censorship

American Civil Liberties Union (ACLU)
125 Broad Street, 18th Floor
New York, NY 10004-2400
Phone: 212-549-2500
www.aclu.org

The American Civil Liberties Union is the nation's foremost advocate of individual rights—litigating, lobbying, and educating the public on a broad array of issues affecting individual freedom in the United States. The ACLU is a 50-state network with staffed affiliate offices in most major cities, more than 300 chapters in smaller towns, and regional offices in Denver and Atlanta. Work is coordinated by a national office in New York, aided by a legislative office in Washington that lobbies Congress. The ACLU has more than a dozen national projects devoted to specific civil liberties issues, including education reform and workplace rights. If you believe your civil liberties have been violated, contact the local ACLU office listed in your telephone directory.

American Library Association (ALA)
Office For Intellectual Freedom
50 East Huron Street
Chicago, IL 60611
Phone: 800-545-2433, Ext. 4223
Fax: 312-280-4227
www.ala.org

The American Library Association provides leadership for the development, promotion, and improvement of library and information services and the profession of librarianship in order to enhance learning and ensure access to information for all. The ALA supports intellectual freedom and the freedom to read. For many years, the organization has fought censorship for both adults and children. The ALA Office for Intellectual

Freedom is charged with implementing ALA policies concerning the concept of intellectual freedom as embodied in the Library Bill of Rights, the association's basic policy on free access to libraries and library materials. The goal of the office is to educate librarians and the general public about the nature and importance of intellectual freedom in libraries.

Center for Democracy and Technology (CDT)
1634 Eye Street NW, Suite 1100
Washington, DC 20006
Phone: 202-637-9800
Fax: 202-637-0968
E-mail: info@cdt.org
www.cdt.org

The Center for Democracy and Technology is a nonprofit public policy organization that works to promote democratic values and constitutional liberties in the digital age. With expertise in law, technology, and policy, CDT seeks practical solutions to enhance free expression and privacy in global communications technologies. CDT is dedicated to building consensus among all parties interested in the future of the Internet and other new communications media. In addition, CDT promotes its own policy positions in the United States and globally through public policy advocacy, online grassroots organizing with the Internet user community and public education campaigns, and litigation, as well as through the development of technology standards and online information resources.

National Coalition Against Censorship (NCAC)
275 7th Avenue
New York, NY 10001
Phone: 212-807-6222
Fax: 212-807-6245
E-mail: ncac@ncac.org
www.ncac.org

The National Coalition Against Censorship is an alliance of more than 40 national, nonprofit organizations. Associations that do not have an anticensorship program participate in NCAC as a means of fulfilling an organizational commitment. The Modern Language Association (MLA), the National Council for the Social Studies (NCSS), and the International Reading Association (IRA) are members of NCAC.

NCAC's program, Countering Censorship in Our Schools and Libraries, provides information and advice to educators, librarians, parents, and "ordinary" citizens fighting efforts to censor materials in schools and libraries. NCAC collaborates with coalition partners to produce educational materials. Currently, with the National Education Association, NCAC is producing materials for parents and teachers about the First Amendment and its role in education.

National Campaign for Freedom of Expression (NCFE)
1429 G Street NW, PMB #416
Washington, DC 20005-2009
Phone: 202-393-2787
E-mail: ncfe@ncfe.net
www.ncfe.net

The National Campaign for Freedom of Expression is an educational and advocacy network of artists, arts organizations, audience members, and concerned citizens formed to protect and extend freedom of artistic expression and fight censorship throughout the United States. The NCFE's work is committed to the understanding that true democracy is dependent on the right to free artistic expression for all, including those censored because of racism, sexism, homophobia, and all other forms of invidious discrimination. NCFE is the only nationwide organization exclusively dedicated to challenging the erosion of First Amendment rights as applied to the support, presentation, and creation of the arts in our culture today.

National Council of Teachers of English (NCTE)
1111 West Kenyon Road
Urbana, IL 61801-1096
Phone: 800-369-6283 or 217-328-3870
Fax: 217-328-9645
www.ncte.org

The National Council of Teachers of English is devoted to improving the teaching and learning of English and the language arts at all levels of education. Since 1911, NCTE has provided a forum for the profession, an array of opportunities for teachers to continue their professional growth throughout their careers, and a framework for cooperation to deal with issues that affect the teaching of English. NCTE works at the national and local levels to support the work of classroom teachers and to combat efforts to restrict their choices of curricular materials and teaching methods. NCTE has a Standing Committee Against Censorship and compiles and distributes rationales for challenged books to help teachers fight censorship attempts.

National Education Association (NEA)
1201 16th St. NW
Washington, DC 20036
Phone: 202-833-4000
www.nea.org

The NEA is America's oldest and largest organization committed to advancing the cause of public education. The NEA has affiliates in every state as well as in more than 13,000 local communities across the United States. At the state level, NEA affiliate activities include filing legal actions to protect academic freedom. The NEA believes that democratic values can best be transmitted in an atmosphere that does not restrain free inquiry and learning and that quality teaching depends on the freedom to select materials and techniques. Challenges to the choice of instructional materials and techniques must be orderly and objective, under procedures mutually adopted by professional associations and school governing boards. The NEA often defends and covers legal costs for its members involved in censorship challenges that become legal battles.

People for the American Way (PFAW)
2000 M Street NW, Suite 400
Washington, DC 20036
Phone: 202-467-4999 or 800-326-7329
E-mail: pfaw@pfaw.org
www.pfaw.org

People For the American Way organizes and mobilizes Americans to fight for fairness, justice, civil rights, and the freedoms guaranteed by the Constitution. PFAW lobbies for progressive legislation and helps to build communities of activists. It protects democracy in Congress and state capitals, in classrooms and in libraries, in courthouses and houses of worship, on the airwaves and on the printed page, on sidewalks and in cyberspace. For many years, PFAW has monitored the censorship of both materials and methods in K–12 schools. It offers advice and pertinent strategies for confronting educational challenges.

About the Editors and the Contributors

James K. Daly is director of secondary education in the College of Education and Human services at Seton Hall University. He is also co-founder and associate director of the New Jersey Center for Law-Related Education at the university. As a middle school teacher of social studies for 16 years, he developed an interest in the political ramifications of teaching and the political nature of schools. He chaired the National Council for the Social Studies committee on Academic Freedom for 2 years and has spoken and written extensively about censorship challenges facing teachers today.

Patricia L. Schall is chair of the Education Department at The College of Saint Elizabeth in Morristown, New Jersey. She teaches secondary education and English education courses. She spent 13 years teaching English in urban and suburban high schools and was the director of the educational media center at Seton Hall University, where she also taught. She serves as vice president of the New Jersey Council of Teachers of English and has presented at conferences nationwide.

Rosemary W. Skeele is director of instructional design, information technologies, and educational media specialist programs in the College of Education and Human Services at Seton Hall University. She is also a consultant and trainer for school districts in New Jersey. As a media specialist, she has had a career-long interest in censorship of teaching materials, intellectual freedom, challenges to teaching methods, and academic freedom. Developing learning strategies and teaching is her favorite activity. She believes that academic and intellectual freedom stimulate "good practice."

CHAPTER AUTHORS

Jack L. Nelson is a professor emeritus after 30 years on the faculty at Rutgers University. His publications include 16 books and more than 150 monographs, chapters, articles, and reviews. Much of his scholarly work is devoted to an examination of academic freedom, censorship, and related issues involving freedom in education. He is a member of the national panel of judges for Project Censored, which identifies the 10 most censored news stories each year.

William B. Stanley is professor of curriculum and social education and dean of the School of Education at the University of Colorado at Boulder. He is a former high school social studies teacher whose publications have appeared in numerous journals. He is the author of *Curriculum for Utopia* (State University of New York Press, 1992). He is a member of John Goodlad's National Network for Educational Renewal, the NCATE Board of Examiners, and the Colorado Partnership for Educational Renewal.

Joan Naomi Steiner, a former president of the National Council of Teachers of English, is the Director of Standards for the West Bend, Wisconsin, School District. A teacher and administrator for more than 23 years, she is the co-founder of the Wisconsin Assessment Consortium. She recently taught reading education at the University of Wisconsin, Oshkosh, before returning to the public schools. A much-sought-after speaker on what reading looks like in the high school, she has a rich background in secondary reading.

VOICES OF THE CHALLENGED

Jan Cole taught elementary school from 1968 to 1998 in Northglenn, Colorado. She received her B.S. and M.A. from the University of Colorado. In 1988, she received the Honored Lion Advocate Award for Standing Up for Teacher's Rights and Academic Freedom from the Colorado Education Association and in 1995 the Central Adams Uniserv Teacher's Hall of Fame Award for enduring attacks by far-right-affiliated groups.

Janet Cooper taught social studies for the Kingsville Independent School District from 1967 through 1972, and from 1980 until retirement in 1988. She specialized in teaching world history, economics, U.S. government, and U.S. history, for which she wrote the curriculum. She succeeded in getting students involved in citizen action projects and a variety of environmental advocacy programs.

Cissy Lacks, a teacher for 25 years in Missouri, was fired for "good teaching." Using the knowledge from her formal education, including a Ph.D. in American Studies, and her teaching experience, she is developing another "life" that includes photography, editing a professional newsletter, and writing a book about her challenge. She has spent the last 4 years living her case, talking to the press, and speaking to groups about teaching and censorship.

Gloria T. Pipkin, an English teacher for more than 20 years, was the head of a middle school English Department named by the National Council of Teachers of English as one of the 150 Centers of Excellence. She received intellectual freedom awards from the Florida Association for Media in Education and the Florida Council of Teachers of English, and her story appeared in *Seconding the First,* a national television show. Currently she is co-authoring a book about school censorship.

Gretchen Klopfer Wing, an educator for 15 years, is now teaching social studies, English, and leadership at a high school in Tacoma, Washington. She is the adviser for the student government and plays a key role on the school's site-based management team. A winner of the National Council for the Social Studies Academic Freedom Award, she advises colleagues to consult their conscience first and then go ahead with their teaching plans.

Index